WORLD THE SERIES ILLUSTRATED ALMANAC

Richard Whittingham

Contemporary Books, Inc.
Chicago

Library of Congress Cataloging in Publication Data

Paige, David.
  The World Series illustrated almanac.

  Includes index.
  1. World series (Baseball)—History.   2. Baseball—
United States—Records.   I. Title.
GV863.A1P34   1984   796.357′782′0973   83-26295
ISBN 0-8092-5489-1

Published by Contemporary Books, Inc.
180 North Michigan Avenue, Chicago, Illinois 60601
Manufactured in the United States of America
Library of Congress Catalog Card Number: 83-26295
International Standard Book Number: 0-8092-5489-1

Published simultaneously in Canada by Beaverbooks, Ltd.
195 Allstate Parkway, Valleywood Business Park
Markham, Ontario L3R 4T8 Canada

CONTENTS

★ ★ ★ CONTENTS ★ ★ ★

Acknowledgment

The author and publisher wish to thank the major league baseball clubs and their respective public relations departments, who so generously aided and cooperated with the author in the compilation of this book. All photographs, unless otherwise credited, were provided by the various baseball clubs and are reprinted with permission.

★ ★ ★ THE EARLY YEARS ★ ★ ★

It all began on a crisp, clear autumn day in Boston not long after the turn of the century. The date was October 1, 1903, and baseball fans queued up early outside the rickety wooden stadium known as Huntington Street Grounds where a sports tradition was about to be established. That afternoon they would watch the premier confrontation between the pennant winners of the National and American leagues, the first modern World Series game.

Attending a baseball game in those days was a rather proper affair. Men wore bowler hats, starched white collars, coats, and ties; their sons were decked out in knickers, jackets, and snap-peak caps. Although there were a few women there for this special event, finding females at a ballgame in those days was ordinarily about as rare as pitchers who did not throw the spitball.

As the Bostonians milled about waiting for the game, there was some talk about the outrageously inflated ticket price, 50¢, twice the admission charged for a regular season game. There was little consolation in the fact that the line had been held at 10¢ for a printed scorecard. In contrast to such economic woes, there were other topics of conversation in which to imbibe and pass the pregame time: the encouraging performance so far of the youthful president Teddy Roosevelt, for example; or the incredible motor car trip someone had just made, all the way from coast to coast for the very first time; or the impressive way in which James J. Jeffries had recently knocked out Gentleman Jim Corbett to retain the world heavyweight boxing crown; or the preposterous announcement from a pair of brothers named Wright that they had built a machine and were planning to fly in it at a place called Kitty Hawk down in North Carolina.

But all those diversions were set aside at two o'clock when the Boston Pilgrims (who would later take the name Red Sox), representing the American League, trotted out onto the field. On the mound for them was their ace, Cy Young, ready to face the heralded bats of the National League champions, the Pittsburgh Pirates. More than 16,000 had paid to attend the game and maybe another thousand clambered over the 10-foot wood fence to watch it for free. There were grandstands behind home plate and along the baselines, but no outfield bleachers as we know them today embraced Huntington Street Grounds; instead spectators simply stood behind ropes in left, center, and right. The dugouts

were nothing more than long, lean-to shacks, each with a wooden bench, and the team's bats were laid in a row on the ground in front of each dugout.

The reason this game and the World Series came about was because Pirate owner Barney Dreyfus had suggested it to Pilgrim owner Henry Killilea earlier in the season, and it seemed like a good idea at the time.

There had been some resentment from other National League club owners and managers because, for the most part, they frowned on the fledgling American League which was only three years old in 1903. The National League had been around since 1876, and its VIPs considered it not merely the senior league but the *only* "major" league. That distinction, however, would shortly be put to rest, because the American League pennant holders were about to establish their credibility by defeating the National League in the first World Series.

The Pilgrims not only had the great Cy Young on their roster but also such other certified stars as Patsy Dougherty, Jimmy Collins, Freddy Parent, and Bill Dinneen. The Pirates claimed the immortal Honus Wagner as well as Fred Clarke, Jimmy Sebring, Deacon Phillippe, and Brickyard

Kennedy. (The Pilgrims also had a first baseman with the unlikely name of Candy LaChance and the Pirates had a pitcher known as Kaiser Wilhelm.)

On that history-making day in Boston, the inaugural crowd got its money's worth in terms of excitement, even if the hometown team did stumble and fall. They cheered Cy Young, despite his giving up four runs in the top of the first inning, and they were shocked in the top of the seventh when Jimmy Sebring blasted the first World Series home run into the crowd behind the rope in center field.

The Pilgrims lost that day, but they would rally to win the Series, five games to three (a best of nine series had been agreed upon for that first championship match). It was a fitting climax to a fine season. The Pilgrims had won their first pennant behind the arms of Cy Young (28–9), Bill Dinneen (21–11), and Long Tom Hughes (20–7); the power of Buck Freeman who, in that era when the long ball hitter was a distinct rarity, led the league in homers with 13 and RBIs, 104; and the steady hitting of Patsy Dougherty, .331 (he also led the league in hits, 195, and runs, 106).

The Pirates had been the favorite, and not just in chauvinistic National League circles. Pittsburgh had won their third consecutive pennant, beating out John "Little Napoleon" McGraw's New York Giants—no mean feat because the New Yorkers sported two 30-game winners that year, Christy Mathewson (30–13) and Iron Man Joe McGinnity (31–20) as well as such great hitters as Dan McGann and Roger Bresnahan. The Pirates were paced by Honus Wagner, who led the league with an average of .355 and who stole 46 bases; Fred Clarke, who hit .351; and Ginger Beaumont, batting .341. They also had the mound services of Sam Leever (25–7) and Deacon Phillippe (24–9). And their performances enabled the Pirates to end up six-and-a-half games ahead of the Giants at the end of the season.

When that first World Series ended, the attendance at the eight games totaled somewhere around 100,000. Everyone involved agreed that the experiment had been a success, especially the players who received a nice bonus for their postseason efforts. There was about $50,000 to divide between the two teams.

There would be no resumption of the World Series the following year, however. The New York Giants won the National League flag but manager John McGraw and club president John T. Brush decided to snub the "inferior league," as they referred to it, and declined a postseason playoff with the Boston Pilgrims, who had won their second consecutive American League pennant.

The Series, however, would be resumed in 1905 and would remain the classic climax to every baseball season thereafter. McGraw and his Giants consented to meet the AL champs, Connie Mack's Philadelphia Athletics, matching two teams who would be dominating forces in major league baseball over the next decade.

It was heralded as a "Pitchers' Series" with good reason. The Giants had the great righthander Christy Mathewson, who had won 32 games and lost only eight during the regular season as well as two other hurlers who had chalked up 22 wins apiece, Iron Man Joe McGinnity and Red Ames. The Philadelphia staff was spearheaded by Rube Waddell, whose 26 wins, 287 strikeouts, and ERA of 1.48 were the best in the American League, and boasted a supporting cast of Eddie Plank (25–12), Andy Coakley (20–7), and Chief Bender (16–11).

The Giants had taken the Na-tional League pennant easily, winning 105 games, one less than they had in capturing the previous year's flag. The Pittsburgh Pirates and the Chicago Cubs, both considered fine teams, trailed by nine and 13 games respectively at season's end. The A's, on the other hand, barely got by the Chicago White Sox, both teams winning 92 games, but the ChiSox lost 60 while the A's dropped only 56 in that era of less than stable schedules.

As predicted, the pitchers truly dominated the 1905 Series. Waddell was not one of them, however, benched by a sore shoulder. Mathewson's arm was fine, so fine in fact he hurled three shut-outs, allowing the A's a meager 14 hits in 27 innings. Eddie Plank pitched another shutout for the Giants, while Chief Bender snuck one in for the Athletics. For the first and only time in Series history all the games were shutouts.

The "Trolley Series" is what sportswriters dubbed the 1906 postseason festivity because it was the first intracity championship. Chicago was the site.

The White Sox were not denied the pennant that year, their success carried chiefly by the arms of their superb pitching staff. Big Ed Walsh (17–13), notorious for both his fastball and his spitball (which was legal then) was to become the most famous of them, but the Sox also boasted of Frank Owen (22-13), Nick Altrock (20-13), and Doc White (18-6). But they had so little offense they were known around the league as the "Hitless Wonders." With a team batting average of only .230 and a team total of just six home runs, the Sox were outhit by all seven of the other American League teams that year. Still, they managed to end up three games ahead of Clark Griffith's New York Yankees and five in front of Nap Lajoie's Cleveland Indians; while the previous year's champions, the A's, sunk to fourth place, 12 games back.

In the National League, the Chicago Cubs proved they could do just about everything with consummate skill. They won 116 games, losing only 36, the best regular season record ever posted in the major leagues. They possessed the game's most famous double play combination—Tinker to Evers to Chance—and they also were a notorious force at the plate, leading the league in batting average, slugging average, runs scored, hits, and RBIs, among other stats. And they had pitching: Mordecai "Three Finger" Brown (26-6), Jack Pfiester

(20-8), and Ed Reulbach (19-4).

As one might imagine, the Cubs were a heavy favorite. And when the Sox could only come up with one lonesome hit in Game 2 off Ed Reulbach, fans throughout Chicago thought the demise of the AL flagbearers was only a few games away. But it wasn't. Proof that there can be as many surprises in baseball as there are in horse racing, the "Hitless Wonders" turned their balsa wood bats into clubs and pounded out wins in three of the next four games to take the Series. In the last two games, they collected eight runs in each and a total of 26 hits to the astonishment of just about everyone in Chicago.

The Cubs were back seeking vengeance the following year. Once again they had thoroughly dominated the National League, taking the pennant by 17 full games. Their hitting in 1907 was not as impressive as in 1906, the team average was only .250, and not a single regular hit .300, nor did anyone hit more than two home runs the entire season. Still, they won 107 games and were never challenged.

Over in the American League, the race had been much closer, decided only in the last few days of the regular season. Connie

Mack's Philadelphia Athletics, relying on the pitching of Eddie Plank, Jimmy Dygert, Rube Waddell, and Chief Bender, fought the Detroit Tigers all the way to the finish. The Tigers were piloted by Hughie Jennings and fueled by the play of 20-year-old sensation Tyrus Cobb, who led the league in batting (.350), slugging (.473), RBIs (119), hits (212), and stolen bases (49). Both teams had outdistanced the White Sox in the final two weeks of the season, with the Tigers finally edging ahead by one-and-a-half games.

Besides the "Georgia Peach," as Cobb was known, the Tigers had Sam Crawford in their outfield, and he was the league's second most productive batter that year with an average of .323. And the Tigers were no slouch in the pitching department either, with Wild Bill Donovan turning in the year's best won-lost percentage, .862 (25–4), while Ed Killian won another 25 games; George Mullin, 20; and Ed Siever, 19.

The Tigers, however, were no match for the Cubs in 1907. The youngsters from Chicago, after a first game that ended in a tie due to darkness, marched through the next four games to become the first team to sweep a World Series. Cub pitchers allowed the Tigers only three runs in those four games, and effectively shut down Cobb (.200) and Crawford (.238). Speedy Cub baserunners stole 18 bases, a Series record, off hapless Tiger catcher Boss Schmidt.

It was a repeat in 1908. The same two teams triumphed in their respective leagues, but it was no easy task for either the Tigers or Cubs that year. The Tigers gained their title on the very last day of the season, ending up with a record of 90–63, .004 percentage points ahead of Nap Lajoie's Cleveland Indians (90–64), and one-and-a-half games ahead of Fielder Jones's White Sox (88–64).

For the Tigers, Cobb again burned up the league with his hitting, taking six crowns: batting average (.324), slugging average (.475), RBIs (108), triples (20), doubles (36), and hits (188). Sam Crawford, with an average of .311, was the league's third best hitter. Ed Summers, a 23-year-old righthander, was Detroit's only 20-game winner (24–12), although he was quite a bit short of the league leader that year—Big Ed Walsh of the White Sox won an amazing 40 games.

The National League pennant race had been just about as close, the Cubs (99–55) sneaking in only a game ahead of both John McGraw's New York Giants and

Fred Clarke's Pittsburgh Pirates. The Cubs still relied on fielding and speed, with such stars as Harry Steinfeldt, Jimmy Sheckard, Joe Tinker, Johnny Evers, and Frank Chance (who was also their manager). And they had 29-game winner Three Finger Brown and 24-game winner Ed Reulbach. Between them, the Chicagoans demolished the Tigers just as they had the year before, only this time they allowed the Tigers one victory.

In 1909, the Tigers were back for the third consecutive time. They managed to hold off the Philadelphia A's, who had now developed some impressive power at the plate generated by the bats of Eddie Collins and Frank "Home Run" Baker. But no one was hitting as well as Ty Cobb (.377), who again led the league in just about every category that year, including home runs (9) and stolen bases (76), which set a major league record. Tiger righthander George Mullin was that year's mound master (29-9), while Ed Willett chalked up 22 wins and Ed Summers, 19.

The Cubs, however, were unable to make it back for a third straight year. The Pittsburgh Pirates proved too tough, racking up 110 wins against 42 defeats,

besting the Chicago franchise by six-and-a-half games. Shortstop Honus Wagner was their star supreme, and he led the NL with an average of .339. He also collected the most RBIs (100) and doubles (39). The Pirates got clutch hitting from Tommy Leach and player-manager Fred Clarke as well. Howie Camnitz won 25 games for them; Vic Willis, 22; and Lefty Leifield, 19.

The game's predominant hitter, Ty Cobb tapped out a meek .231 (6 for 26) in the Series, while Wagner managed a respectable .333 (8 for 24). The Series hero, it turned out, was Pirate pitcher Babe Adams, who went the distance to win three games for the National Leaguers. After seven games, the Tigers went back to Detroit, an also-ran for the third straight year. They would not make another World Series appearance for 25 years.

The Cubs reasserted themselves in 1910, and they did it with flair, virtually sailing through the National League (104–50), 13 games separating them from the second-place New York Giants. For a change, the Cubs could boast some strong hitting. Solly Hofman hit .325; Wildfire Schultz, .301 (his 10 home runs were the most in the league);

Jack Coombs (left), talking with Dodger manager Wilbert "Uncle Robbie" Robertson, hurled in three World Series for the Philadelphia A's in 1910 and 1911 and for the Dodgers in 1916. Robertson managed the Dodgers in two, 1916 and 1920. *(Photo courtesy of the National Baseball Hall of Fame)*

Frank Chance, .298; and Joe Tinker, .288. Three Finger Brown was still their top moundsman, winning 25 games and losing 13, and youthful King Cole turned in an impressive 20–4 season. The Giants still had Christy Mathewson hurling for them, and he remained the best in the league at age 31 (27–9). And the Pirates still had Honus Wagner who, at 36, could still manage to hit .320 and steal 24 bases. But neither team gave the Cubs a scare in 1910. And so for the fourth time in five years, the Chicagoans were the NL representative in the World Series.

Over in the American League, Connie Mack's Philadelphia Athletics had been equally awesome during the regular season. A team of superb hitters, they breezed to the pennant with 102 wins. The second place New York Yankees, under George Stallings, were 14½ games back, and third-place Detroit was a full 18 games out. The A's batting attack was led by Eddie Collins, who hit .322 and set a major league record by stealing 81 bases. Besides Collins, Rube Oldring hit .308 and Danny Murphy, .300. In the pitching department, righthander Jack Coombs led the league with 31 wins against only nine defeats. Chief Bender turned in a 23–5 season, while Cy Morgan won 18 and Eddie Plank, 16.

The Cubs, coming off two national championships in the preceding three years, were decided favorites. Pitching had been what they consistently relied upon, but it failed them against the sharp bats wielded by the A's in 1910. The Philadelphians registered a team average of .316, a Series record that would stand until 1960. With an average of seven runs a game, they annihilated the Cubs in four of their five encounters that Series. The A's, in fact, used only *two* pitchers in the five games, Coombs and Bender, who allowed the Cubs an average of only three runs and seven hits a game.

The 1911 Series brought a reunion between Connie Mack and John McGraw as the Philadelphia A's and the New York Giants faced each other for the first time since the 1905 Series. In that one, McGraw's Giants had prevailed, so now it was time for Philadel-phia's revenge. The A's had coasted to the American League pennant with ease; the Detroit Tigers were a distant second, 13½ games back. Home Run Baker had lived up to his nickname and led the league in round-trippers (11), not bad in that era of the dead ball. Eddie Collins hit a hefty .365, which, however, was only good enough for fourth in the league that year when Ty Cobb of the Tigers batted .420, Shoeless Joe Jackson hit .408 for the Cleveland Indians, and Sam Crawford, .378 for the Tigers. The A's had a host of other fine hitters that year in addition to Collins: Baker hit .334; Danny Murphy, .329; Stuffy McInnis, .321; and Bris Lord, 310. Their hitting was complemented by the league's foremost pitching staff, headed by Jack Coombs, whose 28 wins was the league's top; Eddie Plank rang up another 22 wins while Chief Bender added 17.

The Cubs had been the favorite to take the National League title, but they faltered in midseason and McGraw's Giants steamrolled their way to the pennant. They were a fast, good-fielding team, with mediocre hitting, but their mound staff was the gem of the league. Veteran Christy Mathewson won 26 games and his ERA of 1.99 was the league's best.

Young Rube Marquard, 21, came through with 24 wins against only seven defeats. But the Giants had only two hitters who topped the .300 mark, Chief Meyers (.332) and Larry Doyle (.310). Doyle also led the league with 25 triples. On the basepaths, the Giants were sheer murder, *pilfering 347 bases,* far and away the most in either league and a major league record that has never been topped.

Lack of hitting, however, is what did the Giants in during the 1911 Series. As a team they batted a meek .175, and scored only 13 runs in six games. As a result, Connie Mack had his second consecutive world championship to take back to Philadelphia.

In 1912, the Boston Red Sox made their way to the World Series, the first time since that first postseason meeting back in 1903, when they were known as the Pilgrims. Now they played their games at a place called Fenway Park instead of Huntington Street Grounds, and they won a total of 105 to finish 14 games ahead of Clark Griffith's Washington Senators and 15 above the reigning world champion A's.

The Red Sox, managed by Jake Stahl, were a consummate team. Their pitching staff was spear-headed by Smokey Joe Wood, who won 34 games while losing only five. He hurled 10 shutouts and posted an ERA of 1.91. The BoSox also had Hugh Bedient (20–9) and Buck O'Brien (19–13). As hitters, the team led the American League in runs scored (800), RBIs (654), doubles (269), and slugging average (.380), and they

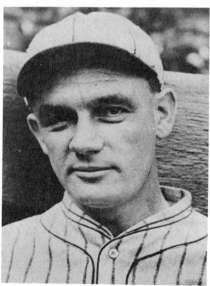

Rube Marquard pitched in three World Series for the New York Giants and two for the Dodgers. His overall record was 2–5. *(Photo courtesy of the National Baseball Hall of Fame)*

drew the most bases on balls (565). Center fielder Tris Speaker hit a resounding .383 and set a major league record with his 53 doubles (which would stand until he would slug 59 some 12 years later).

The Giants had had no more trouble taking the National League pennant than Boston had in the American, finishing 10 games ahead of the Pittsburgh Pirates. Rube Marquard had bettered his previous year's record by winning 26 games while losing only 11. Christy Mathewson, at 33, won another 23 games. Again, Chief Meyers was their most consistent hitter (.358), but Larry Doyle and Fred Merkle turned in good seasons with averages of .330 and .309 respectively.

The 1912 Series turned out to be one of the most exciting ever. The Giants, trailing three games to one, rallied to tie it at three apiece with two resounding wins. But then they virtually handed it over to the Red Sox in the 10th inning of the seventh and deciding game. It was a saga of "Freds flubs," two different Freds. The more infamous was Fred Merkle, who, in the top of the 10th, appeared to be the game, and, for that matter, the Series hero when he drove in the lead run. But instead he became forever the goat of it in the bottom of that inning. He was not alone, however. There was also center fielder Fred Snodgrass, who started it off in the bottom of the 10th by dropping an easy fly ball from the bat of

Harry Hooper was a mainstay on four Boston Red Sox pennant winners, and batted .350 and .300 in two of his four World Series appearances. *(Photo courtesy of the National Baseball Hall of Fame)*

pinch hitter Clyde Engle. So, instead of being credited with the first out of the inning, Engle ended up on second base. Engle tagged up and went to third on a fly out by Harry Hooper. Then Merkle made his fateful blunder. Tris Speaker was at bat, the most feared of the Red Sox hitters; he hit a little looping foul ball down the first base line, an apparent easy out. But first baseman Fred

Merkle, obviously not paying attention, stood transfixed, unaware that the ball was on its way toward him. It dropped about 10 feet from him. Instead of becoming out Number 2, Speaker went back to the batter's box and subsequently rapped out a single to drive in the tying run. Moments later the Red Sox scored the game-winning run and earned the Series title.

The Giants earned a chance to redeem themselves in 1913, and also to avenge their Series loss to the Philadelphia A's in 1911. Once again they had sailed through the National League on the pitching of Mathewson (25–11), Marquard (23–10), and 24-year-old Jeff Tesreau (22–13). And their hitting was much more consistent, the team average of .273 being the best in the league. But John McGraw was to receive neither his redemption nor his revenge.

The Athletics, still under Connie Mack, were back and perhaps stronger than ever. Eddie Collins hit .345 for the season, followed by Home Run Baker, .336 (his 12 homers and 117 RBIs were also AL highs), and Stuffy McInnis, .326. Chief Bender was the only 20-game winner (21–10).

It took the Athletics only five games to dismantle John McGraw's dreams. The Giants' only moment of glory in the 5-game affair was Christy Mathewson's shutout in Game 2. This time they did not have to worry about handing the Series over to their AL opponents, they simply were overwhelmed by the bats of Home Run Baker and Eddie Collins, who hit .450 and .421 in the series, and by pitching that held the Giants to a team average of .201. McGraw's Giants would not be back to the Series until 1917.

By 1914, the time had come for a true Cinderella team to snare the spotlight. The surprise belle of the ball was the hitherto unheralded Boston Braves. The year before they had dwelled in fifth place, 31½ games out of first, with a dismal record of 69–82. And in mid-July of 1914 they were in *last* place in the National League. But George Stallings, their manager, somehow inspired the Braves to reverse the fates and the turn-around was as dramatic as any ever in a professional sport. Suddenly the lowly Braves were winning ballgames and steadily ascending the National League ladder. They moved all the way up to first place and took the pennant from an astounded New York Giants by 10½ games, earning the right to meet the Philadelphia A's, who had won their fifth AL pennant in 11 years.

It was not the Braves hitting. They had only one .300 batter, Joe Connolly (.306), and as a team the Braves hit 14 percentage points less than the Giants. They also scored fewer runs and collected fewer hits than the Giants. They did get some sterling pitching from Dick Rudolph (27–10) and Bill James (26–7); on the other hand, the Giants got 26 wins from Jeff Tesreau and 24 from Christy Mathewson. But the bottom line was the fact that the Braves won 10 more games than the Giants, and therefore they earned the right to represent the National League in the 1914 World Series.

And represent them they did! A four-game sweep. Brave hurlers held the once awesome Athletic offense to a mere six runs in four games, only 22 hits, and a team batting average of just .172. An astonished and somewhat morti-fied Connie Mack was denied his fourth world championship in five years. Meanwhile the Braves, the talk of the baseball world, became the toast of Beantown where they had labored so long under the shadow of the Red Sox.

The same two cities would host the 1915 World Series, only the two teams would be different. In-stead of the Braves it would be the Boston Red Sox, and from Philadelphia it would be the Phil-lies rather than the Athletics.

Under Bill Carrigan, the Red Sox eked out a pennant in the American League, ending up two-and-a-half games ahead of the De-troit Tigers. Connie Mack's pow-erhouse of the last decade had been plucked of all its gems— gone were Eddie Collins, Home Run Baker, Chief Bender, and Ed-die Plank, among others. Without them the A's plummeted to the cellar of the American League, 58½ games out with a record of 43–109.

The Red Sox had five note-worthy pitchers in their regular rotation that year, among them a 20-year-old second-year man named George Herman "Babe" Ruth. (Despite his role as pitcher and his appearance in only 32 games, Ruth led the Red Sox in home runs with four and batted a respectable .315). They also had the game's greatest center fielder of the day, Tris Speaker, who led the team with a .322 average that year, and another Hall of Famer, Harry Hooper, in right field.

The Philadelphia Phillies sur-prised everyone by taking the NL crown, ending up seven games ahead of the previous year's Cin-

Jake Daubert was at first base for the Dodgers in the 1916 Series and for Cincinnati in 1919, and batted .294 and .310. *(Photo courtesy of the National Baseball Hall of Fame)*

derella Braves. The Phils had come in sixth the year before, posting a meager record of 74–80. The biggest sparkle on the Phillies roster was the great right-hander Grover Cleveland "Pete" Alexander, who won 31 games for them in 1915. They also had 21-game winner Erskine Mayer and a first-rate slugger in Gavvy Cravath, who led the league in homers (24), RBIs (115), runs scored (89), walks (86), and slugging average (.510). But the new Cinderella, now of Philadelphia,

didn't get the prince in 1915. Their bats failed them after winning the first game, and the Phillies dropped the next four straight. Boston had its second world champion in two years, that title unselfishly shared between the Red Sox and the Braves.

There had been a National League franchise in Brooklyn since 1890, known variously as the "Brooklyners," "Bridegrooms," "Superbas," and by 1916 as the "Robins." They would not officially take on the now-famous moniker "Dodgers" until the early 1930s. Brooklyn had won three NL pennants in the pre-World Series era, but did not make their debut in the postseason classic until 1916. They got there that year under the guidance of affable Wilbert "Uncle Robbie" Robinson (the team nickname Robins was a derivation of Uncle Robbie's name), and with help from the bats of Jake Daubert (.316) and Zack Wheat (.312, he also led the AL in slugging with an average of .461). Jeff Pfeffer won 25 games for the boys from Brooklyn. The Robins had emerged a winner after a rather close pennant race, and when the season ended the Phillies were only 2½ games behind and the Braves four.

The Red Sox were a repeat winner in the American League, just barely edging out the Chicago White Sox by two games and the Detroit Tigers by four. Southpaw Babe Ruth had become their frontline pitcher in 1916, winning 23 while losing only 12, and his ERA of 1.75 was the best in the league. Hitting was not the forte of the Red Sox, however, and only Larry Gardner broke the .300 mark (.308). Even the Babe could only muster a .272 average and a total of three round-trippers.

But just as they had the Series before, the Red Sox rose to the postseason occasion. They allowed the Robins a single win but that was all. Brooklyn would have to wait another 40 years, until 1955, before they could collect a world championship.

The 1917 Series featured two superb teams, the Chicago White Sox and the New York Giants. The Sox had not been to the Series since that intracity battle back in 1906. Now, in 1917, under

Shoeless Joe Jackson appeared in the 1917 and 1919 Series for the White Sox, batting .304 and .375.

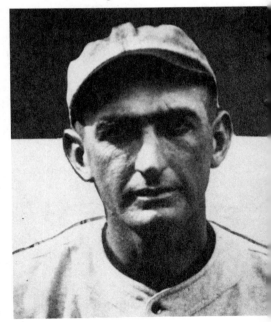

Ray Schalk, a Hall of Famer, was behind the plate for the White Sox in both the 1917 and 1919 Series, and hit .304 in the latter. *(Photo courtesy of the National Baseball Hall of Fame)*

Pants Rowland, they fielded what many believe to be one of the finest all-around baseball teams ever to play the game. Among the greats in the Sox line-up were Eddie Collins, Shoeless Joe Jackson, Ray Schalk, Happy Felsch, and Buck Weaver, as well as such master hurlers as Urban "Red" Faber, Eddie Cicotte, and Lefty Williams. They breezed through the AL, leaving the Red Sox a full nine games behind them.

John McGraw's New York Giants were making their fifth Series appearance. They, too, had experienced little trouble in securing their pennant, beating the Phillies out by 10 games. They had their reserve of stars as well, such as Heinie Zimmerman, Dave Robertson, George Burns, and Ferdie Schupp. But the New Yorkers were no match for the White Sox that year, and they were disposed of in six games.

The 1918 baseball season was an abbreviated one because of the U.S. involvement in World War I. Teams were depleted of players, the grandstands sparsely filled with spectators, and a special government order cut the season short so the World Series was held in early September.

The Red Sox took the American League pennant by winning 75 games while losing only 51. Ed Barrow was now their manager, having replaced Bill Carrigan who had led the BoSox to two world championships in 1915 and 1916. Babe Ruth was now playing in the outfield as well as pitching for the Bostonians, and he led the league with 11 homers. Their chief hurler that year was Carl Mays, who won 21 games and lost 13.

In the National League, the Chicago Cubs won handily, leaving the Giants 10½ games behind. Their batting order contained almost no memorable names, except perhaps the notorious one of Fred Merkle, who now held down first base for them. But they did have two 20-game winners in Hippo Vaughn (22-10) and Claude Hendrix (20-7).

The Series did not draw large crowds, the six games averaging about 21,400. The players on both teams threatened to strike before the fifth game over the amount of their share of the Series revenues, but after a delay they finally took the field and played the game. A day later, the Red Sox chalked up their fourth win of the Series and their fifth world championship.

By the time the 1919 World Series came around, the Armistice had been signed and the fighting in Europe was over. The teams were replenished with the talents they had lost during the 1918 season and baseball was again the popular pastime it had been before the war diverted most Americans' attention. But the Series would turn out to be a tainted one.

The White Sox had practically the same team that had triumphed in 1917, although they were now managed by Kid Gleason. As good as they were, they had had a tough time of it with

Eddie Cicotte hurled for the White Sox in both the 1917 and 1919 World Series, winning two games and losing three.

the Cleveland Indians, who were now managed by Tris Speaker. The ChiSox emerged victorious by a mere three-and-a-half games.

The Chicago team was a power of the first order. Shoeless Joe Jackson batted .351 (and slugged .506), Eddie Collins hit .319, and Nemo Leibold, .302. Righthander Eddie Cicotte turned in a rousing 29-7 season and Lefty Williams 23-11.

Over in the National League, the Cincinnati Reds collected their first pennant ever, leaving

One of the game's all-time greats, Eddie Collins appeared in four World Series for the Philadelphia A's and two for the White Sox, hitting over .400 in three of them. *(Photo courtesy of the National Baseball Hall of Fame)*

Chick Gandil, sliding, is out at second in this game from the 1919 Series. *(Photo courtesy of the Chicago Historical Society)*

the Giants a distant nine games back at the end of the regular season. The Reds were blessed with the fine hitting of Edd Roush (.321) and Heinie Groh (.310) as well as the class pitching of Slim Sallee (21-7), Hod Eller (20-9), and Dutch Ruether (19-6).

Baseball fans turned out in record numbers for the World Series now that the war was over, unaware that the fix was in, that gamblers had gotten to some of the players. They watched the sham in which seven members of the White Sox threw the Series and forever gained for their team the epithet "Black Sox." The seven—Shoeless Joe Jackson, Eddie Cicotte, Lefty Williams, Swede Risberg, Happy Felsch, Chick Gandil, and Fred McMullen—had agreed to manipulate the Series (one in which they were heavily favored) so as to lose it in return for payments alleged to total $100,000. The money was to come from a syndicate of gamblers headed by Arnold Rothstein of New York. Another Sox player, Buck Weaver, would also be involved in that he attended meetings regarding the fix. But even though he did not participate in the actual throwing of the Series, his fate would be the same as the other seven: banned from baseball forever. It took them eight games to throw it in that extended Series (a best of nine trial series), but the infamous seven did it. Cincinnati had its first world crown and the White Sox would not play in another World Series for four decades.

"Baseball's darkest day," is the way one sportswriter described it. The truth of it would not come out for almost a year, and when it did, the baseball world was shaken as it never has been, before or since. But the game, of course, would survive. The stars who took the field would again glisten with rich magnitude, and the fans would continue to turn out to cheer and hoot and enjoy it all.

Manager of the infamous Black Sox of 1919, Kid Gleason. *(Photo courtesy of the Chicago Historical Society)*

1903

Boston Pilgrims (Red Sox)   5
Pittsburgh Pirates   3

Line-ups

	Boston Pilgrims		Pittsburgh Pirates
1b	Candy LaChance	1b	Kitty Bransfield
2b	Hobe Ferris	2b	Claude Ritchey
3b	Jimmy Collins	3b	Tommy Leach
ss	Freddy Parent	ss	Honus Wagner
lf	Patsy Dougherty	lf	Fred Clarke
cf	Chick Stahl	cf	Ginger Beaumont
rf	Buck Freeman	rf	Jimmy Sebring
c	Lou Criger	c	Eddie Phelps
mgr	Jimmy Collins	mgr	Fred Clarke

		R	H	E	Pitching
Game 1	Pittsburgh	7	12	2	Deacon Phillippe (W)
	Boston	3	6	4	Cy Young
Game 2	Pittsburgh	0	3	2	Sam Leever, Bucky Veil (2nd)
	Boston	3	9	0	Bill Dinneen (W)
Game 3	Pittsburgh	4	7	0	Deacon Phillippe (W)
	Boston	2	4	2	Long Tom Hughes, Cy Young (3rd)
Game 4	Boston	4	9	1	Bill Dinneen
	Pittsburgh	5	12	1	Deacon Phillippe (W)
Game 5	Boston	11	14	2	Cy Young (W)
	Pittsburgh	2	6	4	Brickyard Kennedy, Gus Thompson (8th)
Game 6	Boston	6	10	1	Bill Dinneen (W)
	Pittsburgh	2	10	3	Sam Leever
Game 7	Boston	7	11	4	Cy Young (W)
	Pittsburgh	3	10	3	Deacon Phillippe
Game 8	Pittsburgh	0	4	3	Deacon Phillippe
	Boston	3	8	0	Bill Dinneen (W)

Highlights

- Deacon Phillippe started and completed five games for the Pirates (44 innings pitched, a Series record).
- Bill Dinneen started and completed four games for the Pilgrims (35 innings pitched).
- Dinneen's record of 28 strikeouts would stand as the most in a Series until Bob Gibson of the Cardinals fanned 31 batters in 1964.
- Pirate slugger Jimmy Sebring hit the first World Series home run in Game 1. His total of nine singles set a record for an eight-game Series.
- Tommy Leach of the Pirates hit two triples in Game 1, and Patsy Dougherty cracked another two for the Pilgrims in Game 5 to share a Series record.
- Dinneen is credited with pitching the first World Series shutout, Game 2, and the second, Game 8.
- Patsy Dougherty hit two home runs in Game 2.
- Pilgrim batters collected five triples in Game 5, and another five in Game 7, a Series record that still stands.
- Honus Wagner, the Pirates famed shortstop, playing with an injured leg, was tabbed with six errors in the Series.

Best Efforts

Batting

Average	Jimmy Sebring	.367
Home Runs	Patsy Dougherty	2
Triples	Tommy Leach	4
Doubles	Candy LaChance	2
	Fred Clarke	2
Hits	Jimmy Sebring	11
Runs	Freddy Parent	8
RBIs	Tommy Leach	8

Pitching

Wins	Bill Dinneen	3–1
	Deacon Phillippe	3–2
ERA	Cy Young	1.85
Strikeouts	Bill Dinneen	28
Innings Pitched	Deacon Phillippe	44

1905

New York Giants 4
Philadelphia Athletics 1

Line-ups

New York Giants		Philadelphia Athletics	
1b	Dan McGann	1b	Harry Davis
2b	Billy Gilbert	2b	Danny Murphy
3b	Art Devlin	3b	Lave Cross
ss	Bill Dahlen	ss	Monte Cross
lf	Sam Mertes	lf	Topsy Hartsel
cf	Mike Donlin	cf	Bris Lord
rf	George Browne	rf	Socks Seybold
c	Roger Bresnahan	c	Ossee Schreckengost
mgr	John McGraw	mgr	Connie Mack

		R	H	E	Pitching
Game 1	New York	3	10	1	Christy Mathewson (W)
	Philadelphia	0	4	0	Eddie Plank
Game 2	Philadelphia	3	6	2	Chief Bender (W)
	New York	0	4	2	Iron Man Joe McGinnity, Red Ames (9th)
Game 3	New York	9	9	1	Christy Mathewson (W)
	Philadelphia	0	4	5	Andy Caokley
Game 4	Philadelphia	0	5	2	Eddie Plank
	New York	1	4	1	Iron Man Joe McGinnity (W)
Game 5	Philadelphia	0	6	0	Chief Bender
	New York	2	5	1	Christy Mathewson

Highlights

- The Giants pitching staff gave up only three runs in five Series games.
- Christy Mathewson hurled three shutouts for the Giants, the only player in Series history to accomplish that feat.
- All five games in the Series were shutouts.
- The 18 strikeouts thrown by Christy Mathewson remains the record for a five-game Series.
- Dan McGann drove in four runs for the Giants in Game 3 with a double and two singles.

Best Efforts

Batting

Average	Roger Bresnahan	.313
Home Runs	——	
Triples	——	
Doubles	Dan McGann	2
	Roger Bresnahan	2
Hits	Mike Donlin	5
	Roger Bresnahan	5
	Topsy Hartsel	5
Runs	Mike Donlin	4
RBIs	Dan McGann	4

Pitching

Wins	Christy Mathewson	3–0
ERA	Christy Mathewson	0.00
Strikeouts	Christy Mathewson	18
Innings Pitched	Christy Mathewson	27

1906

Chicago White Sox   4
Chicago Cubs   2

Line-ups

Chicago White Sox		Chicago Cubs	
1b	Jiggs Donahue	1b	Frank Chance
2b	Frank Isbell	2b	Johnny Evers
3b	George Rohe	3b	Harry Steinfeldt
ss	George Davis	ss	Joe Tinker
lf	Patsy Dougherty	lf	Jimmy Sheckard
cf	Fielder Jones	cf	Solly Hofman
rf	Eddie Hahn	rf	Wildfire Schulte
c	Billy Sullivan	c	Johnny Kling
mgr	Fielder Jones	mgr	Frank Chance

		R	H	E	Pitching
Game 1	White Sox	2	4	1	Nick Altrock (W)
	Cubs	1	4	2	Three Finger Brown
Game 2	Cubs	7	10	2	Ed Reulbach (W)
	White Sox	1	1	2	Doc White, Frank Owen (4th)
Game 3	White Sox	3	4	1	Ed Walsh (W)
	Cubs	0	2	2	Jack Pfiester
Game 4	Cubs	1	7	1	Three Finger Brown (W)
	White Sox	0	2	1	Nick Altrock
Game 5	White Sox	8	12	6	Ed Walsh (W), Doc White (7th)
	Cubs	6	6	0	Ed Reulbach, Jack Pfiester (3rd), Orvie Overall (4th)
Game 6	Cubs	3	7	0	Three Finger Brown, Orvie Overall (2nd)
	White Sox	8	14	3	Doc White (W)

Highlights

- Ed Reulbach allowed the Sox only one hit in Game 2, a single by Jiggs Donahue in the seventh.
- Big Ed Walsh struck out 12 Cubs in Game 3.
- George Rohe drove in all three Sox runs in Game 3 with a bases-loaded triple in the sixth.
- Sox slugger Frank Isbell clouted four doubles in five at-bats in Game 5, a Series record.
- The eight Sox doubles and the two-team total of 11 in Game 5 both became Series marks.
- Eddie Hahn collected four hits and Jiggs Donahue and George Davis drove in three runs apiece for the Sox in Game 6.

Best Efforts

Batting

Average	Jiggs Donahue	.333
	George Rohe	.333
Home Runs	——	
Triples	George Rohe	2
Doubles	Frank Isbell	4
Hits	Frank Isbell	8
Runs	Frank Isbell	4
	George Davis	4
	Eddie Hahn	4
	Fielder Jones	4
	Joe Tinker	4
RBIs	George Davis	6

Pitching

Wins	Ed Walsh	2–0
ERA	Nick Altrock	1.00
Strikeouts	Ed Walsh	17
Innings Pitched	Three Finger Brown	19⅔

1907

Chicago Cubs   4
Detroit Tigers 0

Line-ups

Chicago Cubs		Detroit Tigers	
1b	Frank Chance	1b	Claude Rossman
2b	Johnny Evers	2b	Germany Schaefer
3b	Harry Steinfeldt	3b	Bill Coughlin
ss	Joe Tinker	ss	Charley O'Leary
lf	Jimmy Sheckard	lf	Davy Jones
cf	Jimmy Slagle	cf	Sam Crawford
rf	Wildfire Schulte	rf	Ty Cobb
c	Johnny Kling	c	Boss Schmidt
mgr	Frank Chance	mgr	Hughie Jennings

		R	H	E	Pitching
Game 1	Detroit	3	9	3	Wild Bill Donovan
	Chicago	3	10	5	Orvie Overall, Ed Reulbach (10th)
Game 2	Detroit	1	9	1	George Mullin
	Chicago	3	9	1	Jack Pfiester (W)
Game 3	Detroit	1	6	1	Ed Siever, Ed Killian (5th)
	Chicago	5	10	1	Ed Reulbach (W)
Game 4	Chicago	6	7	2	Orvie Overall (W)
	Detroit	1	5	2	Wild Bill Donovan
Game 5	Chicago	2	7	1	Three Finger Brown (W)
	Detroit	0	7	2	George Mullin

Highlights

- The first game of the Series ended in a 3–3 tie after 12 innings of play, called due to darkness.
- The Cubs became the first team to sweep a World Series.
- Wild Bill Donovan struck out 12 Tigers in Game 1.
- Cub baserunners stole seven bases in the first Series game.

- The Cubs tied Game 1 in the ninth inning when Harry Steinfeldt, with two outs, scored on a dropped third strike by catcher Boss Schmidt.
- The Cubs stole a total of 16 bases in the five games of the Series.
- In the four games the Cubs won, their pitching staff gave up only three runs.
- Cub centerfielder Jimmy Slagle stole a Series record six bases during the five games. No one would steal more until Lou Brock's seven thefts in the 1967 Series.

Best Efforts

Batting

Average	Harry Steinfeldt .471
Home Runs	——
Triples	Harry Steinfeldt 1
	Claude Rossman 1
	Ty Cobb 1
Doubles	Johnny Evers 2
	Jimmy Sheckard 2
Hits	Harry Steinfeldt 8
	Claude Rossman 8
Runs	Joe Tinker 4
RBIs	Jimmy Slagle 4

Pitching

Wins	Orvie Overall 1–0
	Ed Reulbach 1–0
	Three Finger Brown 1–0
	Jack Pfiester 1–0
ERA	Three Finger Brown 0.00
Strikeouts	Wild Bill Donovan 16
Innings Pitched	Wild Bill Donovan 21

1908

Chicago Cubs 4
Detroit Tigers 1

Line-ups

Chicago Cubs		Detroit Tigers	
1b	Frank Chance	1b	Claude Rossman
2b	Johnny Evers	2b	Germany Schaefer
3b	Harry Steinfeldt	3b	Bill Coughlin
ss	Joe Tinker	ss	Charley O'Leary
lf	Jimmy Sheckard	lf	Matty McIntyre
cf	Solly Hofman	cf	Sam Crawford
rf	Wildfire Schulte	rf	Ty Cobb
c	Johnny Kling	c	Boss Schmidt
mgr	Frank Chance	mgr	Hughie Jennings

		R	H	E	Pitching
Game 1	Chicago	10	14	2	Ed Reulbach, Orvie Overall (7th),
					Three Finger Brown (8th, W)
	Detroit	6	10	4	Ed Killian, Ed Summers (3rd)
Game 2	Detroit	1	4	1	Wild Bill Donovan
	Chicago	6	7	1	Orvie Overall (W)
Game 3	Detroit	8	11	4	George Mullin (W)
	Chicago	3	7	2	Jack Pfiester, Ed Reulbach (9th)
Game 4	Chicago	3	10	0	Three Finger Brown (W)
	Detroit	0	4	1	Ed Summers, George Winter (9th)
Game 5	Chicago	2	10	0	Orvie Overall (W)
	Detroit	0	3	0	Wild Bill Donovan

Highlights

- Ty Cobb rapped out a double and three singles in five at-bats for the Tigers during Game 3.
- Cub hurler Orvie Overall set a Series record of *four* strikeouts in the first inning of Game 5 (the third strike of one got away from the catcher).
- Orvie Overall allowed only three hits and no runs in Game 5, and four hits and one run in Game 2.
- Johnny Evers and Frank Chance each got three hits and drove in a run to account for the Cubs 2–0 victory in Game 5.
- Game 5, played in Detroit, was the shortest in all Series history (1 hour, 25 minutes), and drew the all-time smallest crowd (6,210).
- Frank Chance's eight singles for the Cubs set a record for a five-game Series. He also stole five bases.

Best Efforts

Batting

Average	Frank Chance .421
Home Runs	Joe Tinker 1
Triples	Wildfire Schulte 1
	Solly Hofman 1
Doubles	Jimmy Sheckard 2
Hits	Frank Chance 8
Runs	Johnny Evers 5
RBIs	Joe Tinker 4
	Solly Hofman 4
	Ty Cobb 4

Pitching

Wins	Orvie Overall 2–0
	Three Finger Brown 2–0
ERA	Three Finger Brown 0.00
Strikeouts	Orvie Overall 15
Innings Pitched	Orvie Overall 18⅓

1909

Pittsburgh Pirates 4
Detroit Tigers 3

Line-ups

Pittsburgh Pirates		Detroit Tigers	
1b	Bill Abstein	1b	Tom Jones
2b	Dots Miller	2b	Jim Delahanty
3b	Bobby Byrne	3b	George Moriarty
ss	Honus Wagner	ss	Donie Bush
lf	Fred Clarke	lf	Davy Jones
cf	Tommy Leach	cf	Sam Crawford
rf	Owen Wilson	rf	Ty Cobb
c	George Gibson	c	Boss Schmidt
mgr	Fred Clarke	mgr	Hughie Jennings

		R	H	E	Pitching
Game 1	Detroit	1	6	4	George Mullin
	Pittsburgh	4	5	0	Babe Adams (W)
Game 2	Detroit	7	9	3	Wild Bill Donovan (W)
	Pittsburgh	2	5	1	Howie Camnitz, Vic Willis (3rd)
Game 3	Pittsburgh	8	10	3	Nick Maddox (W)
	Detroit	6	10	5	Ed Summers, Ed Willett (1st), Ralph Works (8th)
Game 4	Pittsburgh	0	5	6	Lefty Leifield, Deacon Phillippe (5th)
	Detroit	5	8	0	George Mullin (W)
Game 5	Detroit	4	6	1	Ed Summers, Ed Willett (8th)
	Pittsburgh	8	10	2	Babe Adams (W)
Game 6	Pittsburgh	4	7	3	Vic Willis, Howie Camnitz (6th), Deacon Phillippe (7th)
	Detroit	5	10	3	George Mullin (W)
Game 7	Pittsburgh	8	7	0	Babe Adams (W)
	Detroit	0	6	3	Wild Bill Donovan, George Mullin (4th)

Highlights

- Babe Adams went the distance in each of his three wins, allowing the Tigers a total of only five runs.
- Honus Wagner stole six bases for the Pirates to tie the Series record set by Jimmy Slagle in 1907.
- Tiger base thief Ty Cobb stole home in Game 2.
- In Game 3, Honus Wagner got three hits, stole three bases (a Series record), and drove in two runs.
- Pirate slugger Fred Clarke hit a three-run homer in the 7th inning of Game 5 to shatter a 3–3 tie.
- The eight runs scored by Tommy Leach of the Pirates set a record for a seven-game Series.

Best Efforts

Batting

Average	Tommy Leach	.360
Home Runs	Fred Clarke	2
Triples	Honus Wagner	1
Doubles	Tommy Leach	4
Hits	Tommy Leach	9
	Jim Delahanty	9
Runs	Tommy Leach	8
RBIs	Fred Clarke	7

Pitching

Wins	Babe Adams	3–0
ERA	Nick Maddox	1.00
Strikeouts	George Mullin	20
Innings Pitched	George Mullin	32

1910

Philadelphia Athletics 4
Chicago Cubs 1

Line-ups

Philadelphia Athletics		Chicago Cubs	
1b	Harry Davis	1b	Frank Chance
2b	Eddie Collins	2b	Heinie Zimmerman
3b	Home Run Baker	3b	Harry Steinfeldt
ss	Jack Barry	ss	Joe Tinker
lf	Bris Lord	lf	Jimmy Sheckard
cf	Amos Strunk	cf	Solly Hofman
rf	Danny Murphy	rf	Wildfire Schulte
c	Ira Thomas	c	Johnny Kling
mgr	Connie Mack	mgr	Frank Chance

		R	H	E	Pitching
Game 1	Chicago	1	3	1	Orvie Overall, Harry McIntire (4th)
	Philadelphia	4	7	2	Chief Bender (W)
Game 2	Chicago	3	8	3	Three Finger Brown, Lew Richie (8th)
	Philadelphia	9	14	4	Jack Coombs (W)
Game 3	Philadelphia	12	15	1	Jack Coombs (W)
	Chicago	5	6	5	Ed Reulbach, Harry McIntire (3rd), Jack Pfiester (3rd)
Game 4	Philadelphia	3	11	3	Chief Bender
	Chicago	4	9	1	King Cole, Three Finger Brown (9th, W)
Game 5	Philadelphia	7	9	1	Jack Coombs (W)
	Chicago	2	9	2	Three Finger Brown

Highlights

- Jack Coombs won three games for the Athletics, going the distance in each.

- Chief Bender hurled a three-hitter against the Cubs in Game 1.
- The 12 runs scored by the Athletics in Game 3 was the most scored in a World Series game up to that time.
- The Athletics scored six runs in the seventh inning of Game 2 on five hits, four of which were doubles.
- Danny Murphy hit a three-run homer to blow open Game 3 for the A's.
- The Cubs were saved from a Philadelphia sweep in Game 4 when Frank Chance tripled in the tying run and Jimmy Sheckard drove in the winner in the tenth.
- Eddie Collins contributed two doubles, a single, two RBIs, and two stolen bases to the A's Series-clinching victory in Game 5.
- The following records (still standing) were set for a five-game Series by Philadelphia players:
    - —six runs scored, by Home Run Baker and Danny Murphy
    - —eight RBIs, by Danny Murphy
    - —nine hits, by Home Run Baker and Eddie Collins
    - —four doubles, by Eddie Collins.

Best Efforts

Batting

Average	Eddie Collins	.429
Home Runs	Danny Murphy	1
Triples	Amos Strunk	1
	Frank Chance	1
Doubles	Eddie Collins	4
Hits	Home Run Baker	9
	Eddie Collins	9
Runs	Home Run Baker	6
	Danny Murphy	6
RBIs	Danny Murphy	9

Pitching

Wins	Jack Coombs	3–0
ERA	Chief Bender	1.93
Strikeouts	Jack Coombs	17
Innings Pitched	Jack Coombs	27

1911

Philadelphia Athletics   4
New York Giants   2

Line-ups

Philadelphia Athletics		**New York Giants**	
1b	Harry Davis	1b	Fred Merkle
2b	Eddie Collins	2b	Larry Doyle
3b	Home Run Baker	3b	Buck Herzog
ss	Jack Barry	ss	Art Fletcher
lf	Bris Lord	lf	Josh Devore
cf	Rube Oldring	cf	Fred Snodgrass
rf	Danny Murphy	rf	Red Murray
c	Ira Thomas	c	Chief Meyers
mgr	Connie Mack	mgr	John McGraw

		R	H	E	Pitching
Game 1	Philadelphia	1	6	2	Chief Bender
	New York	2	5	0	Christy Mathewson (W)
Game 2	New York	1	5	3	Rube Marquard, Doc Crandall (8th)
	Philadelphia	3	4	0	Eddie Plank (W)
Game 3	Philadelphia	3	9	2	Jack Coombs (W)
	New York	2	3	5	Christy Mathewson
Game 4	New York	2	7	3	Christy Mathewson, Hooks Wiltse (8th)
	Philadelphia	4	11	1	Chief Bender (W)
Game 5	Philadelphia	3	7	1	Jack Coombs, Eddie Plank (10th)
	New York	4	9	2	Rube Marquard, Red Ames (4th), Doc Crandall (8th, W)
Game 6	New York	2	4	3	Red Ames, Hooks Wiltse (5th), Rube Marquard (7th)
	Philadelphia	13	13	5	Chief Bender (W)

Highlights

- Chief Bender, the A's ace righthander, struck out 11 batters in Game 1.
- Home Run Baker smashed a two-run homer to provide the winning margin for Philadelphia in Game 2, and hit another four-bagger to tie the score in the ninth inning of Game 3.
- Danny Murphy of the A's slapped a double and three singles in four at-bats in Game 6 and scored three runs.
- The seven runs scored by the Athletics in the seventh inning of Game 6 were the most by one team in any Series inning up to that time, and their total of 13 runs were the most in a single game.
- Chief Bender's 20 strikeouts stands as the all-time record for a six-game Series. He went the distance in each of his three starts.

Best Efforts

Batting

Average	Home Run Baker	.375
Home Runs	Home Run Baker	2
Triples	Larry Doyle	1
Doubles	Jack Barry	4
Hits	Home Run Baker	9
Runs	Home Run Baker	7
RBIs	Home Run Baker	5
	Harry Davis	5

Pitching

Wins	Chief Bender	2–1
ERA	Chief Bender	1.04
Strikeouts	Chief Bender	20
Innings Pitched	Christy Mathewson	27

1912

Boston Red Sox   4
New York Giants   3

Line-ups

Boston Red Sox		**New York Giants**	
1b	Jake Stahl	1b	Fred Merkle
2b	Steve Yerkes	2b	Larry Doyle
3b	Larry Gardner	3b	Buck Herzog
ss	Heinie Wagner	ss	Art Fletcher
lf	Duffy Lewis	lf	Josh Devore
cf	Tris Speaker	cf	Fred Snodgrass
rf	Harry Hooper	rf	Red Murray
c	Hick Cady	c	Chief Meyers
mgr	Jake Stahl	mgr	John McGraw

		R	H	E	Pitching
Game 1	Boston	4	6	1	Smokey Joe Wood (W)
	New York	3	8	1	Jeff Tesreau, Doc Crandall (8th)
Game 2	New York	6	11	5	Christy Mathewson
	Boston	6	10	1	Ray Collins, Charley Hall (8th), Hugh Bedient (11th)
Game 3	New York	2	7	1	Rube Marquard (W)
	Boston	1	7	0	Buck O'Brien, Hugh Bedient (9th)
Game 4	Boston	3	8	1	Smokey Joe Wood (W)
	New York	1	9	1	Jeff Tesreau, Red Ames (8th)
Game 5	New York	1	3	1	Christy Mathewson
	Boston	2	5	1	Hugh Bedient (W)
Game 6	Boston	2	7	2	Buck O'Brien, Ray Collins (2nd)
	New York	5	11	2	Rube Marquard (W)
Game 7	New York	11	16	4	Jeff Tesreau (W)
	Boston	4	9	3	Smokey Joe Wood, Charley Hall (2nd)
Game 8	New York	2	9	2	Christy Mathewson
	Boston	3	8	5	Hugh Bedient, Smokey Joe Wood (8th, W)

Highlights

- Game 2 was declared a stalemate (6–6) after 11 innings because of darkness.
- Smokey Joe Wood of the Red Sox was credited with three wins in the Series, and he struck out 11 in Game 1.
- Hugh Bedient pitched a three-hitter for the Red Sox in Game 5.
- Harry Hooper and Steve Yerkes hit back-to-back triples in Game 5 and scored the Red Sox two runs for the day.
- Christy Mathewson, the Giants' masterful righthander, set down 15 consecutive Boston batters in Game 5 but still lost the game.
- The Giants handed the Series to the Red Sox in the tenth inning of Game 8 when Fred Snodgrass dropped an easy fly ball and then Fred Merkle failed to go after Tris Speaker's easy foul pop-up. (Speaker then singled in the tying run and Larry Gardner drove in the winning run.)
- Buck Herzog's batting average of .400 (12 for 30), slugging average of .600, 12 hits, and four doubles (shared that year with teammate Red Murray) are all records for an eight-game Series.
- The nine singles collected by Giant catcher Chief Meyers was a record for an eight-game Series.

Best Efforts

Batting

Average	Buck Herzog	.400
Home Runs	Larry Gardner	1
	Larry Doyle	1
Triples	Steve Yerkes	2
	Tris Speaker	2
Doubles	Buck Herzog	4
	Red Murray	4
Hits	Buck Herzog	12
Runs	Buck Herzog	6
RBIs	Red Murray	5

Pitching

Wins	Smokey Joe Wood	3–1
ERA	Rube Marquard	0.50
Strikeouts	Smokey Joe Wood	21
Innings Pitched	Christy Mathewson	28⅔

1913

Philadelphia Athletics 4
New York Giants 1

Line-ups

Philadelphia Athletics		New York Giants	
1b	Stuffy McInnis	1b	Fred Merkle
2b	Eddie Collins	2b	Larry Doyle
3b	Home Run Baker	3b	Buck Herzog
ss	Jack Barry	ss	Art Fletcher
lf	Rube Oldring	lf	George Burns
cf	Amos Strunk	cf	Tillie Shafer
rf	Eddie Murphy	rf	Red Murray
c	Wally Schang	c	Larry McLean
mgr	Connie Mack	mgr	John McGraw

		R	H	E	Pitching
Game 1	Philadelphia	6	11	1	Chief Bender (W)
	New York	4	11	0	Rube Marquard, Doc Crandall (6th) Jeff Tesreau (8th)
Game 2	New York	3	7	2	Christy Mathewson (W)
	Philadelphia	0	8	2	Eddie Plank
Game 3	Philadelphia	8	12	1	Joe Bush (W)
	New York	2	5	1	Jeff Tesreau, Doc Crandall (7th)
Game 4	New York	5	8	2	Al Demaree, Rube Marquard (5th)
	Philadelphia	6	9	0	Chief Bender (W)
Game 5	Philadelphia	3	6	1	Eddie Plank (W)
	New York	1	2	2	Christy Mathewson

Highlights

- Home Run Baker got three hits (one a homer) and drove in three runs for the Athletics in Game 1.
- Neither Christy Mathewson nor Eddie Plank gave up a single run in nine full innings of play in Game 2, but Mathewson singled in what proved to be the game-winning run for the Giants in the tenth.
- Eddie Collins collected three hits and three RBIs in Game 3 for Philadelphia.
- A's ace southpaw Eddie Plank hurled a two-hitter in Game 5 and gave up only one base on balls.
- Larry McLean's batting average of .500 (6 for 12) for the Giants is a record for a five-game Series.
- The nine hits by Home Run Baker tied his own record (shared with teammate Eddie Collins) for a five-game Series.
- The two triples clubbed by Eddie Collins set another five-game Series mark.

Best Efforts

Batting

Average	Larry McLean	.500
Home Runs	Home Run Baker	1
	Wally Schang	1
	Fred Merkle	1
Triples	Eddie Collins	2
Doubles	Jack Barry	3
Hits	Home Run Baker	9
Runs	Eddie Collins	5
	Rube Oldring	5
RBIs	Home Run Baker	7

Pitching

Wins	Chief Bender	2–0
ERA	Eddie Plank	0.95
	Christy Mathewson	0.95
Strikeouts	Chief Bender	9
Innings Pitched	Eddie Plank	19
	Christy Mathewson	19

1914

Boston Braves   4
Philadelphia Athletics 0

Line-ups

Boston Braves		**Philadelphia Athletics**	
1b	Butch Schmidt	1b	Stuffy McInnis
2b	Johnny Evers	2b	Eddie Collins
3b	Charlie Deal	3b	Home Run Baker
ss	Rabbit Maranville	ss	Jack Barry
lf	Joe Connolly	lf	Rube Oldring
cf	Possum Whitted	cf	Amos Strunk
rf	Herbie Moran	rf	Eddie Murphy
c	Hank Gowdy	c	Wally Schang
mgr	George Stallings	mgr	Connie Mack

		R	H	E	Pitching
Game 1	Boston	7	11	2	Dick Rudolph (W)
	Philadelphia	1	5	0	Chief Bender, Weldon Wyckoff (6th)
Game 2	Boston	1	7	1	Bill James (W)
	Philadelphia	0	2	1	Eddie Plank
Game 3	Philadelphia	4	8	2	Joe Bush
	Boston	5	9	1	Lefty Tyler, Bill James (11th, W)
Game 4	Philadelphia	1	7	0	Bob Shawkey, Herb Pennock (6th)
	Boston	3	6	0	Dick Rudolph (W)

Highlights

- Braves pitchers allowed only six runs in the four Series games.
- Bill James pitched a two-hit shutout in Game 2 for the Braves, but struck out himself in each of his four appearances at bat.
- Braves catcher Hank Gowdy had a Series slugging average of 1.273, the result of his three doubles, one home run, one triple, and a single. He also collected five walks.
- Joe Bush of the A's went 11 innings in Game 3 but then made a wild throw to third after fielding a bunt in the 12th, allowing the winning run to score.
- The three doubles from the bat of Braves slugger Hank Gowdy set a record for a four-game Series.

Best Efforts

Batting

Average	Hank Gowdy	.545
Home Runs	Hank Gowdy	1
Triples	Hank Gowdy	1
	Possum Whitted	1
Doubles	Hank Gowdy	3
Hits	Johnny Evers	7
Runs	Hank Gowdy	3
RBIs	Hank Gowdy	3
	Rabbit Maranville	3

Pitching

Wins	Dick Rudolph	2–0
	Bill James	2–0
ERA	Bill James	0.00
Strikeouts	Dick Rudolph	15
Innings Pitched	Dick Rudolph	18

1915

Boston Red Sox   4
Philadelphia Phillies   1

Line-ups

Boston Red Sox		**Philadelphia Phillies**	
1b	Dick Hoblitzell	1b	Fred Luderus
2b	Jack Barry	2b	Bert Viehoff
3b	Larry Gardner	3b	Milt Stock
ss	Everett Scott	ss	Dave Bancroft
lf	Duffy Lewis	lf	Possum Whitted
cf	Tris Speaker	cf	Dode Paskert
rf	Harry Hooper	rf	Gavvy Cravath
c	Hick Cady	c	Ed Burns
mgr	Bill Carrigan	mgr	Pat Moran

		R	H	E	Pitching
Game 1	Boston	1	8	1	Ernie Shore
	Philadelphia	3	5	1	Grover Alexander (W)
Game 2	Boston	2	10	0	Rube Foster (W)
	Philadelphia	1	3	1	Erskine Mayer
Game 3	Philadelphia	1	3	0	Grover Alexander
	Boston	2	6	1	Dutch Leonard (W)
Game 4	Philadelphia	1	7	0	George Chalmers
	Boston	2	8	1	Ernie Shore (W)
Game 5	Boston	5	10	1	Rube Foster (W)
	Philadelphia	4	9	1	Erskine Mayer, Eppa Rixey (3rd)

Highlights

- Boston pitchers Rube Foster and Dutch Leonard hurled back-to-back three-hitters in Games 2 and 3.
- Red Sox hurler Rube Foster won Game 2 for himself when he singled in the winning run in the ninth.
- The batting hero of Game 3 was Duffy Lewis whose three hits for the Red Sox included a ninth inning, game-winning single.
- Harry Hooper hit two home runs in Game 5 for the Red Sox, the second of which proved to be the game-winning run in the ninth inning.

Best Efforts

Batting

Average	Duffy Lewis .444
Home Runs	Harry Hooper 2
Triples	Larry Gardner 1
	Tris Speaker 1
	Gavvy Cravath 1
Doubles	Fred Luderus 2
Hits	Duffy Lewis 8
Runs	Harry Hooper 4
RBIs	Fred Luderus 6

Pitching

Wins	Rube Foster 2–0
ERA	Dutch Leonard 1.00
Strikeouts	Rube Foster 13
Innings Pitched	Rube Foster 18

1916

	Boston Red Sox	4
	Brooklyn Robins (Dodgers)	1

Line-ups

	Boston Red Sox		**Brooklyn Robins**
1b	Dick Hoblitzell	1b	Jake Daubert
2b	Hal Janvrin	2b	George Cutshaw
3b	Larry Gardner	3b	Mike Mowrey
ss	Everett Scott	ss	Ivy Olson
lf	Duffy Lewis	lf	Zack Wheat
cf	Tilly Walker	cf	Hy Myers
rf	Harry Hooper	rf	Casey Stengel
c	Pinch Thomas	c	Chief Meyers
mgr	Bill Carrigan	mgr	Wilbert Robinson

		R	H	E	Pitching
Game 1	Brooklyn	5	10	4	Rube Marquard, Jeff Pfeffer (8th)
	Boston	6	8	1	Ernie Shore (W), Carl Mays (9th)
Game 2	Brooklyn	1	6	2	Sherry Smith
	Boston	2	7	1	Babe Ruth (W)
Game 3	Boston	3	7	1	Carl Mays, Rube Foster (6th)
	Brooklyn	4	10	0	Jack Coombs (W), Jeff Pfeffer (7th)
Game 4	Boston	6	10	1	Dutch Leonard (W)
	Brooklyn	2	5	4	Rube Marquard, Larry Cheney (5th), Nap Rucker (8th)
Game 5	Brooklyn	1	3	3	Jeff Pfeffer, Wheezer Dell (8th)
	Boston	4	7	2	Ernie Shore (W)

Highlights

- The Robins rallied with four runs in the ninth inning of Game 1 to come within one run of the Red Sox, but with the bases loaded Brooklyn shortstop Everett Scott made a great play and threw Jake Daubert out from deep short to end the threat.
- Babe Ruth, in his first World Series start (Game 2), went 0 for 5 at bat but did pitch the Red Sox to a one-run, six-hit victory.
- No two pitchers in World Series history opposed each other as long as Babe Ruth and Sherry Smith did in a single game (14 innings in Game 2).
- Game 2 was decided on a pinch-hit single in the bottom of the 14th inning by Del Gainer of the Red Sox (his only at-bat in the Series).
- Larry Gardner hit a three-run, inside-the-park homer to put the Red Sox ahead for good in Game 4.
- Ernie Shore allowed the Brooklyners only three hits in Game 5.
- The six runs scored by Harry Hooper of the Red Sox tied the record for a five-game Series.

Best Efforts

Batting

Average	Casey Stengel	.364
Home Runs	Larry Gardner	2
Triples	(nine players)	1
Doubles	Hal Janvrin	3
Hits	Harry Hooper	7
Runs	Harry Hooper	6
RBIs	Larry Gardner	6

Pitching

Wins	Ernie Shore	2–0
ERA	Babe Ruth	0.64
Strikeouts	Ernie Shore	9
	Rube Marquard	9
Innings Pitched	Ernie Shore	17⅔

1917

Chicago White Sox 4
New York Giants 2

Line-ups

Chicago White Sox		New York Giants	
1b	Chick Gandil	1b	Walter Holke
2b	Eddie Collins	2b	Buck Herzog
3b	Fred McMullin	3b	Heinie Zimmerman
ss	Buck Weaver	ss	Art Fletcher
lf	Shoeless Joe Jackson	lf	George Burns
cf	Happy Felsch	cf	Benny Kauff
rf	Shano Collins	rf	Dave Robertson
c	Ray Schalk	c	Bill Rariden
mgr	Pants Rowland	mgr	John McGraw

		R	H	E	Pitching
Game 1	New York	1	7	1	Slim Sallee
	Chicago	2	7	1	Eddie Cicotte (W)
Game 2	New York	2	8	1	Ferdie Schupp, Fred Anderson (2nd), Pol Perritt (4th), Jeff Tesreau (5th)
	Chicago	7	14	1	Red Faber (W)
Game 3	Chicago	0	5	3	Eddie Cicotte
	New York	2	8	2	Rube Benton (W)
Game 4	Chicago	0	7	0	Red Faber, Dave Danforth (8th)
	New York	5	10	0	Ferdie Shupp (W)
Game 5	New York	5	12	3	Slim Sallee, Pol Perritt (8th)
	Chicago	8	14	6	Reb Russell, Eddie Cicotte (1st), Lefty Williams (7th), Red Faber (8th, W)
Game 6	Chicago	4	7	1	Red Faber (W)
	New York	2	6	3	Rube Benton, Pol Perritt (6th)

Highlights

- White Sox ace Red Faber was credited with three Series wins, including two in a row.
- White Sox batters rapped out 14 hits in both Games 2 and 5.
- Shoeless Joe Jackson went three for three, Buck Weaver three for four, and Eddie Collins stole two bases for the Sox in Game 2.
- Benny Kauff belted two home runs and drove in three runs for the Giants in Game 4.
- The Sox broke a 5–5 tie in the eighth inning of Game 5 when runs were scored consecutively by Shano Collins, Eddie Collins, and Shoeless Joe Jackson.
- Dave Robertson of the Giants had a batting average of .500 (11 for 22), a record for a six-game Series.

Best Efforts

Batting

Average	Dave Robertson .500
Home Runs	Benny Kauff 2
Triples	(four players) 1
Doubles	Walter Holke 2
Hits	Dave Robertson 11
Runs	Eddie Collins 4
	Shoeless Joe Jackson 4
	Happy Felsch 4
RBIs	Chick Gandil 5
	Benny Kauff 5

Pitching

Wins	Red Faber 3–1
ERA	Rube Benton 0.00
Strikeouts	Eddie Cicotte 13
Innings Pitched	Red Faber 27

1918

Boston Red Sox 4
Chicago Cubs 2

Line-ups

Boston Red Sox		Chicago Cubs	
1b	Stuffy McInnis	1b	Fred Merkle
2b	Dave Shean	2b	Charlie Pick
3b	Fred Thomas	3b	Charlie Deal
ss	Everett Scott	ss	Charlie Hollocher
lf	George Whiteman	lf	Les Mann
cf	Amos Strunk	cf	Dode Paskert
rf	Harry Hooper	rf	Max Flack
c	Sam Agnew	c	Bill Killefer
mgr	Ed Barrow	mgr	Fred Mitchell

		R	H	E	Pitching
Game 1	Boston	1	5	0	Babe Ruth (W)
	Chicago	0	6	0	Hippo Vaughn
Game 2	Boston	1	6	1	Joe Bush
	Chicago	3	7	1	Lefty Tyler (W)
Game 3	Boston	2	7	0	Carl Mays (W)
	Chicago	1	7	1	Hippo Vaughn
Game 4	Chicago	2	7	1	Lefty Tyler, Phil Douglas (8th)
	Boston	3	4	0	Babe Ruth (W), Joe Bush (9th)
Game 5	Chicago	3	7	0	Hippo Vaughn (W)
	Boston	0	5	0	Sad Sam Jones
Game 6	Chicago	1	3	2	Lefty Tyler, Claude Hendrix (8th)
	Boston	2	5	0	Carl Mays (W)

Highlights

- Red Sox hurler Babe Ruth shut the Cubs out in Game 1, giving up only six hits.
- Ruth set a World Series mark when he extended his number of scoreless innings pitched to 29⅔.
- With two outs in the ninth of Game 3, Charlie Pick, representing the tying run for the Cubs, stole second, then went to third on a passed ball, but in trying to stretch it to a run-scored was tagged out at the plate.
- Carl Mays allowed the Cubs only three hits in the final game of the Series.
- Although the Red Sox won the Series, they scored only nine runs in six games, one less than the Cubs.

Best Efforts

Batting

Average	Charlie Pick .389
Home Runs	——
Triples	(four players) 1
Doubles	Les Mann 2
Hits	Charlie Pick 7
Runs	(seven players) 2
RBIs	(four players) 2

Pitching

Wins	Carl Mays 2–0
	Babe Ruth 2–0
ERA	Carl Mays 1.00
	Hippo Vaughn 1.00
Strikeouts	Hippo Vaughn 17
Innings Pitched	Hippo Vaughn 27

1919

Cincinnati Reds 5
Chicago White Sox 3

Line-ups

	Cincinnati Reds		Chicago White Sox
1b	Jake Daubert	1b	Chick Gandil
2b	Morrie Rath	2b	Eddie Collins
3b	Heinie Groh	3b	Buck Weaver
ss	Larry Kopf	ss	Swede Risberg
lf	Pat Duncan	lf	Shoeless Joe Jackson
cf	Edd Roush	cf	Happy Felsch
rf	Greasy Neale	rf	Nemo Leibold
c	Bill Rariden	c	Ray Schalk
mgr	Pat Moran	mgr	Kid Gleason

		R	H	E	Pitching
Game 1	Chicago	1	6	1	Eddie Cicotte, Roy Wilkinson (4th), Grover Lowdermilk (8th)
	Cincinnati	9	14	1	Dutch Ruether (W)
Game 2	Chicago	2	10	1	Lefty Williams
	Cincinnati	4	4	2	Slim Sallee (W)
Game 3	Cincinnati	0	3	1	Ray Fisher, Dolf Luque (8th)
	Chicago	3	7	0	Dickie Kerr (W)
Game 4	Cincinnati	2	5	2	Jimmy Ring (W)
	Chicago	0	3	2	Eddie Cicotte
Game 5	Cincinnati	5	4	0	Hod Eller (W)
	Chicago	0	3	3	Lefty Williams, Erskine Mayer (9th)
Game 6	Chicago	5	10	3	Dickie Kerr (W)
	Cincinnati	4	11	0	Dutch Ruether, Jimmy Ring (6th)
Game 7	Chicago	4	10	1	Eddie Cicotte (W)
	Cincinnati	1	7	4	Slim Sallee, Ray Fisher (5th), Dolf Luque (6th)
Game 8	Cincinnati	10	16	2	Hod Eller (W)
	Chicago	5	10	1	Lefty Williams, Bill James (1st), Roy Wilkinson (6th)

Highlights

- Dutch Ruether of the Reds tied a Series record in Game 1 when he slugged two triples (the only pitcher ever to do that). He was also three for three and credited with three RBIs.
- Cincinnati got only four hits to the White Sox 10 in Game 2 but still won.
- Jimmy Ring pitched Cincinnati to a three-hit shutout in Game 4.
- Edd Roush of Cincinnati broke a scoreless tie in the sixth inning of Game 5 by driving in two runs with a triple.
- Hod Eller hurled a three-hit shutout against the Sox in Game 5.
- Chick Gandil drove in what proved to be the Sox winning run in the top of the tenth of Game 6 with a single.
- Edd Roush cracked two doubles and a single, drove in four runs, and scored another two in Game 8 for the Reds. Cincinnati collected a total of 16 hits that game.
- Dickie Kerr won two games for the Sox, one a three-hit shutout, despite the efforts of some of his teammates to throw the games.
- Pat Duncan's eight RBIs for the Reds tied the record for an eight-game Series.

Best Efforts

Batting

Average	Shoeless Joe Jackson	.375
Home Runs	Shoeless Joe Jackson	1
Triples	Larry Kopf	2
	Dutch Ruether	2
Doubles	Buck Weaver	4
Hits	Shoeless Joe Jackson	12
Runs	Heinie Groh	6
	Edd Roush	6
RBIs	Pat Duncan	8

Pitching

Wins	Hod Eller	2–0
	Dickie Kerr	2–0
ERA	Jimmy Ring	0.64
Strikeouts	Hod Eller	15
Innings Pitched	Eddie Cicotte	21⅔

THE TWENTIES ★ ★ ★

The turn of the decade signaled one of the most vivacious periods in American history, and the 1920s was a true age of extremes. It began with Prohibition and ended with the stock market crash. In between, it was the era of flappers and bootleggers, of jazz, speakeasies, and the Charleston, of Harding and Coolidge. People were listening to the music of George Gershwin and Jerome Kern, reading the novels of F. Scott Fitzgerald and Ernest Hemingway, watching on flickering movie screens the antics of Charlie Chaplin and the radiance of Mary Pickford. The talk of the time moved through a variety of topics, some chilling, others hopeful: the Sacco-Vanzetti trial, Ku Klux Klan terrorism in the South, the violent labor strikes, Clarence Darrow's defense of John Scopes in the "Monkey Trial," Dr. Robert Goddard's rocket, Charles Lindberg's flight from New York to Paris aboard the *Spirit of St. Louis,* the new motion picture "talkies," the St. Valentine's Day Massacre in Chicago.

In sports, it was an age of superstars. Reports filled the sportspages with the exploits and triumphs of such greats as Jack Dempsey, Gene Tunney, Red Grange, Notre Dame's Four Horsemen, Bill Tilden, Bobby Jones, Paavo Nurmi, and Johnny Weissmuller. In baseball, of course, there was Babe Ruth who would christen the decade by blasting 54 home runs, more than the *total* hit by any other *team* but one in the major leagues that year. The immortal Sultan of Swat would lead the majors in homers in eight of the 10 years of the 20s. But while Ruth was building his legend, there was a plethora of other sensations playing the game, great hitters like Rogers Hornsby, Ty Cobb, George Sisler, Harry Heilmann, Tris Speaker, Eddie Collins, Pie Traynor, Frankie Frisch, Hack Wilson, and Lou Gehrig, and such masterful hurlers as Walter Johnson, Grover Cleveland Alexander, Lefty Grove, Red Faber, Dazzy Vance, and Ted Lyons.

For baseball devotees, the decade did not begin on the proverbial right foot, however. Instead, in the waning days of the 1920 regular season, the Black Sox scandal was revealed and suddenly the integrity of the sport and of those playing it was shrouded under the darkest of clouds. Baseball, however, surmounted the crisis, much the result of the guidance of Judge Kennesaw Mountain Landis, the baronial overlord who had been appointed commissioner in 1920.

The White Sox were in the thick of the American League pennant race before they were turned Black in September 1920. Midway through that last month of the season, eight of their players were suspended—as it would turn out later, for life—and the team disintegrated. Among the Sox ousted were Shoeless Joe Jackson (hitting .382), Happy Felsh (.338), and Buck Weaver (.333), and pitchers Lefty Williams who had a record of 22–14 and Ed Cicotte, 21–10. Cleveland, under manager/center fielder Tris Speaker, glided in, taking the pennant by two games.

Hall of Famer Zack Wheat, one of the best hitters in all Dodger history, played in the 1916 and 1920 Series for Brooklyn. He batted .333 in the latter.

Zack Wheat
L.F. Brooklyn
Nat'ls

Speaker at 32, was still the Indians best batsman, cracking an impressive .388, only good enough for runner-up in the AL, however, in a year when George Sisler of the St. Louis Browns hit .407. The Indians also had five others batting above the .300 mark: Steve O'Neill (.321), Charlie Jamieson (.319), Elmer Smith (.316), Larry Gardner (.310), and Ray Chapman (.303). (Chapman, however, was killed late in the season when he was hit in the head by a pitch from Yankee hurler Carl Mays.) Cleveland's Jim Bagby was the winningest pitcher in the majors that year (31–12), and Stan Coveleski won 24 and Ray Caldwell, 20, for the Indians.

The Dodgers were back for their second appearance in the Series, having outlasted the Giants to take the flag by seven games. The boys from Brooklyn were not a hard-hitting club; in fact, as a team they batted 26 percentage points below the Indians and had scored 197 fewer runs. Their chief offensive threats were Zack Wheat (.328) and Ed Konetchy (.302). Heading the mound staff for the Dodgers was Burleigh "Ol' Stubblebeard" Grimes who won 23 and lost 11.

Again, it was to be a best-of-nine Series, but it took the Indians only seven games to do away with the Dodgers. Brooklyn batted a meek .205 as a team, averaging only a little over a run a game, and were thoroughly mesmerized by Stan Coveleski who went the distance in three Indian wins, allowing the Dodgers only two runs and 15 hits in 27 innings.

Burleigh "Ol Stubblebeard" Grimes was on the mound for the Dodgers in the 1920 Series, for the St. Louis Cardinals in 1930 and 1931, and for the Chicago Cubs in 1932. His overall record was 3–4. *(Photo courtesy of the National Baseball Hall of Fame)*

The World Series of 1921 saw the beginning of a grand tradition, the New York Yankees were making their maiden appearance. The team that would come to play in and win more World Series by far than any other baseball club had managed to edge past the Cleveland Indians by 4½ games to earn the AL flag. Miller Huggins was manager of the Yankees and Babe Ruth was their focal point. The Bambino had broken his own home run record of 54 that year when he clouted 59 out of various ballparks, had shattered his previous RBI record of 137 by driving in 171 runs, and missed tying his record slugging average of .847 (still the all-time high) by a single percentage point. His batting average of .378 was good enough for third in the AL that year, trailing Tiger su-

A familiar scene—Babe Ruth crosses home plate after swatting a home run. The Sultan of Swat played in three World Series for the Boston Red Sox and seven for the Yanks, posted an overall average of .326, and slammed 15 home runs.

per-bats Harry Heilmann (.394) and Ty Cobb (.389). Ruth also stole 17 bases and pitched the Yankees to a pair of victories.

The Yankees also had .300 hitters in Bob Meusel (.318), Wally Schang (.316), and Aaron Ward (.306). Carl Mays won 27 games while losing only nine for the Yanks, while Waite Hoyt registered 19 wins and Bob Shawkey won 18.

In the National League, John McGraw got his Giants back into postseason play after a three-year hiatus. The Little Napoleon's team overtook the Pittsburgh Pirates and won the pennant by four games. Frankie Frisch was their best hitter in 1921 (.341) and the most successful base thief in either league (49). Also for the Giants, Irish Meusel hit .329, Ross Youngs .327, Frank Snyder .320, Dave Bancroft .318, and George Kelly .308. Art Nehf was the only 20-game winner (20–10).

It was the first Series in which the two pennant winners represented the same city since the Cubs and White Sox went at it in Chicago back in 1906. And it was the very first time that all the games would be played in the same stadium, the Polo Grounds, which was home turf to both teams that year.

The Yankees looked like a cinch to win it after back-to-back shutouts in the first two games. They got their third win in Game 5, but it was a pyrrhic victory because in the battle they lost the services of the Babe due to an injured elbow. The Yankees then proceeded to lose the next three games, giving the Giants their second world championship.

The same two teams were back in 1922, and once again the stadium at the foot of Coogan's Bluff would be the site of all games. The Yankees found it much tougher to get there than the Giants in 1922, however. They had to hold off a fierce-hitting St. Louis Browns team (George Sisler hit .420, the third-highest batting average in major league history, and five other players hit .312 or better). But the Yanks managed to do it, and won the pennant by a single game. Ruth, who had been suspended for the first month of the season by Commissioner Landis for having gone on a postseason barnstorming tour the year before, hit only .315 and 35 homers. Wally Pipp led the Yanks with an average of .329, while Bob Meusel and Wally Schang hit .319 each. Joe Bush won 26 games against only seven losses, Bob Shawkey racked up 20 wins, and Waite Hoyt, 19.

McGraw's Giants had little trouble, taking the NL crown a full seven games ahead of the Cincinnati Reds. The Giants did not have a single 20-game winner in 1922, but they had seven batters who hit above .300: Casey Stengel (.368), Frank Snyder (.343), Ross Youngs and Irish Meusel (.331 each), George Kelly (.328), Frankie Frisch (.327), and Dave Bancroft (.321).

The Series was returned to a seven-game affair in 1922, but it did not go that distance. The Giants swept it four games to zip, although there was a tie game called due to darkness in Game 2. The Giants did it with their hitting, a team average of .309, 103 percentage points above that of the Yanks. Ruth had his worst Series ever, tapping out a weak .118 and no homers. The Giants, however, would not win another world championship for 11 years.

No one came close to the Yankees in 1923. Playing in brandnew Yankee Stadium, "the house that Ruth built," as it was dubbed because of the great power he had in drawing fans out to watch him perform, New York roared through the regular season. They won 98 games and ended up 16 ahead of the second-place Detroit Tigers at the end of the season.

Casey Stengel played for Brooklyn in the 1916 World Series and for the New York Giants in 1922 and 1923. In the latter two he hit .400 and .417 respectively. *(Photo courtesy of the National Baseball Hall of Fame)*

Ruth once again came close to winning the triple crown. His 41 homers and 131 RBIs were league highs, but his average of .393 was 10 points less than the .403 posted by Detroit Tiger Harry Heilmann. Other Yankee hitting was provided by Whitey Witt (.314), Bob Meusel (.313), and Wally Pipp (.304). Sad Sam Jones was the only pitcher to exceed 20 wins (21–8), but Herb Pennock and Joe Bush mustered 19 apiece.

The Giants had a bit tougher go of it in '23 but still managed to take the NL flag by 4½ games over the Cincinnati Reds. At the plate, Frankie Frisch was the most consistent batter, hitting .348. Other notables included Ross Youngs (.336), George Kelly (.307), and Dave Bancroft (.304). No Giant pitcher won more than 16 games that year, however.

John McGraw was thirsting for his third consecutive world championship, Miller Huggins searching for his first. It took the Yanks six games to fulfill Huggins' dream and justify the building of the Bronx edifice known as Yankee Stadium. The 301,430 fans who showed up for the six games was the largest attendance at a Series up to that time.

Despite the power of Ruth and the promise of a young Lou Gehrig, the managerial wisdom of Miller Huggins, and the friendly confines of Yankee Stadium, the Yanks would take a two-year leave of absence from the postseason pageant after the 1923 Series. The reason: The Washington Senators. Under 27-year-old manager/second baseman Bucky Harris, the Senators had surprised everybody and beat the Yankees to the wire by two games. They were paced by 36-year-old Walter Johnson (23–7), who led the league in both strikeouts (158) and shut-outs (6). Washington also had a raft of good hitters: Goose Goslin (.344), Sam Rice (.334), and Joe Judge (.324), among them. None were as awesome as Ruth, however, who again barely missed the triple crown, this time failing in RBIs, his total eight short of Goslin's 129. Ruth led the league with an average of .378, and in four-baggers with 46.

In the National League, the Giants became the first team to win four consecutive pennants. It was an especially close race that year, and when it was over Wilbert Robinson's Brooklyn Dodgers were a scant one-and-a-half games out and Bill McKechnie's Pittsburgh Pirates just three behind. Once again it was New York's consistent hitting that brought them the NL title, their team average of .300 the best in either league. Tops was Ross Youngs, who recorded a career high .356, impressive enough, but far below the .424 hit by St. Louis Cardinal Rogers Hornsby, which stands as the best single season batting average in modern major league history. Frankie Frisch hit .328 for the Giants, and George Kelly, .324; Irish Meusel, .310; and Travis Jackson and Frank Snyder, .302 each. But again they had no hurler who chalked up more than 16 victories.

It was to be John McGraw's last appearance at a World Series, and the memory of it would be a bittersweet one. The Giants played well through the first six games and through 11½ innings of the seventh and final game, only to see it all implode in the bottom of the 12th inning. A bounding ball took a crazy hop and careened over the head of Giant third baseman Freddie Lindstrom, enabling Muddy Ruel to score the game- and series-winning run. It was one of the most exciting, evenly matched clashes in World Series history.

For the first time in the decade, the Yankees, in 1925, were not a part of the AL pennant race, finishing a dismal seventh. In fact, no one was there to trouble the Washington Senators as they easily copped a second straight flag. Connie Mack and his Philadelphia Athletics had come the closest, but they were 8½ games back. Sam Rice batted .350 for the Senators and Goose Goslin, .334; as a whole the team hit .303. Stan Coveleski posted the best record for the Washingtonians, 20–5, with Walter Johnson right behind at 20–7, while Dutch Ruether won 18 and lost only seven.

In the National League the Giants finally fell from grace. De-throning them were the Pittsburgh Pirates, a team that batted .307 and stole a total of 159 bases, both major league highs in 1925. They scored 912 runs, 176 more than the second-place Giants who trailed them by eight-and-a-half games at season's end.

The *lowest* batting average among the Pirates' starting eight was .298 that year, hit by Eddie Moore. The .300 hitters were: Kiki Cuyler (.357), Max Carey (.343), George Grantham (.326), Clyde Barnhart (.325), Pie Traynor (.320), Earl Smith (.313), and Glen Wright (.308). Lee Meadows was the top hurler, 19–10.

It certainly looked like the Senators would take their second straight world championship. They won three of the first four games, but then watched with chagrin as a determined Pirate team surged back to take the remaining three games and the Series cup. It was the Pirates' first world title since 1909.

In 1926, the St. Louis Cardinals had finally gotten their act in order. Under Branch Rickey, they had been bumbling along in the second division for most of the decade, even though they possessed the NL's premier hitter, Rogers Hornsby. Just the year before Hornsby had won the triple crown with a batting average of .403 and totals of 39 home runs and 143 RBIs. Hornsby had also taken the managerial reins from Rickey during the 1925 season, and now in his first full year as skipper had brought St. Louis its first NL pennant. It had not been easy, however, and the Cards got a run for it all the way from the Cincinnati Reds and the Pittsburgh Pirates.

Apparently the extended duties of managing the team detracted from Hornsby's traditional hitting, because his average fell 86 points in 1926 to .317. It was the first time in seven years that he did not win the NL batting crown. The most consistent Cardinal hitter that year was Les Bell with an average of .325, and the most productive slugger was Jim Bottomley who led the league in RBIs (120) and doubles (40) and ran second in home runs with 19. Flint Rhem won 20 games and lost only seven. And Rogers Hornsby had made a crucial acquisition during the season when he obtained 39-year-old Grover Cleveland Alexander, who was still going strong, intimidating batters during the day and bartenders at night.

The Yankees were back in 1926. Babe Ruth had regained his form: .372 average, 47 homers, 145 RBIs, and 139 runs scored, all but the average the best in the AL that year. Lou Gehrig, in his second full season at first base, was coming into his own, batting .313, leading the league with 20 triples, and driving in 107 runs. Herb Pennock knocked down 23 wins against 11 losses and Urban Shocker won another 19. The Cleveland Indians had been the main threat, coming in three games behind the Yanks.

The oddsmakers liked the Yankees, but the sportswriters were not taking Hornsby's Cardinals lightly. And, as it turned out everyone was richly entertained because it was an exciting series, with the momentum exchanged several times. It went the full seven games, and it was in that seventh game that old Grover Cleveland Alexander, after pitching a full game the day before, came out of the bullpen to dramatically save the final one for the Cardinals. More than 328,000 spectators had witnessed the seven games, a record attendance at the time.

The year 1927, however, belonged solely to the Yankees, who put on one of the most memorable displays of baseball magnificence ever. It was not just the year that Babe Ruth hit 60 home runs, drove in 164 runs, scored another 158, and batted .356. It was also the year that Lou Gehrig hit 47 homers, 52 doubles, drove in 175 runs, and batted .373. And the year that Earl Coombs hit .356; Bob Meusel, .337; and Tony Lazzeri, .309. The Yankees bludgeoned their way to the pennant, winning 110 games and leaving all seven of the other AL teams in the debris. The Philadelphia A's were the nearest at the end of the season, a distant 19 games back.

The Pittsburgh Pirates won the dubious honor of meeting the Yankees in the Series by taking the NL flag, one-and-a-half games ahead of the St. Louis Cardinals. The Pirates also had a bevy of good hitters. Paul Waner led the league with an average of .380, his brother Lloyd hit .355, while Pie Traynor slapped a respectable .342. And Carmen Hill won 22 games for them. But they were no match for the awesome New Yorkers and their gilded bats, who took the series in four straight games.

The Yankees fielded virtually

The great Lou Gehrig starred in seven World Series for the Yankees, batted .361, and hit a total of 10 homers.

the same team in 1928 as they had the year before. But they did not sail through the regular season as they had in 1927. The Philadelphia A's gave them a battle royal down to the last days of the season, and came within two-and-a-half games of upsetting the mighty Yankees.

Ruth whacked 54 homers and Gehrig 27; they drove in 142 runs apiece. Gehrig batted .374; Tony Lazzeri, .332; and Ruth, .323. George Pipgras won 24 games for the Yanks and Waite Hoyt, 23.

The Yankees were a heavy favorite to dispose of the St. Louis Cardinals, who had staved off both the New York Giants and the Chicago Cubs for that year's NL flag.

The Cards, now under Bill McKechnie, still had some big names. Grover Cleveland Alexander was there, but he was 41 now. They also had Rabbit Maranville at shortstop, but he was 36. Frankie Frisch was 29, but he only batted .300 that year, the lowest since his first full season back in 1920. Jim Bottomley, on the other hand, had one of his most memorable years and led the league in homers (31), RBIs (136), triples (20), and also batted .325. St. Louis had two 20-game winners, Bill Sherdel (21–10) and Jesse Haines (20–8).

The Series, however, was a repeat of the year before. The Yankees won it easily in four straight, in fact the closest the Cards ever got to them was a 4–1 loss in Game 1. The Yankees became the first team to sweep two consecutive World Series.

But the seemingly invincible Yankees were humbled in the last year of the fabled 20s. And the demeaning process was carried out by baseball elder statesman Connie Mack and his Philadelphia Athletics.

The A's with a pair of great sluggers of their own, Al Simmons and Jimmie Foxx, stunned the reigning champion Yankees by winning 104 games and outdistancing them by a full 18 games. Simmons hit .365 that year as well as contributing 34 home runs and 157 RBIs; Foxx was credited with an average of .354, 33 four-baggers, and 117 runs driven in. In addition, Bing Miller hit .335; Mickey Cochrane, 331; and Mule Haas, .313. George Earnshaw posted a record of 24–8 and Lefty Grove came in with 20–6.

In 1929, the Chicago Cubs finally made it back to the World Series where they had not appeared since 1918. Managed by Joe McCarthy, the Cubbies had added a few bejewelled names to

Two of the game's all-time greats, Rabbit Maranville (left) and Babe Ruth, opposed each other in the 1928 World Series. Maranville hit .308 and Ruth batted .625.

their roster in the two years previous, most prominent of which were Rogers Hornsby and Kiki Cuyler. Hornsby hit .380, swatted 39 homers, and drove in 149 runs for the Cubs of 1929, while Cuyler batted .360 and accounted for 102 RBIs and a league-high 43 stolen bases. The Chicagoans also had hefty slugger Hack Wilson who belted 39 homers, drove in 159 runs, and batted .345; and Riggs Stephenson who batted .362. Pat Malone won 22 games and Charlie Root garnered 19 for the Cubs.

Mack's Athletics, however, silenced the clamorous Cub bats in the '29 Series. Philadelphia pitchers held them to a team average of just .249, 54 percentage points below their regular season average. After five games it was all over, and Connie Mack had his fourth world championship. And with it came to a close one of the most dazzling decades of baseball ever to be played.

1920

Cleveland Indians　　　　5
Brooklyn Robins (Dodgers)　2

Line-ups

Cleveland Indians		**Brooklyn Robins**
1b	Doc Johnston	1b	Ed Konetchy
2b	Bill Wambsganss	2b	Pete Kilduff
3b	Larry Gardner	3b	Jimmy Johnston
ss	Joe Sewell	ss	Ivy Olson
lf	Charlie Jamieson	lf	Zack Wheat
cf	Tris Speaker	cf	Hy Myers
rf	Elmer Smith	rf	Tommy Griffith
c	Steve O'Neill	c	Otto Miller
mgr	Tris Speaker	mgr	Wilbert Robinson

		R	H	E	Pitching
Game 1	Cleveland	3	5	0	Stan Coveleski (W)
	Brooklyn	1	5	1	Rube Marquard, Al Mamaus (7th), Leon Cadore (9th)
Game 2	Cleveland	0	7	1	Jim Bagby, George Uhle (7th)
	Brooklyn	3	7	0	Burleigh Grimes (W)
Game 3	Cleveland	1	3	1	Ray Caldwell, Duster Mails (1st), George Uhle (8th)
	Brooklyn	2	6	1	Sherry Smith (W)
Game 4	Brooklyn	1	5	1	Leon Cadore, Al Mamaux (2nd), Rube Marquard (3rd), Jeff Pfeffer (6th)
	Cleveland	5	12	2	Stan Coveleski (W)
Game 5	Brooklyn	1	13	1	Burleigh Grimes, Clarence Mitchell (4th)
	Cleveland	8	12	2	Jim Bagby (W)
Game 6	Brooklyn	0	3	0	Sherry Smith
	Cleveland	1	7	3	Duster Mails (W)
Game 7	Brooklyn	0	5	2	Burleigh Grimes, Al Mamaux (8th)
	Cleveland	3	7	3	Stan Coveleski (W)

Highlights

- Stan Coveleski hurled three victories for the Indians, tying a Series record. He went the distance in each game and gave up a total of only two runs, 15 hits, and two walks.
- Indian second baseman Bill Wambsganss pulled off the only unassisted triple play in World Series history in Game 5. With runners on first and second, he grabbed Clarence Mitchell's line drive for the first out, stepped on second to retire Pete Kilduff, and then tagged Otto Miller in the basepath between first and second.
- Sherry Smith hurled a three-hitter for the Robins in Game 3, and Duster Mails pitched another for the Indians in Game 6.
- Elmer Smith of the Indians hit the first grand slam homer in Series history in Game 5.
- Jim Bagby of the Indians became the first pitcher to clout a home run in a World Series game when he knocked one out of the park with two men on base in Game 5.

Best Efforts

Batting

Average	Steve O'Neill .333
	Charlie Jamieson .333
	Zack Wheat .333
Home Runs	Elmer Smith 1
	Jim Bagby 1
Triples	Elmer Smith 1
	Tris Speaker 1
	Ed Konetchy 1
Doubles	Steve O'Neill 3
Hits	Zack Wheat 9
Runs	Tris Speaker 6
RBIs	Elmer Smith 5

Pitching

Wins	Stan Coveleski 3–0
ERA	Duster Mails 0.00
Strikeouts	Stan Coveleski 8
Innings Pitched	Stan Coveleski 27

1921

New York Giants 5
New York Yankees 3

Line-ups

New York Giants		**New York Yankees**	
1b	George Kelly	1b	Wally Pipp
2b	Johnny Rawlings	2b	Aaron Ward
3b	Frankie Frisch	3b	Mike McNally
ss	Dave Bancroft	ss	Roger Peckinpaugh
lf	Irish Meusel	lf	Babe Ruth
cf	George Burns	cf	Elmer Miller
rf	Ross Youngs	rf	Bob Meusel
c	Frank Snyder	c	Wally Schang
mgr	John McGraw	mgr	Miller Huggins

		R	H	E	Pitching
Game 1	Yankees	3	7	0	Carl Mays (W)
	Giants	0	5	0	Phil Douglas, Jesse Barnes (9th)
Game 2	Giants	0	2	3	Art Nehf
	Yankees	3	3	0	Waite Hoyt (W)
Game 3	Yankees	5	8	0	Bob Shawkey, Jack Quinn (3rd), Rip Collins (7th), Tom Rogers (7th)
	Giants	13	20	0	Fred Toney, Jesse Barnes (3rd, W)
Game 4	Giants	4	9	1	Phil Douglas (W)
	Yankees	2	7	1	Carl Mays
Game 5	Yankees	3	6	1	Waite Hoyt (W)
	Giants	1	10	1	Art Nehf
Game 6	Giants	8	13	0	Fred Toney, Jesse Barnes (1st, W)
	Yankees	5	7	2	Harry Harper, Bob Shawkey (2nd), Bill Piercy (9th)
Game 7	Yankees	1	8	1	Carl Mays
	Giants	2	6	0	Phil Douglas (W)
Game 8	Giants	1	6	0	Art Nehf (W)
	Yankees	0	4	1	Waite Hoyt

Highlights

- For the first time, a team that won the first two games went on to lose the Series.
- Another first: all games were played in the same ballpark, the Polo Grounds, which in 1921 was serving as the home park for both the Giants and the Yankees in the days before Yankee Stadium was built.
- Waite Hoyt of the Yankees pitched 27 innings without allowing a single earned run, tying the mark set by Christy Mathewson in 1905. Hoyt, however, lost one of the games (Game 8) on an unearned run, scored on an error by shortstop Roger Peckinpaugh.
- The total attendance at eight games—269,976—set a Series mark.
- For the Yankees, Mike McNally stole home in Game 1 and Bob Meusel pilfered it in Game 2.
- Frankie Frisch of the Giants collected a triple and three singles in four at-bats in Game 1, but he neither scored nor drove in a run.
- Babe Ruth tied a Series record when he stole two bases in the same inning, the fifth of Game 2.
- Waite Hoyt gave up only two hits, both singles, in his shutout victory in Game 2.
- The Giants scored eight runs in the seventh inning of Game 3 on eight hits, including a triple and a double from Ross Youngs and a double by Irish Meusel. Their total of 20 hits in the game is a Series mark which still stands.
- Babe Ruth hit the first of his 15 career World Series home runs in Game 4.

Best Efforts

Batting

Average	Frank Snyder	.364
Home Runs	(four players)	1
Triples	(five players)	1
Doubles	George Burns	4
Hits	George Burns	11
Runs	Frankie Frisch	5
RBIs	Irish Meusel	7

Pitching

Wins	Jesse Barnes	2–0
	Phil Douglas	2–1
	Waite Hoyt	2–1
ERA	Waite Hoyt	0.00
Strikeouts	Jesse Barnes	18
	Waite Hoyt	18
Innings Pitched	Waite Hoyt	27

1922

New York Giants 4
New York Yankees 0

Line-ups

New York Giants		New York Yankees	
1b	George Kelly	1b	Wally Pipp
2b	Frankie Frisch	2b	Aaron Ward
3b	Heinie Groh	3b	Joe Dugan
ss	Dave Bancroft	ss	Everett Scott
lf	Irish Meusel	lf	Bob Meusel
cf	Bill Cunningham	cf	Whitey Witt
rf	Ross Youngs	rf	Babe Ruth
c	Frank Snyder	c	Wally Schang
mgr	John McGraw	mgr	Miller Huggins

		R	H	E	Pitching
Game 1	Yankees	2	7	0	Joe Bush, Waite Hoyt (8th)
	Giants	3	11	3	Art Nehf, Rosy Ryan (8th, W)
Game 2	Giants	3	8	1	Jesse Barnes
	Yankees	3	8	0	Bob Shawkey
Game 3	Yankees	0	4	1	Waite Hoyt, Sad Sam Jones (8th)
	Giants	3	12	1	Jack Scott (W)
Game 4	Giants	4	9	1	Hugh McQuillan (W)
	Yankees	3	8	0	Carl Mays, Sad Sam Jones (9th)
Game 5	Yankees	3	5	0	Joe Bush
	Giants	5	10	0	Art Nehf (W)

Highlights

- The Giants became the third team in history to sweep the Series (the others: Chicago Cubs, 1907, and Boston Braves, 1914).
- Babe Ruth turned in his worst Series ever, hitting a paltry .118 (2 for 17), no homers, and only one RBI.

- Aaron Ward hit two home runs to tie the Series standard.
- The nine hits collected by Giant third baseman Heinie Groh tied the mark for a five-game Series (he had one hit in the tie-game).
- The Series marked Giant manager John "Little Napoleon" McGraw's third and last world championship.
- Game 2 ended in a 3–3 tie, called because of darkness after 10 full innings (it was not all that dark, however, and after protests by the fans, baseball commissioner Kenesaw Landis ordered that the game's proceeds ($120,000) be given to charity.
- Jack Scott allowed the Yanks only four hits and one base on balls in his shutout victory in Game 3.

Best Efforts

Batting

Average	Heinie Groh	.474
Home Runs	Aaron Ward	2
Triples	Heinie Groh	1
	Whitey Witt	1
Doubles	(eight players)	1
Hits	Heinie Groh	9
Runs	Heinie Groh	4
	Dave Bancroft	4
	Joe Dugan	4
RBIs	Irish Meusel	7

Pitching

Wins	Art Nehf	1–0
	Jack Scott	1–0
	Hugh McQuillan	1–0
	Rosy Ryan	1–0
ERA	Jack Scott	0.00
Strikeouts	Art Nehf	6
	Jesse Barnes	6
	Joe Bush	6
Innings Pitched	Art Nehf	16

1923

New York Yankees 4
New York Giants 2

Line-ups

New York Yankees		New York Giants	
1b	Wally Pipp	1b	George Kelly
2b	Aaron Ward	2b	Frankie Frisch
3b	Joe Dugan	3b	Heinie Groh
ss	Everett Scott	ss	Dave Bancroft
lf	Bob Meusel	lf	Irish Meusel
cf	Whitey Witt	cf	Casey Stengel
rf	Babe Ruth	rf	Ross Youngs
c	Wally Schang	c	Frank Snyder
mgr	Miller Huggins	mgr	John McGraw

		R	H	E	Pitching
Game 1	Giants	5	8	0	Mule Watson, Rosy Ryan (3rd, W)
	Yankees	4	12	1	Waite Hoyt, Joe Bush (3rd)
Game 2	Yankees	4	10	0	Herb Pennock (W)
	Giants	2	9	2	Hugh McQuillan, Jack Bentley (4th)
Game 3	Giants	1	4	0	Art Nehf (W)
	Yankees	0	6	1	Sad Sam Jones, Joe Bush (9th)
Game 4	Yankees	8	13	1	Bob Shawkey (W), Herb Pennock (8th)
	Giants	4	13	1	Jack Scott, Rosy Ryan, (2nd), Hugh McQuillan (2nd), Claude Jonnard (8th), Virgil Barnes (9th)
Game 5	Giants	1	3	2	Jack Bentley, Jack Scott (2nd), Virgil Barnes (4th), Claude Jonnard (8th)
	Yankees	8	14	0	Joe Bush (W)
Game 6	Yankees	6	5	0	Herb Pennock (W), Sad Sam Jones (8th)
	Giants	4	10	1	Art Nehf, Rosy Ryan (8th)

1923

New York Yankees 4
New York Giants 2

Highlights

- For the first time in history, the same two teams played in their third consecutive World Series.
- The Yankees won the first of a record 22 world championships.
- Babe Ruth became the first batter to hit three home runs in a single Series. Two of them were in Game 2, both solos.
- Bob Meusel of the Yankees set a record for a six-game Series with his eight RBIs.
- Casey Stengel hit an inside-the-park home run in the ninth inning to win Game 1 for the Giants.
- Stengel hit one out of the park in the seventh inning of Game 3 to give the Giants another victory.
- The Yankees scored six runs in the second inning of Game 4 on five hits and a walk, including a triple by Bob Meusel and a double from Whitey Witt.
- Joe Bush hurled a three-hitter for the Yanks in Game 5 (all three were from the bat of Irish Meusel, including a triple and a double).
- Joe Dugan collected a homer and three singles in five at-bats and drove in three runs for the Yankees in Game 5.
- Game 5, played at Yankee Stadium, which had just opened that spring, drew the largest crowd for a Series game up to that time, 62,817.
- Giant first baseman George Kelly set a Series record with 19 put-outs in Game 6.

Best Efforts

Batting

Average	Aaron Ward	.417
Home Runs	Babe Ruth	3
Triples	Bob Meusel	2
Doubles	Joe Dugan	2
	Whitey Witt	2
Hits	Aaron Ward	10
	Frankie Frisch	10
Runs	Babe Ruth	8
RBIs	Bob Meusel	8

Pitching

Wins	Herb Pennock	2–0
ERA	Sad Sam Jones	0.90
Strikeouts	Herb Pennock	8
Innings Pitched	Herb Pennock	17⅓

1924

Line-ups

Washington Senators		New York Giants	
1b	Joe Judge	1b	Bill Terry
2b	Bucky Harris	2b	Frankie Frisch
3b	Ossie Bluege	3b	Freddie Lindstrom
ss	Roger Peckinpaugh	ss	Travis Jackson
lf	Goose Goslin	lf	Hack Wilson
cf	Earl McNeely	cf	George Kelly
rf	Sam Rice	rf	Ross Youngs
c	Muddy Ruel	c	Hank Gowdy
mgr	Bucky Harris	mgr	John McGraw

		R	H	E	Pitching
Game 1	New York	4	14	1	Art Nehf (W)
	Washington	3	10	1	Walter Johnson
Game 2	New York	3	6	0	Jack Bentley
	Washington	4	6	1	Tom Zachary (W), Firpo Marberry (9th)
Game 3	Washington	4	9	2	Firpo Marberry, Allen Russell (4th), Joe Martina (7th), By Speece (8th)
	New York	6	12	0	Hugh McQuillan (W), Rosy Ryan (4th), Claude Jonnard (9th), Mule Watson (9th)
Game 4	Washington	7	13	3	George Mogridge (W), Firpo Marberry (8th)
	New York	4	6	1	Virgil Barnes, Harry Baldwin (6th), Wayland Dean (8th)
Game 5	Washington	2	9	1	Walter Johnson
	New York	6	13	0	Jack Bentley (W), Hugh McQuillan (8th)

		R	H	E	Pitching
Game 6	New York	1	7	1	Art Nehf, Rosy Ryan (8th)
	Washington	2	4	0	Tom Zachary (W)
Game 7	New York	3	8	3	Virgil Barnes, Art Nehf (8th), Hugh McQuillan (9th), Jack Bentley (11th)
	Washington	4	10	4	Curly Odgen, George Mogridge (1st), Firpo Marberry (6th), Walter Johnson (9th, W)

Highlights

- This Series marked the ninth in which Giant pilot John McGraw managed, a service record that stood until Casey Stengel managed the Yankees to ten between 1949 and 1960. It was also the sixth Series McGraw would lose, an unprized record which still stands.
- Goose Goslin hit three home runs for the Senators to tie the mark set by Babe Ruth the year before.
- Giant third baseman Freddie Lindstrom, at 18 years of age, gained the distinction of being the youngest player ever to appear in a World Series game.
- Walter Johnson, after 18 years in the major leagues, made his first Series appearance in Game 1; he struck out 12 Giants, pitched 12 full innings, but lost by a run.
- Homers by Goslin and Bucky Harris and a ninth inning RBI from Roger Peckinpaugh in Game 2 gave the Senators their first World Series win ever.
- Goslin smacked a homer and three singles in four at-bats, drove in four runs, and scored two others in Game 4 for the Senators.
- Freddie Lindstrom rapped out four singles in five at-bats in Game 5 for the Giants.
- The Series was decided in the bottom of the 12th inning of Game 7 when Senator Muddy Ruel, who had doubled, scored when a high hopper hit by Earl McNeely bounced over the head of Giant third baseman Freddie Lindstrom.

Best Efforts

Batting

Average	Bill Terry	.429
Home Runs	Goose Goslin	3
Triples	Bill Terry	1
	Frankie Frisch	1
Doubles	Frankie Frisch	4
Hits	Bucky Harris	11
	Goose Goslin	11
Runs	George Kelly	7
RBIs	Bucky Harris	7
	Goose Goslin	7

Pitching

Wins	Tom Zachary	2–0
ERA	Firpo Marberry	1.13
Strikeouts	Walter Johnson	20
Innings Pitched	Walter Johnson	24

1925

Pittsburgh Pirates   4
Washington Senators   3

Line-ups

Pittsburgh Pirates		Washington Senators	
1b	George Grantham	1b	Joe Judge
2b	Eddie Moore	2b	Bucky Harris
3b	Pie Traynor	3b	Ossie Bluege
ss	Glenn Wright	ss	Roger Peckinpaugh
lf	Clyde Barnhart	lf	Goose Goslin
cf	Max Carey	cf	Sam Rice
rf	Kiki Cuyler	rf	Joe Harris
c	Earl Smith	c	Muddy Ruel
mgr	Bill McKechnie	mgr	Bucky Harris

		R	H	E	Pitching
Game 1	Washington	4	8	1	Walter Johnson (W)
	Pittsburgh	1	5	0	Lee Meadows, Johnny Morrison (9th)
Game 2	Washington	2	8	2	Stan Coveleski
	Pittsburgh	3	7	0	Vic Aldridge (W)
Game 3	Pittsburgh	3	8	3	Ray Kremer
	Washington	4	10	1	Alex Ferguson (W), Firpo Marberry (8th)
Game 4	Pittsburgh	0	6	1	Emil Yde, Johnny Morrison (3rd), Babe Adams (8th)
	Washington	4	12	0	Walter Johnson (W)
Game 5	Pittsburgh	6	13	0	Vic Aldridge (W)
	Washington	3	8	1	Stan Coveleski, Win Ballou (7th), Tom Zachary (8th), Firpo Marberry (9th)

1925

Pittsburgh Pirates   4
Washington Senators   3

		R	H	E	Pitching
Game 6	Washington	2	6	2	Alex Ferguson, Win Ballou (8th)
	Pittsburgh	3	7	1	Ray Kremer (W)
Game 7	Washington	7	7	2	Walter Johnson
	Pittsburgh	9	15	2	Vic Aldridge, Johnny Morrison (1st), Ray Kremer (5th, W), Red Oldham (9th)

Highlights

- The Pirates, after losing three of the first four Series games, rallied to win the major league crown, the first time any team had staged such a comeback.
- Two home run records were set in the Series: the two-team total of 12 and the Senators one-team total of eight.
- The 12 singles rapped out by Senator slugger Sam Rice is still the most ever in a seven-game Series.
- Goose Goslin hit three homers for the Senators, tying the Series mark and becoming the first player ever to do it twice (in back-to-back years).
- Moon Harris also clouted three home runs for the Senators to share in the record.
- Senator shortstop Roger Peckinpaugh set an unenviable record when he committed a total of eight errors in the Series.
- Walter Johnson struck out 10 Pirate batters in Game 1.
- Kiki Cuyler hit a two-run homer in the bottom of the eighth of Game 2 to give the Pirates their first World Series victory since 1909.
- Sam Rice dove into the bleachers and caught Earl Smith's would-be home run in the bottom of the eighth to preserve the lead (and the win) for the Senators in Game 3.
- Cuyler was the hero of the hour again in Game 7 when, with two outs, he doubled to drive in the two winning runs in the bottom of the eighth.
- Max Carey collected four hits in five at-bats, including three doubles, in Game 7 and scored three of the Pirate runs that day.
- The eight doubles swatted by Pirate batters in Game 7 tied a Series record.

Best Efforts

Batting

Average	Max Carey .458
Home Runs	Goose Goslin 3
	Moon Harris 3
Triples	Pie Traynor 2
Doubles	Max Carey 4
Hits	Sam Rice 12
Runs	Eddie Moore 7
RBIs	Kiki Cuyler 6
	Goose Goslin 6
	Moon Harris 6

Pitching

Wins	Vic Aldridge 2–0
	Ray Kremer 2–1
	Walter Johnson 2–1
ERA	Walter Johnson 2.08
Strikeouts	Walter Johnson 15
Innings Pitched	Walter Johnson 26

1926

St. Louis Cardinals 4
New York Yankees 3

Line-ups

St. Louis Cardinals		New York Yankees	
1b	Jim Bottomley	1b	Lou Gehrig
2b	Rogers Hornsby	2b	Tony Lazzeri
3b	Les Bell	3b	Joe Dugan
ss	Tommy Thevenow	ss	Mark Koenig
lf	Chick Hafey	lf	Bob Meusel
cf	Taylor Douthit	cf	Earl Combs
rf	Billy Southworth	rf	Babe Ruth
c	Bob O'Farrell	c	Hank Severeid
mgr	Rogers Hornsby	mgr	Miller Huggins

		R	H	E	Pitching
Game 1	St. Louis	1	3	1	Bill Sherdel, Jesse Haines (8th)
	New York	2	6	0	Herb Pennock (W)
Game 2	St. Louis	6	12	1	Pete Alexander (W)
	New York	2	4	0	Urban Shocker, Bob Shawkey, (8th) Sad Sam Jones (9th)
Game 3	New York	0	5	1	Dutch Ruether, Bob Shawkey (5th), Myles Thomas (8th)
	St. Louis	4	8	0	Jesse Haines (W)
Game 4	New York	10	14	1	Waite Hoyt (W)
	St. Louis	5	14	0	Flint Rhem, Art Reinhart (5th), Hi Bell (5th), Wild Bill Hallahan (7th), Vic Keen (9th)
Game 5	New York	3	9	1	Herb Pennock (W)
	St. Louis	2	7	1	Bill Sherdel
Game 6	St. Louis	10	13	2	Pete Alexander (W)
	New York	2	8	1	Bob Shawkey, Urban Shocker (7th), Myles Thomas (8th)
Game 7	St. Louis	3	8	0	Jesse Haines (W), Pete Alexander (7th)
	New York	2	8	3	Waite Hoyt, Herb Pennock (7th)

Highlights

- Babe Ruth set two Series home run marks: a grand total of four and three in a single contest (Game 4). The 11 walks he drew was also a Series record.
- Grover Cleveland "Pete" Alexander, 39, acquired by the Cardinals in midseason, was credited with two wins and a save.
- Lou Gehrig's first World Series hit, a single, drove in the winning run for the Yanks in Game 1.
- Herb Pennock allowed the Cardinals only three hits in the nine innings of Game 1.
- Alexander, in Game 2, retired the last 21 Yankee batters in a row, striking out 10, and recording his second Series victory (the first was for the Philadelphia Phillies back in 1915).
- Jesse Haines hurled a shutout and hit a two-run homer to beat the Yanks in Game 3.
- In Game 4, Babe Ruth, besides his three homers, drove in four runs and scored another four (the latter a Series record).
- Ruth also became the first player in a World Series to reach first base safely five times in a single game (Game 4: three homers, two walks), and repeated that feat four days later in Game 7 with one homer and four walks.
- Les Bell drove in four runs and Rogers Hornsby three as the Cardinals clobbered the Yankees in Game 6.
- Old pro Pete Alexander, with the Cards clinging to a 3–2 lead, came on in relief in the seventh inning of the final game with the bases loaded, two outs, and clutch hitter Tony Lazzeri at bat. Alexander struck him out and then gave up only a lone base on balls in the eighth and ninth innings to earn for St. Louis their first world championship.

Best Efforts

Batting
Average	Tommy Thevenow .417
Home Runs	Babe Ruth 4
Triples	Billy Southworth 1
	Bob Meusel 1
Doubles	Jim Bottomley 3
Hits	(four players) 10
Runs	Babe Ruth 6
	Billy Southworth 6
RBIs	Les Bell 6

Pitching
Wins	Pete Alexander 2–0
	Jesse Haines 2–0
	Herb Pennock 2–0
ERA	Jesse Haines 1.08
Strikeouts	Pete Alexander 17
Innings Pitched	Herb Pennock 22

1927

New York Yankees 4
Pittsburgh Pirates 0

Line-ups

New York Yankees	Pittsburgh Pirates
1b Lou Gehrig	1b Joe Harris
2b Tony Lazzeri	2b George Grantham
3b Joe Dugan	3b Pie Traynor
ss Mark Koenig	ss Glenn Wright
lf Bob Meusel	lf Clyde Barnhart
cf Earle Combs	cf Lloyd Waner
rf Babe Ruth	rf Paul Waner
c Pat Collins	c Earl Smith
mgr Miller Huggins	mgr Donie Bush

		R	H	E	Pitching
Game 1	New York	5	6	1	Waite Hoyt (W), Wilcy Moore (8th)
	Pittsburgh	4	9	2	Ray Kremer, Johnny Miljus (6th)
Game 2	New York	6	11	0	George Pipgras (W)
	Pittsburgh	2	7	2	Vic Aldridge, Mike Cvengros (8th), Joe Dawson (9th)
Game 3	Pittsburgh	1	3	1	Lee Meadows, Mike Cvengros (7th)
	New York	8	9	0	Herb Pennock (W)
Game 4	Pittsburgh	3	10	1	Carmen Hill, Johnny Miljus (7th)
	New York	4	12	2	Wiley Moore (W)

Highlights

- The Yankees became the first American League team ever to sweep the Series (the Cubs, Braves, and Giants had done it for the National League).
- Lou Gehrig's two triples for the Yanks set a record for a four-game Series.
- Herb Pennock retired 22 Pirate batters in a row in Game 3 before his perfect game was ruptured in the top of the eighth by Pie Traynor's single. He allowed only two more hits in the game.
- Babe Ruth drove in three runs with a homer and Lou Gehrig another two with a triple to pace the Yankee offense in Game 3.
- Pirate reliever John Miljus, with the score tied 3–3 in the bottom of the ninth of Game 4, walked Babe Ruth intentionally to load the bases. He then struck out both Lou Gehrig and Bob Meusel, only to lose it all by throwing a wild pitch while facing Tony Lazzeri which enabled Earle Combs to score the game- and Series-winning run.

Best Efforts

Batting

Average	Mark Koenig	.500
Home Runs	Babe Ruth	2
Triples	Lou Gehrig	2
Doubles	Lou Gehrig	2
	Mark Koenig	2
Hits	Mark Koenig	9
Runs	Earle Combs	6
RBIs	Babe Ruth	7

Pitching

Wins	Wilcy Moore	1–0
	Herb Pennock	1–0
	George Pipgras	1–0
	Waite Hoyt	1–0
ERA	Wilcy Moore	0.84
Strikeouts	Johnny Miljus	6
	Lee Meadows	6
	Carmen Hill	6
Innings Pitched	Wilcy Moore	$10\frac{2}{3}$

1928

Line-ups

New York Yankees		**St. Louis Cardinals**	
1b	Lou Gehrig	1b	Jim Bottomley
2b	Tony Lazzeri	2b	Frankie Frisch
3b	Gene Robertson	3b	Andy High
ss	Mark Koenig	ss	Rabbit Maranville
lf	Bob Meusel	lf	Chick Hafey
cf	Ben Paschal	cf	Taylor Douthit
rf	Babe Ruth	rf	George Harper
c	Benny Bengough	c	Jimmie Wilson
mgr	Miller Huggins	mgr	Bill McKechnie

		R	H	E	Pitching
Game 1	St. Louis	1	3	1	Bill Sherdel, Syl Johnson (8th)
	New York	4	7	0	Waite Hoyte (W)
Game 2	St. Louis	3	4	1	Pete Alexander, Clarence Mitchell (3rd)
	New York	9	8	2	George Pipgras (W)
Game 3	New York	7	7	2	Tom Zachary (W)
	St. Louis	3	9	3	Jesse Haines, Syl Johnson (7th), Flint Rhem (8th)
Game 4	New York	7	15	2	Waite Hoyt (W)
	St. Louis	3	11	0	Bill Sherdel, Pete Alexander (7th)

Highlights

- The Yankees became the first team to sweep two World Series in succession.
- The nine home runs by the Yanks is still the club mark for a four-game Series.

- Babe Ruth's batting average of .625 was (and is) the highest ever recorded in Series history. His nine runs scored, 10 hits, and 22 total bases all stand as the most in a four-game Series.
- Lou Gehrig's slugging average of 1.727 remains the all-time tops in any Series. His nine RBIs is also a record for a four-game Series.
- Gehrig hit four homers to tie Ruth's record for a single Series (it also established a record for a four-game Series).
- Waite Hoyt hurled a three-hitter for New York in Game 1, with his cause aided by Ruth's two doubles and a single and Gehrig's two RBIs.
- Gehrig drove in three runs in both Games 2 and 3. In the latter, he hit two home runs.
- Babe Ruth hit three homers in Game 4 to tie the mark he originally set in 1926. He also accounted for four RBIs and two runs-scored in that game.
- The five Yankee home runs in Game 4—besides Ruth's three, there was one from Gehrig and another from Cedric Durst—is still the most hit by one team in any Series game.
- Hoyt's win in Game 4 was his sixth career Series victory, tying the record set by Chief Bender of the Philadelphia Athletics between 1905 and 1914.

Best Efforts

Batting

Average	Babe Ruth	.625
Home Runs	Lou Gehrig	4
Triples	Jim Bottomley	1
Doubles	Babe Ruth	3
Hits	Babe Ruth	10
Runs	Babe Ruth	9
RBIs	Lou Gehrig	9

Pitching

Wins	Waite Hoyt	2-0
ERA	Waite Hoyt	1.50
Strikeouts	Waite Hoyt	14
Innings Pitched	Waite Hoyt	18

1929

Philadelphia Athletics   4
Chicago Cubs   1

Line-ups

Philadelphia Athletics		**Chicago Cubs**	
1b	Jimmy Foxx	1b	Charlie Grimm
2b	Max Bishop	2b	Rogers Hornsby
3b	Jimmy Dykes	3b	Norm McMillan
ss	Joe Boley	ss	Woody English
lf	Al Simmons	lf	Riggs Stephenson
cf	Mule Haas	cf	Hack Wilson
rf	Bing Miller	rf	Kiki Cuyler
c	Mickey Cochrane	c	Zack Taylor
mgr	Connie Mack	mgr	Joe McCarthy

		R	H	E	Pitching
Game 1	Philadelphia	3	6	1	Howard Ehmke (W)
	Chicago	1	8	2	Charlie Root, Guy Bush (8th)
Game 2	Philadelphia	9	12	0	George Earnshaw (W), Lefty Grove (5th)
	Chicago	3	11	1	Pat Malone, Sheriff Blake (4th), Hal Carlson (6th), Art Nehf (9th)
Game 3	Chicago	3	6	1	Guy Bush (W)
	Philadelphia	1	9	1	George Earnshaw
Game 4	Chicago	8	10	2	Charlie Root, Art Nehf (7th), Sheriff Blake (7th), Pat Malone (7th), Hal Carlson (8th)
	Philadelphia	10	15	2	Jack Quinn, Rube Walberg (6th), Eddie Rommell (7th, W), Lefty Grove (8th)
Game 5	Chicago	2	8	1	Pat Malone
	Philadelphia	3	6	0	Howard Ehmke, Rube Walberg (4th, W)

1929

Philadelphia Athletics   4
Chicago Cubs   1

Highlights

- The Philadelphia Athletics had five players who hit .300 or better in the Series: Jimmy Dykes (.421), Mickey Cochrane (.400), Bing Miller (.368), Jimmy Foxx (.350), and Al Simmons (.300).
- The Cubs, whose batters struck out 50 times in the five-game Series, set a club record for whiffs, while Rogers Hornsby, who fanned eight times in 21 at-bats, set an individual mark.
- The 59 put-outs by the A's Mickey Cochrane was the most ever for a catcher in a five-game Series.
- The six runs scored by Al Simmons also tied a record for a five-game Series.
- Howard Ehmke struck out 13 Cub batters in Game 1 to set a Series record.
- Jimmie Foxx hit home runs in both Games 1 and 2 for the A's.
- Al Simmons drove in four runs in Game 2 with a homer and a single.
- George Earnshaw, who pitched 4⅔ innings, and Lefty Grove, who hurled the other 4⅓ innings for the A's, combined to strike out 13 Cubs in Game 2.
- Earnshaw struck out another 10 Cub batters in Game 3, went the distance, but lost the game.
- The A's, losing 8–0 in Game 4, rallied with 10 runs in the bottom of the seventh, the most ever scored in one Series inning (the record would be tied by the Detroit Tigers in 1968). The A's got 10 hits during the inning, including a home run by Al Simmons and a three-run, inside-the-park homer from Mule Haas. Pinch hitter George Burns got to bat twice in the inning and accounted for two of the A's three outs.
- Losing 2–0 in the bottom of the ninth of Game 5, the A's again came back, this time with three runs to win the game and the Series. The runs were the result of a homer by Mule Haas with Max Bishop on base, then a double by Al Simmons and another to drive him in by Bing Miller.

Best Efforts

Batting

Average	Hack Wilson .471
Home Runs	Jimmy Foxx 2
	Mule Haas 2
	Al Simmons 2
Triples	Rogers Hornsby 1
	Hack Wilson 1
Doubles	Woody English 2
Hits	Hack Wilson 8
	Jimmy Dykes 8
Runs	Al Simmons 6
RBIs	Mule Haas 6

Pitching

Wins	(five players) 1 each
ERA	Guy Bush 0.82
Strikeouts	George Earnshaw 17
Innings Pitched	George Earnshaw 13$\frac{2}{3}$

THE THIRTIES

America went from the passionate and prosperous era of the twenties to the impoverished life of the thirties with incredible speed. The stock market crash of October 1929 hurtled the nation into the Great Depression where it would struggle through a long and desperate decade. Suddenly the jobs were gone and the stores and banks were closing. Bread lines were formed and there were street corner apple peddlers, hobo camps and Hoovervilles, Okies trudging to California, and FDR with his New Deal and fireside chats.

In one dark corner of American society lurked the likes of Al Capone, John Dillinger, Machine Gun Kelly, Pretty Boy Floyd, Ma Barker, and Bonnie and Clyde Barrow. In another there was the glitter and indulgence of the world of Elsa Maxwell, Barbara Hutton, the Vanderbilts, and the teenage debutantes who hung out at the Stork Club and El Morocco and had $150,000 coming-out parties.

But for most, the times were bad. To compensate, there were a variety of things to keep minds off the economy. The golden age of radio entertained with Amos and Andy, Kate Smith, Fred Allen, and Edgar Bergen and Charley McCarthy; while the platinum age of the movies produced such stars of the first magnitude as Will Rogers, Shirley Temple, Clark Gable, Joan Crawford, Fred

Astaire and Ginger Rogers, and the Marx Brothers. There was the music of Irving Berlin and Rodgers and Hart and the swing of the Big Bands of Benny Goodman, Glenn Miller, and the Dorsey brothers.

In the sports world, professional football was gaining a following because greats like Red Grange, Bronko Nagurski, Dutch Clark, and Don Hutson were bringing the fans out to the stadiums. There were famous boxers like Maxey Rosenbloom, Max Schmeling, Jack Sharkey, Barney Ross, and, of course, Joe Louis; great runners like Eddie Tolan, Jesse Owens, and Glenn Cunningham; and other sports celebrities from Babe Didrickson Zaharias to Bobby Riggs.

Still, baseball was the nation's premier pastime. In the first half of the decade there were many fine teams. Connie Mack's Philadelphia A's took a pair of pennants, the Gas House Gang made the St. Louis Cardinals a constant threat, and Mickey Cochrane's Detroit Tigers were always at or near the top. But the second half of the decade belonged solely to the New York Yankees. Under manager Joe McCarthy, the Bronx Bombers took *four* consecutive world championships, winning 16 World Series games while losing just three.

The Yankees were also a force to contend with in 1930. They were playing under new manager Bob Shawkey, hired after the death of Miller Huggins. They led the American League in just about every offensive category: batting average (.309), slugging average (.488), runs (1,062), hits (1,683), homers (152), triples (110), and RBIs (986). Babe Ruth hit 49 homers himself, drove in 153 runs, and batted .359. Lou Gehrig hit .379, batted in 174 runs, and clouted 41 round-trippers. Earle Combs had an average of .344; Bill Dickey, .339; Ben Chapman, .316; and Tony Lazzeri, .303. But remarkably the Yanks, despite all this, ended up in third place, 16 games behind the Phildelphia A's at the end of the season.

The Athletics had clout power, too, although as a team they hit 15 percentage points less than the Yankees. Al Simmons led the league with an average of .381 and he also contributed 36 home runs and 165 RBIs. Jimmie Foxx knocked 37 out of the ballpark, drove in 156 runs, and had a batting average of .335. Catcher Mickey Cochrane hit .357. Where the A's outshone the Yankees was on the pitcher's mound. Lefty Grove was the league's top pitcher that year (28–5) and he chalked up AL highs of 209 strike-

Joe McCarthy managed the Yankees in eight World Series and the Chicago Cubs in one from 1929 through 1943.

outs and nine saves. George Earnshaw also had an impressive year, winning 22 while dropping only 13.

Over in the National League, the Cardinals, now under Gabby Street, beat out Rogers Hornsby's Chicago Cubs by a mere two games to take the flag. As a team,

St. Louis batted .314 and all eight starting hitters were above .300, keynoted by the .373 average of George Watkins. Frankie Frisch hit .346 and Chick Hafey, .336.

But for all the hitting that went on during the regular season, it quickly evaporated in the Series. The Cards hit .200, three percentage points better than the A's, but they lost four of the six games, outscored a total of 21 to 12.

The same two teams were back in 1931, under the same managers. Both had traveled relatively easy roads to get there. The A's won 107 games that year and ended up 13½ ahead of the Yankees, while the Cards, with 101 wins to their credit, beat out the New York Giants by 13 games.

Once again it was Connie Mack's pitching staff that made the difference. Lefty Grove had a fabulous year (31–4), and was named the American League's first MVP. But the A's also had George Earnshaw (21–7), Rube Walberg (20–12), and Roy Mahaffey (15–4) to round out the mound corps. Again Al Simmons led all AL hitters, this time with an average of .390. Mickey Cochrane batted .349 and Mule Haas, .323, while Jimmie Foxx led the club in homers with 30.

The Cardinal pitching staff had improved considerably in 1931. Bill Hallahan was the biggest winner (19–9), while Paul Derringer won 18 and Burleigh Grimes, 17. Chick Hafey led the league with an average of .349 and Jim Bottomley was only a single percentage point behind him. Frankie Frisch stole the most bases in

the NL, 28, and was named MVP, and Sparky Adams hit the most doubles, 46.

And once again it was pitching that determined the baseball world title, only this time the laurels would be strewn on the Cardinal staff, with Hallahan and Grimes rising admirably to the occasion. Pepper Martin's marvelous hitting (.500) was also a crucial factor. And so the Gas House Gang gave Gabby Street his first, and what would prove to be his only, world title, and in so doing denied Connie Mack and his Athletics an unprecedented three straight titles.

In 1932, the Yankees gave more than a hint as to what was in store for major league baseball later in the thirties. Under the pilotship of Joe McCarthy, in his second year, the New Yorkers unseated the Philadelphia A's from the American League throne. Although they were outhit as a team by the A's, both in batting and slugging averages, the Yanks managed to win 13 more games than the Philadelphians. And it was not Babe Ruth and Lou Gehrig who led the league in home runs and RBIs, although the Babe swatted 41 and the Iron Horse drove in 151; instead it was Jimmie Foxx who clouted 58 four-baggers,

Another of the great Yankee sluggers was Tony Lazzeri who played in seven World Series from 1926 through 1938. He batted .262 overall.

inating NL play, found themselves far back in the pack, ending up in a tie for sixth place, 18 games out. It was the Chicago Cubs who held off a challenge from the Pittsburgh Pirates and emerged victorious in the National League. They were managed by their first baseman Charlie Grimm, who replaced Rogers Hornsby at the helm in midseason. The Cubs were far from the best hitting team in the league but they got some consistency in that department from Riggs Stephenson (.324), Billy Herman (.314), Grimm (.307), and Johnny Moore (.305). Pitching was their forte and as a team they produced the lowest ERA in the league (3.44). The staff was spearheaded by Lon Warneke (22-6) and Guy Bush (19-11) and had two 15-game winners in Charlie Root and Pat Malone.

drove 169 runs across the plate, and earned the MVP award for 1932. What prevailed was the steady hitting of Gehrig (.349), Ruth (.341), Earl Combs (.321), Bill Dickey (.321), and Tony Lazzeri (.300), and a well-balanced pitching staff that consisted of Lefty Gomez (24-7), Red Ruffing (18-7), Johnny Allen (17-4), and George Pipgras (16-9).

The Cardinals collapsed in 1932 and, after two years of dom-

Cub pitching, however, was battered to an awful pulp by the heavy bats of the Yanks in the Series. Averaging more than nine runs a game and hitting at a collective clip of .313, the Bronx Bombers sailed through in four straight games, leaving for the record books one of the most lopsided Series ever played. And Joe McCarthy wore the first of what would prove to be seven Series crowns earned in Yankee pinstripes.

In 1933, it was a New York team of a different face that would triumph. The Giants edged the Pirates and the Cubs in a heated pennant race. They had the league's premier pitcher and MVP in Carl Hubbell (23–12), and also got some fine hurling from Hal Schumacher (19–12) and Freddie Fitzsimmons (16–11). But the Giants had only one .300 hitter, first baseman/manager Bill Terry (.322), although they got some power from Mel Ott, who cracked 23 homers and drove in 103 runs.

Their neighbors across the Harlem River did not fare so well. The Yankees lost out to the Washington Senators, who functioned under 26-year-old shortstop/manager Joe Cronin. The Senators had the highest team batting average in the majors that year (.287) and four regulars batted above the .300 mark: Heinie Manush (.336), Joe Kuhel (.322), Cronin (.309), and Buddy Myer (.302). They were also the only team in the majors to sport two 20-game winners, General Crowder (24–15) and Earl Whitehill (22–8).

For all their offensive prowess, however, the Senators could not cope in the Series with "King" Carl Hubbell, who did not give up a single earned run in 20 innings. The Giants breezed through the first two games at the Polo Grounds, suffered a single setback down in Washington, then rebounded to hand the Senators two straight losses before the eyes of their fans in the nation's capital. It was the Giant's fourth world championship and their first since 1922 and the days of John McGraw.

1934 was the year of Dizzy, Daffy, Ducky, Pepper, Ripper, the Lip, and the Fordham Flash. Not the seven dwarfs, they were in reality the core of the St. Louis Cardinals, a team that would come to be known as the Gas House Gang. They were Dizzy and Daffy Dean, Ducky Medwick, Pepper Martin, Ripper Collins, Leo Durocher, and Frankie Frisch. In his first full year as manager, Frisch had raised the club from the second division to the pennant with a sparkling blend of pitching and hitting. Dizzy Dean won 30 games against only seven losses, the first 30-game winner in the National League since Grover Cleveland Alexander chalked up that many for the Phillies back in 1917. Brother Daffy, or Paul, brought in another 19 wins and Tex Carleton, 16. The Diz also led both leagues with his 195 strikeouts and seven shutouts, and was the National League's MVP. Ripper Collins batted .333; Ducky Medwick, .319; Frankie Frisch, .305; and Spud

Davis and Ernie Orsati, .300 apiece. Collins also tied Mel Ott of the Giants for the home run crown that year with 35, and Pepper Martin pilfered the most bases in the NL, 23.

But the Cardinals almost didn't make it to the Series. They had to come from behind in the last few days of the regular season to overtake the reigning champion New York Giants. But they did, and it earned them the right to meet the Detroit Tigers, who were making their first postseason appearance since 1909.

Detroit, too, had a rookie manager, Mickey Cochrane, who brought them out of the second division and all the way to the top in a single year. The Yankees had been the AL favorite; they still had Murderer's Row—Gehrig won the triple crown in 1934, batting .363 with 49 home runs and 165 RBIs, and a 39-year-old Ruth managed 22 four-baggers. But as a team the Yanks hit 22 percentage points less than the .300 posted by the Tigers and as a result ended up second, seven games behind.

For Detroit, six sluggers topped the .300 mark. Best was Charlie Gehringer (.356), followed by Hank Greenberg (.339), Mickey Cochrane (.320), Marv Owen (.317), Jo-Jo White (.313), and

One of Brooklyn's greatest pitchers, Dazzy Vance got to only one World Series, 1934, and that was with the St. Louis Cardinals at the age of 43.

Goose Goslin (.305). Greenberg was also the team's power hitter, contributing 26 home runs and 139 RBIs. The Tiger pitching staff was also the league's finest. There were two 20-game winners in Schoolboy Rowe (24–8) and Tommy Bridges (22–11), and Firpo Marberry and Eldon Auker toted up 15 wins each.

It was an exciting Series, one of the closest ever, at least through the first six games. The Cards and Tigers were even at one game apiece, two games, and three games. The Tigers were a slight favorite in the finale because the game was being played in Detroit.

But, as it turned out, there was no home field advantage. Quite the contrary, the Cardinals exploded for 11 runs on 17 hits, while Dizzy Dean shut out the Tigers, allowing only six well-scattered hits. It was the Cardinals' third world championship.

Detroit would be back the following year, once again humbling the Yankees, although in 1935 they did it by only three games at season's end. Babe Ruth was gone from the Yankees; at 40 he would play part of the season for the Boston Braves in the town where it all began for him 21 years earlier and then retire. But Gehrig, Lazzeri, and Dickey were still clobbering the ball for the Yanks and Gomez and Ruffing were still hurling it. Despite that they just couldn't quite catch the hot-hitting Tigers who once again led the majors with a team batting average of .290.

Hank Greenberg, now 24, truly came into his own for the Tigers in 1935, tying for home run honors with Jimmie Foxx by clouting 36, leading the league with 170 RBIs, while batting .328. He was the game's first unanimous selection as MVP. Also for Detroit, Charlie Gehringer hit .330; Pete Fox, .321; and Mickey Cochrane, .319. Tommy Bridges was the only 20-game winner (21–10) but Schoolboy Rowe accounted for 19 wins; Eldon Auker, 18; and General Crowder, 16.

In the National League, there was a bit of a surprise. Most baseball pundits were predicting either a repeat pennant for the Cardinals or perhaps one for Bill Terry's ever-strong Giants. But neither got the bid to the Series; a darkhorse Chicago Cubs overtook both of them in the last month of the season and, with 100 wins, snatched the flag.

Still under Charlie Grimm, the Cubs had a decidedly different starting line-up from the one he led into the 1932 Series. Gabby Hartnett and Billy Herman still took to the batter's box for them, and Lon Warneke and Charlie Root to the mound, but most of the rest were new faces. Chief among them were Stan Hack, Chuck Klein, Frank Demaree, Augie Galan, Phil Cavarretta, and Bill Lee. Hartnett led the club with a .344 average and Billy Herman was close behind with .341; other .300 hitters included Demaree (.325), Galan (.314), and Hack (.311). Both Lee and Warneke registered 20 wins for the Cubbies and Larry French got 17.

The Tigers, with a well-paced attack, won the Series four games to two, although it should be noted that three of their four wins were decided by a single run. But it was enough and manager/catcher Mickey Cochrane gave Detroit its very first baseball championship.

The Yankees of the first half of the 1930s were a great team but they were impaired under the decline and retirement of an aging Babe Ruth—at least enough to assign them to the ranks of runner-up in all but one of those years. In 1936, they rectified that situation by sending a 21-year-old rookie named Joe DiMaggio into the outfield. Joltin' Joe, as he would come to be known, impressed everybody that first year, at bat and in the field. He hit .323 and batted in 125 runs. His 15 triples tied with teammate Red Rolfe for the best in the majors, his 44 doubles were the most slapped by a Yankee that year, and his 29 homers were exceeded in the AL only by MVP Lou Gehrig (49), Hal Trosky of the Indians (42), and Jimmie Foxx (41) who had moved to the Red Sox.

With DiMaggio joining the lineup, the Yankees, as they would prove during the last four years of the thirties, were unconquerable. The 1936 Yanks were never threatened during the regular season and when it was over the sec-ond-place Detroit Tigers were a distant 19½ games behind them. Bill Dickey's .362 was the club's best; Gehrig hit .354; Red Rolfe, .319; George Selkirk, .308; and Jake Powell, .306. Red Ruffing won 20 games and Monte Pearson, 19.

Bill Dickey was the backstop for the Yankees in eight World Series, from 1932 through 1943, then came back as a coach.

In the National League, the Giants earned the right to make their eleventh postseason appearance and set the stage for the fourth New York intracity Series. The Giants had won two of the three previous encounters, but their dreams for 1936 rested on the arms of their pitchers, who manager Bill Terry hoped could somehow defy the mighty Yankee bats. Key to it was the game's best pitcher, southpaw Carl Hubbell, who had won 26 games for the Giants that year against only six losses, and was the NL MVP. Providing the most offensive punch was Mel Ott, whose 33 homers were the most in the NL that year. He also batted .328 and drove in 135 runs. Other respectable hitters included Joe Moore (.316) and Gus Mancuso (.301).

The Giants had to work to get to the Series, fighting off both the defending pennant holders, the Cubs, and the volatile Cardinals, but they outlasted both and won the flag by five games.

Terry's hopes found some substantiation in the first game of the Series, which was played in the friendly confines of the Polo Grounds. King Carl snuffed the Yanks, allowing them only one run and seven hits, while the Giants sent six runs across the plate. But the next day, in the same ballpark, the Bombers from the Bronx ran ruts into the basepaths as they scored 18 runs on 17 hits. The final score, 18-4, is still the largest margin ever in a Series game. From that point on, it was a cakewalk for the Yanks as they took three of the next four games.

There was no sophomore jinx to plague Joe DiMaggio in 1937; to the contrary, his 46 homers were the most in either league, his 167 RBIs was second only to Tiger Hank Greenberg's 183, and his average of .346 was below only the .371 hit by Detroit's Charley Gehringer and the .351 posted by teammate Lou Gehrig. DiMag's slugging average of .673 was the highest in either league.

The Tigers came a little closer to the Yanks in 1937, but were by no means a threat, finishing up 13 games to the rear. Besides the splendid hitting of DiMaggio and Gehrig, the Yanks got consistency from Bill Dickey (.332) and Myril Hoag (.301), and had two 20-game winners in Lefty Gomez (21-11) and Red Ruffing (20-7).

The Giants also had two 20-game winners in 1937, predictably Carl Hubbell (22-8) and Cliff Melton (20-9). And again Mel Ott was their big stick, rapping out a NL high of 31 home runs, but there were only three .300 hitters that year: Jimmy Ripple (.317), Joe Moore (.310), and Dick Bartell (.306). It was ample, however, to enable them to squeeze ahead of the Cubs and win the pennant by two games.

The oddsmakers, with good cause, leaned heavily toward the Yanks in this fifth World Series to be played within the municipal boundaries of New York City. Carl Hubbell was Bill Terry's choice again to first face the Yankee bats. But unlike the year before, he held little sway, and was knocked out in a seven-run 6th inning. He did come back to win a game for the Giants, but not until the Yanks had already collected three victories. After Hubbell's respite, the Yankees cleaned it up the next day. In total, they outscored the Giants 28-12. It gave manager Joe McCarthy his third world championship and the Yankees their sixth.

The following year, the Yankees would have to travel out to Chicago to collect the title. In one of the great comebacks in major league history, the Cubs, winning 21 of their last 25 games, overtook the Pittsburgh Pirates and claimed the 1938 pennant. Pitching was the name of the game with the Cubs, who were now being managed by their catcher Gabby Hartnett. Bill Lee won 22 and lost only nine while Clay Bryant posted a record of 19-11. They had also acquired Dizzy Dean from the Cardinals but the great righthander was plagued with a troubled arm. Only two Cubs batted over .300, Stan Hack (.320) and Carl Reynolds (.302).

The Yankees, on the other hand, who had encountered nothing resembling a threat in taking their third straight flag, were a veritable powerhouse. As a team, they hit 174 home runs to the Cubs' 65, they outscored the Cubs 966 to 713, and their slugging average was 69 percentage points higher. Seven of the eight batters in the Yankee line-up had home run totals in the double figures; tops among them was DiMaggio with 32, while Gehrig contributed 29; Dickey, 27; Joe Gordon, 25; and Tommy Henrich, 22. DiMag was also the most reliable hitter with an average of .324, while Dickey hit .313 and Red Rolfe, .311. In '38, Red Ruffing headed the pitching roster with a record of 21-7, while Lefty Gomez won 18 games; Monte Pearson, 16; and Spud Chandler, 14. They also had a superb reliever in Johnny Murphy.

The Yankees took the train out to the Windy City and easily dis-

Slugger Tommy Henrich played in four World Series from 1938 through 1949 for New York and was highly respected as a clutch hitter.

posed of the Cubs in the first two Series games, then rode the rails back to New York where they defeated them again in two straight. The Yanks collectively outscored the Cubs 22–9, and the closest the Chicagoans ever came in the four-game Series was their 3–1 loss in Game 1. It was the first time a team had swept the Se-

ries since the Yankees had done it to the Cubs in 1932. The Yankees had now extended their record of Series sweeps to four.

In 1939, for the first time since the early 1920s, Lou Gehrig, at 36, was not in the Yankee line-up. The Iron Horse, after playing in a record 2,130 consecutive games— one that is certain to endure— retired because of an illness that would in two years take his life. Still, the Yankees were as awesome as ever. They virtually sailed through the American League; the second-place Boston Red Sox were 17 games behind at the end of the season. DiMaggio led both leagues with an average of .381, led the Yanks in homers with 30 and 126 RBIs, and was named American League MVP. Rookie Charlie "King Kong" Keller joined DiMag in the outfield and hit .334. Other .300 hitters included Red Rolfe (.329), George Selkirk (.306), and Bill Dickey (.302). Red Ruffing was the only 20-game winner (21–7), and Johnny Murphy saved 19 games, at that time the second most in major league history (Firpo Marberry recorded 22 saves for the Senators in 1926).

In the National League, the Cincinnati Reds won their first pennant in 21 years, beating out the

Cardinals by 4½ games. The Reds were managed by Bill McKechnie and were blessed with two of the most effective pitchers in the game, the league's MVP Bucky Walters, who rang up a record of 27–11, and Paul Derringer, 25–7. The Reds had only two hitters above .300, Frank McCormick (.332) and Ival Goodman (.323). They also got some long-ball hitting from Ernie Lombardi, who smacked 20 home runs.

It had gotten to be routine by 1939. Going into the Series, the only National League hope was to somehow silence the Yankee bats.

And Cincinnati found out quickly and surely, just as the Giants and the Cubs had, that that was not possible. They were able to quiet them somewhat, holding the Yankees to an unprecedentedly low average of .206, but New York still outscored the Reds 20–8 in the four games they played. It was the Yankees fourth world championship in a row, their eighth ever, and their fifth Series sweep.

The era of Ruth and Gehrig was over, but the age of Joltin' Joe DiMaggio, The Yankee Clipper, was just getting underway.

The Yankee Clipper, Joe DiMaggio, laces a hit here. Joltin' Joe starred in 10 World Series for the Yanks, batting overall .271.

1930

Philadelphia Athletics   4
St. Louis Cardinals   2

Line-ups

Philadelphia Athletics		St. Louis Cardinals	
1b	Jimmie Foxx	1b	Jim Bottomley
2b	Max Bishop	2b	Frankie Frisch
3b	Jimmy Dykes	3b	Sparky Adams
ss	Joe Boley	ss	Charlie Gelbert
lf	Al Simmons	lf	Chick Hafey
cf	Mule Haas	cf	Taylor Douthit
rf	Bing Miller	rf	George Watkins
c	Mickey Cochrane	c	Jimmie Wilson
mgr	Connie Mack	mgr	Gabby Street

		R	H	E	Pitching
Game 1	St. Louis	2	9	0	Burleigh Grimes
	Philadelphia	5	5	0	Lefty Grove (W)
Game 2	St. Louis	1	6	2	Flint Rhem, Jim Lindsey (4th), Syl Johnson (7th)
	Philadelphia	6	7	2	George Earnshaw (W)
Game 3	Philadelphia	0	7	0	Rube Walberg, Bill Shores (5th), Jack Quinn (7th)
	St. Louis	5	10	0	Wild Bill Hallahan (W)
Game 4	Philadelphia	1	4	1	Lefty Grove
	St. Louis	3	5	1	Jesse Haines (W)
Game 5	Philadelphia	2	5	0	George Earnshaw, Lefty Groves (8th, W)
	St. Louis	0	3	1	Burleigh Grimes
Game 6	St. Louis	1	5	1	Wild Bill Hallahan, Syl Johnson (3rd), Jim Lindsey (6th), Hi Bell (8th)
	Philadelphia	7	7	0	George Earnshaw (W)

Highlights

- The Athletics, by winning their fifth world championship, tied the Boston Red Sox for the most Series titles.
- As a team, the A's batted only .197, while the Cards hit .200.
- Cardinal slugger Chick Hafey set a six-game Series record by collecting five doubles.
- Frankie Frisch of the Cards broke the record for career World Series hits when he got his 43rd in Game 2, eclipsing Eddie Collins' mark of 42 which had stood since 1919.
- Jimmie Foxx hit a two-run homer in the ninth inning of Game 5 to break open a dual shutout and give the A's a victory.
- George Earnshaw hurled back-to-back wins in Games 5 and 6, pitching a total of 16 innings with only one day's rest.

Best Efforts

Batting

Average	Al Simmons .364	
Home Runs	Al Simmons	2
	Mickey Cochrane	2
Triples	Jimmie Foxx	1
	Mule Haas	1
	Charlie Gelbert	1
Doubles	Chick Hafey	5
Hits	Al Simmons	8
Runs	Max Bishop	5
	Mickey Cochrane	5
RBIs	Jimmy Dykes	5

Pitching

Wins	George Earnshaw	2–0
	Lefty Grove	2–1
ERA	George Earnshaw	0.72
Strikeouts	George Earnshaw	19
Innings Pitched	George Earnshaw	25

1931

St. Louis Cardinals 4
Philadelphia Athletics 3

Line-ups

St. Louis Cardinals		Philadelphia Athletics	
1b	Jim Bottomley	1b	Jimmie Foxx
2b	Frankie Frisch	2b	Max Bishop
3b	Andy High	3b	Jimmy Dykes
ss	Charlie Gelbert	ss	Dib Williams
lf	Chick Hafey	lf	Al Simmons
cf	Pepper Martin	cf	Mule Haas
rf	George Watkins	rf	Bing Miller
c	Jimmie Wilson	c	Mickey Cochrane
mgr	Gabby Street	mgr	Connie Mack

		R	H	E	Pitching
Game 1	Philadelphia	6	11	0	Lefty Grove (W)
	St. Louis	2	12	0	Paul Derringer, Syl Johnson (8th)
Game 2	Philadelphia	0	3	0	George Earnshaw
	St. Louis	2	6	1	Wild Bill Hallahan (W)
Game 3	St. Louis	5	12	0	Burleigh Grimes (W)
	Philadelphia	2	2	0	Lefty Grove, Roy Mahaffey (9th)
Game 4	St. Louis	0	2	1	Syl Johnson, Jim Lindsey (6th), Paul Derringer (8th)
	Philadelphia	3	10	0	George Earnshaw (W)
Game 5	St. Louis	5	12	0	Wild Bill Hallahan (W)
	Philadelphia	1	9	0	Waite Hoyt, Rube Walberg (7th), Eddie Rommel (9th)
Game 6	Philadelphia	8	8	1	Lefty Grove (W)
	St. Louis	1	5	2	Paul Derringer, Syl Johnson (5th), Jim Lindsey (7th), Flint Rhem (9th)

		R	H	E	Pitching
Game 7	Philadelphia	2	7	1	George Earnshaw, Rube Walberg (8th)
	St. Louis	4	5	0	Burleigh Grimes (W), Wild Bill Hallahan (9th)

Highlights

- Pepper Martin of the Cardinals set a standard for a seven-game Series when he batted .500 (12 for 24). Martin also stole five bases.
- The Series was the ninth and last in which Connie Mack managed the A's (his record: 5 wins, 4 defeats).
- Bill Hallahan pitched a three-hit shutout for the Cards in Game 2.
- Burleigh Grimes hurled a two-hitter for the Cardinals in Game 3, and got two hits and drove in two runs to aid his cause.
- George Earnshaw chalked up a two-hit shutout for the A's in Game 4.
- Pepper Martin drove in four of the Cardinals five runs in Game 5 with three hits, including a two-run homer.
- George Watkins hit a two-run round-tripper to provide the winning margin for the Cardinals in Game 7.

Best Efforts

Batting

Average	Pepper Martin	.500
Home Runs	Al Simmons	2
Triples	——	
Doubles	Pepper Martin	4
Hits	Pepper Martin	12
Runs	Pepper Martin	5
RBIs	Al Simmons	8

Pitching

Wins	Burleigh Grimes	2–0
	Bill Hallahan	2–0
	Lefty Grove	2–1
ERA	Bill Hallahan	0.49
Strikeouts	George Earnshaw	20
Innings Pitched	Lefty Grove	26

1932

New York Yankees 4
Chicago Cubs 0

Line-ups

New York Yankees		**Chicago Cubs**	
1b	Lou Gehrig	1b	Charlie Grimm
2b	Tony Lazzeri	2b	Billy Herman
3b	Joe Sewell	3b	Woody English
ss	Frank Crosetti	ss	Billy Jurges
lf	Ben Chapman	lf	Riggs Stephenson
cf	Earle Combs	cf	Johnny Moore
rf	Babe Ruth	rf	Kiki Cuyler
c	Bill Dickey	c	Gabby Hartnett
mgr	Joe McCarthy	mgr	Charlie Grimm

		R	H	E	Pitching
Game 1	Chicago	6	10	1	Guy Bush, Burleigh Grimes (6th), Bob Smith (8th)
	New York	12	8	2	Red Ruffing (W)
Game 2	Chicago	2	9	0	Lon Warneke
	New York	5	10	1	Lefty Gomez (W)
Game 3	New York	7	8	1	George Pipgras (W), Herb Pennock (9th)
	Chicago	5	9	4	Charlie Root, Pat Malone (5th), Jackie May (8th), Bud Tinning (9th)
Game 4	New York	13	19	4	Johnny Allen, Wilcy Moore (1st, W), Herb Pennock (7th)
	Chicago	6	9	1	Guy Bush, Lon Warneke (1st), Jakie May (4th), Bud Tinning (7th), Burleigh Grimes (9th)

1932

New York Yankees 4
Chicago Cubs 0

Highlights

- Yankee manager Joe McCarthy won the first of a record seven world championships (only Casey Stengel would ever manage as many winners).
- The Yankees batted a collective .313, a four-game Series record, and averaged 9.25 runs per game.
- The nine runs scored by Lou Gehrig tied the record for a four-game Series set by Babe Ruth in 1928.
- The Yanks' 45 hits and 36 RBIs set marks for a four-game Series.
- Frank Crosetti's four errors was the most ever in a four-game Series.
- Red Ruffing struck out 10 Cubs in Game 1.
- In Game 3, Ruth and Gehrig hit two home runs each. One of Ruth's, in the fifth inning, was the now legendary blast in which he allegedly pointed to the center field bleachers at Wrigley Field and then belted the next pitch into them.
- The four homers from Ruth and Gehrig in Game 3, along with two others from Kiki Cuyler and Gabby Hartnett of the Cubs, set a single-game record of six four-baggers.
- Yankee pitcher George Pipgras struck out in each of his five at-bats in Game 3, an all-time Series record.
- The 19 hits the Yankees got in Game 4 was one shy of the all-time Series record.
- The Yanks' 32 total bases in Game 4 tied a Series record.
- Four Yankee batters got three hits apiece in Game 4: Earle Combs, Joe Sewell, Tony Lazzeri, and Bill Dickey. Lazzeri drove in four runs, and Combs scored four, the latter tying a Series record.

Best Efforts

Batting

Average	Lou Gehrig	.529
Home Runs	Lou Gehrig	3
Triples	Kiki Cuyler	1
	Mark Koenig	1
Doubles	Ben Chapman	2
	Charlie Grimm	2
Hits	Lou Gehrig	9
Runs	Lou Gehrig	9
RBIs	Lou Gehrig	8

Pitching

Wins	(four players)	1 each
ERA	Lefty Gomez	1.00
Strikeouts	Red Ruffing	10
Innings Pitched	Lon Warneke	10⅔

1933

New York Giants 4
Washington Senators 1

Line-ups

New York Giants		**Washington Senators**	
1b	Bill Terry	1b	Joe Kuhel
2b	Hughie Critz	2b	Buddy Myer
3b	Travis Jackson	3b	Ossie Bluege
ss	Blondy Ryan	ss	Joe Cronin
lf	Joe Moore	lf	Heinie Manush
cf	Kiddo Davis	cf	Fred Schulte
rf	Mel Ott	rf	Goose Goslin
c	Gus Mancuso	c	Luke Sewell
mgr	Bill Terry	mgr	Joe Cronin

		R	H	E	**Pitching**
Game 1	Washington	2	5	3	Lefty Stewart, Jack Russell (3rd), Tommy Thomas (8th)
	New York	4	10	2	Carl Hubbell (W)
Game 2	Washington	1	5	0	General Crowder, Tommy Thomas (6th), Alex McColl (7th)
	New York	6	10	0	Hal Schumacher (W)
Game 3	New York	0	5	0	Freddie Fitzsimmons, Hi Bell (8th)
	Washington	4	9	1	Earl Whitehill (W)
Game 4	New York	2	11	1	Carl Hubbell (W)
	Washington	1	8	0	Monty Weaver, Jack Russell (11th)
Game 5	New York	4	11	1	Hal Schumacher, Dolf Luque (6th, W)
	Washington	3	10	0	General Crowder, Jack Russell (6th)

Highlights

- The Series marked the tenth in which the New York Giants had participated (4–6) and the first they played without John McGraw as their manager.
- Carl Hubbell struck out 10 Senators in Game 1.
- Giant slugger Mel Ott went four for four in Game 1, including a two-run homer, and accounted for three RBIs.
- Lefty O'Doul drove in two runs with a pinch-hit single to give the Giants the lead and trigger a six-run inning in Game 2.
- Blondy Ryan singled in the 11th inning of Game 4 to drive in Travis Jackson with the game-winning run for the Giants.
- Cliff Bolton, pinch hitting for the Senators, grounded into a double play with the bases loaded in the bottom of the 11th of Game 4 to end Washington's chances.
- Fred Schulte hit a three-run homer in the sixth inning of Game 5 to tie the match for the Senators.
- Mel Ott homered into the center field seats in the tenth inning of Game 5 to clinch the Series for the Giants.

Best Efforts

Batting

Average	Mel Ott	.389
Home Runs	Mel Ott	2
Triples	——	
Doubles	(nine players)	1 each
Hits	Mel Ott	7
	Kiddo Davis	7
	Joe Cronin	7
	Fred Schulte	7
Runs	Mel Ott	3
	Travis Jackson	3
RBIs	Mel Ott	4
	Fred Schulte	4

Pitching

Wins	Carl Hubbell	2–0
ERA	Carl Hubbell	0.00
Strikeouts	Carl Hubbell	15
Innings Pitched	Carl Hubbell	20

1934

St. Louis Cardinals 4
Detroit Tigers 3

Line-ups

St. Louis Cardinals		Detroit Tigers	
1b	Ripper Collins	1b	Hank Greenberg
2b	Frankie Frisch	2b	Charlie Gehringer
3b	Pepper Martin	3b	Marv Owen
ss	Leo Durocher	ss	Billy Rogell
lf	Ducky Medwick	lf	Goose Goslin
cf	Ernie Orsatti	cf	Jo-Jo White
rf	Jack Rothrock	rf	Pete Fox
c	Bill DeLancey	c	Mickey Cochrane
mgr	Frankie Frisch	mgr	Mickey Cochrane

		R	H	E	Pitching
Game 1	St. Louis	8	13	2	Dizzy Dean (W)
	Detroit	3	8	5	General Crowder, Firpo Marberry (6th), Chief Hogsett (6th)
Game 2	St. Louis	2	7	3	Bill Hallahan, Bill Walker (9th)
	Detroit	3	7	0	Schoolboy Rowe (W)
Game 3	Detroit	1	8	2	Tommy Bridges, Chief Hogsett (5th)
	St. Louis	4	9	1	Paul Dean (W)
Game 4	Detroit	10	13	1	Eldon Auker (W)
	St. Louis	4	10	5	Tex Carleton, Dazzy Vance (3rd), Bill Walker (5th), Jesse Haines (8th), Jim Mooney (9th)
Game 5	Detroit	3	7	0	Tommy Bridges (W)
	St. Louis	1	7	1	Dizzy Dean, Tex Carleton (9th)
Game 6	St. Louis	4	10	2	Paul Dean (W)
	Detroit	3	7	1	Schoolboy Rowe

		R	H	E	Pitching
Game 7	St. Louis	11	17	1	Dizzy Dean (W)
	Detroit	0	6	3	Eldon Auker, Schoolboy Rowe (3rd), Chief Hogsett (3rd), Tommy Bridges (3rd), Firpo Marberry (8th), General Crowder (9th)

Highlights

- This was the third seven-game World Series in which the Cardinals played, and they won all three.
- The Cards had four players who batted .300 or better in the Series: Ducky Medwick (.379), Ripper Collins (.367), Pepper Martin (.355), and Ernie Orsatti (.318).
- The eight runs scored by Pepper Martin tied the record for a seven-game Series.
- The six doubles whacked by Tiger Pete Fox set a standard for a seven-game Series.
- The Tigers committed a total of five errors in Game 1. Two were by third baseman Marv Owen.
- Medwick got four hits in five at-bats, including a home run, in Game 1.
- Tiger pinch hitter Gene Walker drove in Pete Fox with the tying run in the bottom of the ninth of Game 2. In the bottom of the 12th, Goose Goslin singled to drive in Charlie Gehringer with the game-winning Tiger run.
- Schoolboy Rowe pitched 12 full innings for the Tigers in Game 2.
- Hank Greenberg was four for five in Game 4, including two doubles. He drove in three runs and stole a base as well.
- Leo Durocher got a double and two singles and scored two runs to pace the Cardinals in Game 6.
- Cardinal hurler Paul "Daffy" Dean singled to drive Leo Durocher in with the game-winning run of Game 6.
- The Cards got seven runs in the third inning of Game 7, three of them scoring on Frankie Frisch's bases-loaded double.

Best Efforts

Batting

Average	Ducky Medwick .379
	Charlie Gehringer .379
Home Runs	(four players) 1 each
Triples	(six players) 1 each
Doubles	Pete Fox 6
Hits	Ducky Medwick 11
	Charlie Gehringer 11
	Pepper Martin 11
	Ripper Collins 11
Runs	Pepper Martin 8
RBIs	Hank Greenberg 7

Pitching

Wins	Paul Dean 2–0
	Dizzy Dean 2–1
ERA	Paul Dean 1.00
Strikeouts	Dizzy Dean 17
Innings Pitched	Dizzy Dean 26

1935

Detroit Tigers 4
Chicago Cubs 2

Line-ups

Detroit Tigers		**Chicago Cubs**	
1b	Marv Owen	1b	Phil Cavarretta
2b	Charlie Gehringer	2b	Billy Herman
3b	Flea Clifton	3b	Stan Hack
ss	Billy Rogell	ss	Billy Jurges
lf	Goose Goslin	lf	Augie Galan
cf	Jo-Jo White	cf	Freddie Lindstrom
rf	Pete Fox	rf	Frank Demaree
c	Mickey Cochrane	c	Gabby Hartnett
mgr	Mickey Cochrane	mgr	Charlie Grimm

		R	H	E	Pitching
Game 1	Chicago	3	7	0	Lon Warneke (W)
	Detroit	0	4	3	Schoolboy Rowe
Game 2	Chicago	3	6	1	Charlie Root, Roy Henshaw (1st), Fabian Kowalik (4th)
	Detroit	8	9	2	Tommy Bridges (W)
Game 3	Detroit	6	12	2	Eldon Auker, Chief Hogsett (7th), Schoolboy Rowe (8th, W)
	Chicago	5	10	3	Bill Lee, Lon Warneke (8th), Larry French (10th)
Game 4	Detroit	2	7	0	General Crowder (W)
	Chicago	1	5	2	Tex Carleton, Charlie Root (8th)
Game 5	Detroit	1	7	1	Schoolboy Rowe
	Chicago	3	8	0	Lon Warneke (W), Bill Lee (7th)
Game 6	Chicago	3	12	0	Larry French
	Detroit	4	12	1	Tommy Bridges (W)

Highlights

- The Detroit Tigers won their first world championship after having failed to take the cup in four previous Series appearances. Two of those Series setbacks had been administered by the Cubs (1907 and 1908).
- Lon Warneke hurled a four-hit shutout for the Cubs in Game 1.
- The Tigers scored four runs in the bottom of the first inning of Game 2 on singles from Jo-Jo White and Charlie Gehringer, a double by Mickey Cochrane, and a two-run homer from Hank Greenberg.
- The Cubs scored two runs in the bottom of the ninth of Game 3 to send it into extra innings. The first run came when pinch hitter Ken O'Dea singled to drive in Stan Hack and the second when Chuck Klein scored on a sacrifice fly. The Tigers won it, however, in the 11th when Jo-Jo White got a hit which sent Marv Owen across with the game-winning run.
- Chuck Klein's two-run homer was enough to provide the winning margin in Game 5.
- Goose Goslin singled in the bottom of the ninth of Game 6 to drive in Mickey Cochrane and win the game and the Series for the Tigers.

Best Efforts

Batting

Average	Pete Fox	.385
Home Runs	Frank Demaree	2
Triples	Pete Fox	1
	Billy Herman	1
	Stan Hack	1
Doubles	Charlie Gehringer	3
	Pete Fox	3
Hits	Pete Fox	10
Runs	Charlie Gehringer	4
RBIs	Billy Herman	6

Pitching

Wins	Tommy Bridges	2-0
	Lon Warneke	2-0
ERA	Lon Warneke	0.54
Strikeouts	Schoolboy Rowe	14
Innings Pitched	Schoolboy Rowe	21

1936

New York Yankees 4
New York Giants 2

Line-ups

New York Yankees		New York Giants	
1b	Lou Gehrig	1b	Bill Terry
2b	Tony Lazzeri	2b	Burgess Whitehead
3b	Red Rolfe	3b	Travis Jackson
ss	Frank Crosetti	ss	Dick Bartell
lf	Jake Powell	lf	Joe Moore
cf	Joe DiMaggio	cf	Jimmy Ripple
rf	George Selkirk	rf	Mel Ott
c	Bill Dickey	c	Gus Mancuso
mgr	Joe McCarthy	mgr	Bill Terry

		R	H	E	Pitching
Game 1	Yankees	1	7	2	Red Ruffing
	Giants	6	9	1	Carl Hubbell (W)
Game 2	Yankees	18	17	0	Lefty Gomez (W)
	Giants	4	6	1	Hal Schumacher, Al Smith (3rd), Dick Coffman (3rd), Frank Gabler (5th), Harry Gumbert (9th)
Game 3	Giants	1	11	0	Freddie Fitzsimmons
	Yankees	2	4	0	Bump Hadley (W), Pat Malone (9th)
Game 4	Giants	2	7	1	Carl Hubbell, Frank Gabler (8th)
	Yankees	5	10	1	Monte Pearson (W)
Game 5	Giants	5	8	3	Hal Schumacher (W)
	Yankees	4	10	1	Red Ruffing, Pat Malone (7th)
Game 6	Yankees	13	17	2	Lefty Gomez (W), Johnny Murphy (7th)
	Giants	5	9	1	Freddie Fitzsimmons, Slick Castleman (4th), Dick Coffman (9th), Harry Gumbert (9th)

1936

New York Yankees   4
New York Giants   2

Highlights

- The Yankees and the Giants met for the fourth time in an intracity Series, and the Yanks' triumph evened the record at two successes apiece.
- Red Rolfe's 10 singles for the Yankees set a record for a six-game Series.
- The Yankees' 43 runs scored and 41 RBIs set marks for a six-game Series.
- The Yankee loss in Game 1 ended their 12-game Series winning streak.
- Rookie Joe DiMaggio got the first of what would be 54 career World Series hits when he singled in Game 1.
- The Yankees set a Series standard when they scored 18 runs in Game 2, one that has never been bettered.
- In Game 2, Tony Lazzeri became the second slugger to hit a grand-slam homer in the World Series (Elmer Smith of the Cleveland Indians hit the first back in 1920). Lazzeri and Bill Dickey also drove in five runs each in the massacre of the Giants.
- The four runs Frank Crosetti scored for the Yanks in Game 2 tied a Series mark.
- Crosetti singled to drive in Jake Powell with the game-winning run in the bottom of the eighth of Game 3 to give the Yankees a two-to-one edge in the Series.
- In Game 4, the Yankees scored three runs in the third, two of them off a Lou Gehrig homer, to gain the winning margin.
- Hal Schumacher fanned 10 Yankee batters in Game 5.
- Bill Terry's sacrifice fly in the tenth inning of Game 5 scored Joe Moore and won the game for the Giants.
- The Yankees exploded for seven runs in the top of the ninth of Game 6 to clinch the Series. Their 17 hits matched the total they ran up in Game 2.
- Four Yanks got three hits apiece in Game 6: Red Rolfe, Joe DiMaggio, Jake Powell, and Tony Lazzeri.

Best Efforts

Batting

Average	Jake Powell .455
Home Runs	Lou Gehrig 2
	George Selkirk 2
Triples	George Selkirk 1
Doubles	Joe DiMaggio 3
Hits	Jake Powell 10
	Red Rolfe 10
Runs	Jake Powell 8
RBIs	Lou Gehrig 7
	Tony Lazzeri 7

Pitching

Wins	Lefty Gomez 2–0
ERA	Bump Hadley 1.12
Strikeouts	Red Ruffing 12
Innings Pitched	Carl Hubbell 16

1937

New York Yankees 4
New York Giants 1

Line-ups

New York Yankees		**New York Giants**	
1b	Lou Gehrig	1b	Johnny McCarthy
2b	Tony Lazzeri	2b	Burgess Whitehead
3b	Red Rolfe	3b	Mel Ott
ss	Frank Crosetti	ss	Dick Bartell
lf	Myril Hoag	lf	Joe Moore
cf	Joe DiMaggio	cf	Hank Leiber
rf	George Selkirk	rf	Jimmy Ripple
c	Bill Dickey	c	Harry Danning
mgr	Joe McCarthy	mgr	Bill Terry

		R	H	E	Pitching
Game 1	Giants	1	6	2	Carl Hubbell, Harry Gumbert (6th), Dick Coffman (6th), Al Smith (8th)
	Yankees	8	7	0	Lefty Gomez (W)
Game 2	Giants	1	7	0	Cliff Melton, Harry Gumbert (5th), Dick Coffman (6th)
	Yankees	8	12	0	Red Ruffing (W)
Game 3	Yankees	5	9	0	Monte Pearson (W), Johnny Murphy (9th)
	Giants	1	5	4	Hal Schumacher, Cliff Melton (7th), Don Brennan (9th)
Game 4	Yankees	3	6	0	Bump Hadley, Ivy Andrews (2nd), Kemp Wicker (8th)
	Giants	7	12	3	Carl Hubbell (W)
Game 5	Yankees	4	8	0	Lefty Gomez (W)
	Giants	2	10	0	Cliff Melton, Al Smith (6th), Don Brennan (8th)

Highlights

- The Yankees became the first team to win six world championships with their triumph over the Giants.
- Yank Joe Moore's nine hits tied the record for a five-game Series.
- The Yankees erupted for seven runs in the bottom of the sixth of Game 1, the result of five singles, four walks, and two Giant errors.
- Red Ruffing went the distance for the Yanks in Game 2, striking out eight Giants, and helping his pitching efforts with a double, single, and three RBIs.
- Lou Gehrig hit his tenth and last World Series homer in Game 4. Only four players have ever belted more in the postseason (Mickey Mantle, Babe Ruth, Yogi Berra, and Duke Snider).
- In Game 6, Tony Lazzeri tripled in the fifth and scored what proved to be the game- and Series-winning run when pitcher Lefty Gomez cracked a single.

Best Efforts

Batting

Average	Tony Lazzeri	.400
Home Runs	(five players)	1 each
Triples	(four players)	1 each
Doubles	Red Rolfe	2
	Burgess Whitehead	2
Hits	Joe Moore	9
Runs	George Selkirk	5
RBIs	George Selkirk	6

Pitching

Wins	Lefty Gomez	2–0
ERA	Red Ruffing	1.00
Strikeouts	Lefty Gomez	8
	Red Ruffing	8
Innings Pitched	Lefty Gomez	18

1938

New York Yankees 4
Chicago Cubs 0

Line-ups

New York Yankees		Chicago Cubs	
1b	Lou Gehrig	1b	Ripper Collins
2b	Joe Gordon	2b	Billy Herman
3b	Red Rolfe	3b	Stan Hack
ss	Frank Crosetti	ss	Billy Jurges
lf	George Selkirk	lf	Frank Demaree
cf	Joe DiMaggio	cf	Joe Marty
rf	Tommy Henrich	rf	Phil Cavarretta
c	Bill Dickey	c	Gabby Hartnett
mgr	Joe McCarthy	mgr	Gabby Hartnett

		R	H	E	Pitching
Game 1	New York	3	12	1	Red Ruffing (W)
	Chicago	1	9	1	Bill Lee, Jack Russell (9th)
Game 2	New York	6	7	2	Lefty Gomez (W), Johnny Murphy (8th)
	Chicago	3	11	0	Dizzy Dean, Larry French (9th)
Game 3	Chicago	2	5	1	Clay Bryant, Jack Russell (6th), Larry French (7th)
	New York	5	7	2	Monte Pearson (W)
Game 4	Chicago	3	8	1	Bill Lee, Charlie Root (4th), Vance Page (7th), Larry French (8th), Tex Carleton (8th), Dizzy Dean (8th)
	New York	8	11	1	Red Ruffing (W)

Highlights

- For the fourth time, the Yankees swept the World Series. In their six Series appearances during the span from 1927 through 1938, the Bronx Bombers won 24 of 27 Series games.
- Yankee pilot Joe McCarthy became the first manager ever to win three consecutive World Series.
- The 18 innings Red Ruffing pitched for the Yanks tied the record for a four-game Series.
- Bill Dickey rapped out four singles for the New Yorkers in Game 1.
- The Yankees clinched a victory in Game 2 with two-run homers in the eighth and ninth innings from the bats of Frank Crosetti and Joe DiMaggio.
- Joe Gordon drove in three Yankee runs in Game 3 with a homer and a single.
- Tommy Henrich homered in the sixth inning of Game 4 to provide what would be the game- and Series-winning tally.

Best Efforts

Batting

Average	Joe Marty	.500
Home Runs	(seven players)	1 each
Triples	Frank Crosetti	1
	Gabby Hartnett	1
Doubles	Joe Gordon	2
	Frank Crosetti	2
Hits	Stan Hack	8
Runs	Lou Gehrig	4
	Joe DiMaggio	4
RBIs	Joe Gordon	6
	Frank Crosetti	6

Pitching

Wins	Red Ruffing	2-0
ERA	Monte Pearson	1.00
Strikeouts	Red Ruffing	11
Innings Pitched	Red Ruffing	18

1939

New York Yankees 4
Cincinnati Reds 0

Line-ups

New York Yankees		Cincinnati Reds	
1b	Babe Dahlgren	1b	Frank McCormick
2b	Joe Gordon	2b	Lonny Frey
3b	Red Rolfe	3b	Bill Werber
ss	Frank Crosetti	ss	Billy Myers
lf	George Selkirk	lf	Wally Berger
cf	Joe DiMaggio	cf	Harry Craft
rf	King Kong Keller	rf	Ival Goodman
c	Bill Dickey	c	Ernie Lombardi
mgr	Joe McCarthy	mgr	Bill McKechnie

		R	H	E	Pitching
Game 1	Cincinnati	1	4	0	Paul Derringer
	New York	2	6	0	Red Ruffing (W)
Game 2	Cincinnati	0	2	0	Bucky Walters
	New York	4	9	0	Monte Pearson (W)
Game 3	New York	7	5	1	Lefty Gomez, Bump Hadley (2nd, W)
	Cincinnati	3	10	0	Junior Thompson, Lee Grissom (5th), Whitey Moore (7th)
Game 4	New York	7	7	1	Oral Hildebrand, Steve Sundra (5th), Johnny Murphy (7th, W)
	Cincinnati	4	11	4	Paul Derringer, Bucky Walters (8th)

Highlights

- The Yankees increased their record of World Series sweeps to five (no other team in history has swept more than one).
- The Yanks set a Series standard by winning their fourth straight world title.

- Charlie "King Kong" Keller set an all-time Series record for a rookie by belting three home runs.
- As a team, the Yankees batted only .206, three percentage points better than the Reds.
- With the score tied, 1–1, in the bottom of the ninth of Game 1, King Kong Keller tripled and then scored the game-winning run when Bill Dickey singled.
- Monte Pearson pitched the Yankees to a two-hit shutout in Game 2, and had a no-hitter into the eighth inning where it was spoiled by an Ernie Lombardi single.
- Yankee sluggers hit four home runs in Game 3, two by Keller and one each from DiMaggio and Dickey. Keller drove in four runs that game.
- The Reds committed three errors in the top of the tenth inning of Game 4, which enabled the Yankees to score three runs and win the Series. A double error on a single by DiMaggio—fumbled first by outfielder Ival Goodman, then his throw to the plate was dropped by Ernie Lombardi—allowed both Keller and DiMaggio to score.

Best Efforts

Batting

Average	King Kong Keller	.438
Home Runs	King Kong Keller	3
Triples	King Kong Keller	1
	Billy Myers	1
Doubles	Babe Dahlgren	2
Hits	King Kong Keller	7
Runs	King Kong Keller	8
RBIs	King Kong Keller	6

Pitching

Wins	(four players)	1 each
ERA	Monte Pearson	0.00
Strikeouts	Paul Derringer	9
Innings Pitched	Paul Derringer	15⅓

THE FORTIES

Baseball provided one of the nation's more pleasant diversions from the grim goings-on in Europe when the decade of the 1940s began. Somehow the war over there and the worries most Americans had about the United States becoming involved in it seemed remote when one was sitting in a sun-filled ballpark, drinking a beer, and watching Joe DiMaggio, Hank Greenberg, or Ted Williams hit the ball or Bob Feller, Johnny Vander Meer, or Red Ruffing work their wizardry from the pitcher's mound. That is, at least until the bombing of Pearl Harbor so suddenly altered national priorities.

Major league baseball continued despite the war, but most of the game's luminaries were not on the playing fields between 1942 and 1945. Like most other able-bodied young men they became part of the armed services. In addition to the greats mentioned above, the list of ballplayers-turned-soldiers read like the gilded roster of an All-Star game: Rizzuto, Reese, Reiser, Lyons, Henrich, Lemon, Tebbetts, Mize, Slaughter, Hodges, Spahn, Sain, Dickey, Gehringer, Appling, and Pesky, to name just a few of the several hundred who went off to war.

It was not the same quality

game, for obvious reasons, that was played during the war years. Even the St. Louis Browns won a pennant, and the Yankees went for a couple of years *without* winning one. But fans still came out to the ballparks and others listened to the games on the radio. Soldiers in all the war zones, when they were not otherwise preoccupied, followed the pennant races and the World Series and talked and argued baseball just as they had on street corners and in saloons in the summers before the war.

When the fighting finally stopped, the players came back to don their old uniforms and other young men returned to watch explosions from sluggers' bats instead of those from howitzers and bombs. And the post-war fans were treated to some wonderful baseball. There was the reemergence of the Yankees under Casey Stengel. There was also the rise of the Brooklyn Dodgers, or the "Boys of Summer," as Roger Kahn later dubbed them. A host of new faces arrived on the various diamonds of major league baseball, some of whom would leave their own inimitable marks on the game because of the graceful and spectacular way they could play it. And some, for the first time, would be black, because Branch

Rickey signed Jackie Robinson to a Dodger contract in 1947, an act that would forever destroy the color barrier in baseball.

In 1940, before the war and before Jackie Robinson, however, baseball seemed fully in the hands of Joe McCarthy and his magnificent New York Yankees. They had won four consecutive world championships to round out the 1930s, and appeared a seemingly invincible force because they fielded the same star-studded team in 1940. But there were other fine teams in the American League that year and two of them would prove that the Yankees were mortal, that they could indeed be vanquished. Foremost was the Detroit Tigers, who zoomed from fifth place in 1939 to win the 1940 pennant behind the bats of Hank Greenberg, Charlie Gehringer, Rudy York, Barney McCosky, and Pinky Higgins and on the arms of Bobo Newsom and Schoolboy Rowe. They edged the Cleveland Indians, another superb team, by a single game. The Indians gave it a valiant try, riding behind the blazing fastball of Bob Feller (27-11) that year, who hurled a no-hitter and 261 strikeouts, the most in the AL since Walter Johnson fanned 303 back in 1912. The Yankees made a three-way race of it, mostly the result of Joe DiMaggio's efforts, but ended up two games off the pace at season's end.

DiMag was the only regular to hit over .300 for New York (his .352 was the league's best). In fact, the pennant-claiming Tigers as a team outhit the Yanks .286 to .259. Greenberg was their key slugger, leading the league in homers (41) and RBIs (150) while batting a hefty .340. Rudy York hit another 33 homers and drove in 134 runs and turned in an average of .316. Barney McCosky hit a career-high .340 and Charlie Gehringer batted .313. Bobo Newsom was the only 20-game winner (21-6) but Schoolboy Rowe was impressive at 16-3. It was enough to give manager Del Baker his first and only pennant.

There was no race for the pennant in the National League in 1940. Bill McKechnie's Cincinnati Reds, smarting from the sweep the Yankees pounded on them in the previous World Series, got out in front and stayed there, finishing ahead of the Dodgers by 12 games. The Reds had two 20-game winners that year, Bucky Walters (22-10) and Paul Derringer (20-12). Hitting was not necessarily their strong point—four teams in the NL outhit them in '40—but they had three .300 hitters: Ernie Lombardi (.319), Frank McCormick (.309), and Mike McCormick (.300).

The Tigers were a clear favorite, with their awesome hitting and better-than-average pitching. The Series went seven games, and the Tigers outscored the Reds, 28-22, but the Reds managed to win four of the seven games and in so doing became the first National League team to win the world title since 1934.

The Tigers fell in 1941 as mercurially as they had soared in '40, ending up in a tie for fourth place, 26 games out. The Yankees, on the other hand, returned to their station of preeminence, winning their twelfth American League pennant. No one came close. The Boston Red Sox were in second place, but they were 17 games behind. The BoSox were a fine team, however, and had the splendid bat of Ted Williams, who that year batted .406 and hit 37 home runs, both league highs. They also had such good hitters as Jimmie Foxx, Bobby Doerr, Joe Cronin, and Dom DiMaggio.

But it was the Yankees' year, and especially Joe DiMaggio's. He led the league in RBIs with 125, clouted 30 homers and 43 doubles, batted .357, and set a seemingly untouchable record when he hit safely in 56 consecutive games. DiMag edged out Ted Williams in the balloting for MVP. The Yankees had a whole cast of sluggers: King Kong Keller knocked 33 out of the park and drove in 122 runs, Tommy Henrich accounted for 31 homers, and Joe Gordon another 24. Their team total of 151 home runs was far and away the most in the majors. From the mound they got respectable performances from Lefty Gomez (15–5), Red Ruffing (15–6), and Marius Russo (14–10).

In the National League, the Brooklyn Dodgers, under Leo Durocher, snuck in ahead of the St. Louis Cardinals by 2½ games, and as a result set up the first face-off of what would become the most classic and exciting World Series rivalry in the history of the game. The Dodgers and the Yankees would meet in the Series three times in the 1940s, four times in the 1950s, once in the '60s, twice in the '70s, and once thus far in the '80s.

Durocher's Dodgers were a nice blend of pitching and hitting. Kirby Higbe and Whit Wyatt won 22 games apiece for them and Hugh Casey proved to be a strong and effective relief pitcher. Dolph Camilli, the league's MVP, led the NL in home runs (34) and RBIs (120), and Pistol Pete Reiser took

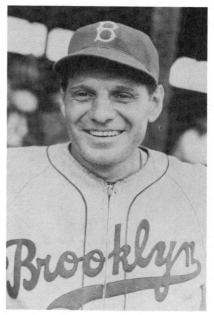

Leo Durocher managed the runner-up Dodgers in the 1941 World Series and the runner-up Giants in 1951. He finally managed the Giants to a championship in 1954.

"Pistol" Pete Reiser played in both the 1941 and 1947 World Series, but the Dodger ace had his best days on the field during the regular seasons.

the batting crown with an average of .343 and also hit the most doubles (39) and triples (17). Ducky Medwick hit .318 and Dixie Walker, .311; and young Pee-Wee Reese was an excellent team leader on the field.

The Yankees, however, were simply too much for them. The Dodgers could barely fetch a hit in the Series, and tapped out a meek .182 team average. The games were close; of the five, three were decided by only a run. But the Yankees were back on top where in the thirties they had gotten so accustomed to being.

It was Boston again in 1942 who gave the Yanks the most pressure. This time they came 10 games closer, but still were nine behind when the season's last out was recorded. The Red Sox even outhit the Yankees by seven percentage points and outslugged them by nine, principally on the bat-swinging of Triple Crown–winner Ted Williams, who led both leagues with an average of .356 and totals of 36 home runs and 137 RBIs.

The Yankees, however, knew how to win ballgames, 103 as a matter of fact. DiMaggio had his poorest year so far in the majors, batting only .305 and drilling a mere 21 home runs, but he led the club in RBIs with 114. Round-trip leader was King Kong Keller who whacked 26, and the team's most consistent hitter was Joe Gordon who recorded an average of .322. Ernie Bonham was the only 20-game winner (21–5), while Spud Chandler turned in a solid performance with a record of 16–5.

The race in the National League was again a close one, and it involved the same two teams as in 1941, the Dodgers and the St. Louis Cardinals. But this time it was the Cards who ended up on top, coming from behind in the late season, holding the lead, and eventually finishing 2½ games better than the "Bums" from Brooklyn, as sportswriters of the time liked to call them.

The descendants of the Gas House Gang had a marvelous line-up, and were now managed by Billy Southworth. In 1942 they had found a wonderful ballplayer in 21-year-old Stan Musial. In his first year as a regular, "the Man," as he would come to be called, batted .315, second only to Enos Slaughter's .318. St. Louis also had All-Star-caliber players in Marty Marion at shortstop, Whitey Kurowski at third, Terry Moore in the outfield, and Walker Cooper behind the plate. Walker's brother, Mort Cooper, hurled the Cards to 22 victories, and earned the National League's MVP award, while Johnny Beazley was just a shade behind with a record of 21–6.

The last time these two teams met in a World Series was back in 1928, when Miller Huggins' Yanks, paced by Ruth and Gehrig, annihilated the Cardinals in four straight games. In '42, the New Yorkers were again the favorite, and when they beat St. Louis in the first game at Sportman's Park it appeared the oddsmakers had called it right. But they hadn't. The Cards turned it around and marched straight through the next four games, leaving a stunned Joe McCarthy in the Yankee dugout—in the six previous World Series that he had managed, the Yankees had won every time. But 1942 belonged to the young stars from St. Louis.

It would be a return engagement for both teams the following year, but the casts would be considerably different because many players had gone off to war. Departed from the Yankee line-up were Joe DiMaggio, Phil Rizzuto, Tommy Henrich, and Red Ruffing most notably. The Cardinals lost Enos Slaughter, Terry Moore, and Johnny Beazley.

Neither team had had any trouble making it back to the postseason classic. The Yanks won their pennant by 13½ games, although they did not have a registered .300 hitter in the starting line-up. Bill Dickey, now 36, had hit .351 but he played in less than half of New York's games that year. King Kong Keller managed to clout an impressive 31 homers, and Spud Chandler won 20 games against only four defeats, to turn in the most noteworthy performances.

The Cards outhit the Yanks by 23 percentage points in 1943, even though they had only two batters above .300. Stan Musial was the biggest show in St. Louis. He led the league in five categories: average (.357), triples (20), doubles (48), hits (220), slugging average (.562); and was named the National League's MVP. Walker Cooper was another .300 hitter with .319. Mort Cooper again headed the staff (21–8) and Max Lanier won 15 for the Cards.

Like the year before, the Series would be decided in five games. But this time it would be with the Yankees back on top, with Joe McCarthy winning his seventh and last world championship. Yankee pitching was overwhelming, allowing the Cardinals an average of less than two runs per game. But now the Yankee dynasty was about to take a four-year recess.

One of the game's great surprises was perpetrated in 1944. The St. Louis Browns, considered a contender by practically no one but their manager Luke Sewell at the beginning of the season, walked off with the AL pennant. The year before the Browns were buried in sixth place, 25 games out at the end of the season. In '44, they were embroiled in one of the hottest flag races ever, battling the Tigers, and they took it on the very last day of the season by a single game.

For the most part, the Browns were a collection of no-names. They did have one .300 hitter, Mike Kreevich (.301). And they possessed a true baseball rarity, a power-hitting shortstop, Vern Stephens, who cracked 20 home runs, second most in the league. Stephens also drove in 109 runs, which was the AL tops that year. Their two most potent forces on the mound were righthanders Nels Potter (19-7) and Jack Kramer (17-13).

The Cardinals made it an intra-city Series by gliding through the National League. They took their second consecutive pennant with no team closer than the Pittsburgh Pirates, who were 14½ games back. The Cards were the first team to win the major league Triple Crown since Connie Mack's Philadelphia A's did it back in 1910, and they did it with team stats of .275 batting average, 2.67 ERA, and .982 fielding average. Stan Musial was the Cardinals' leading hitter with an average of .347, Johnny Hopp hit .336, and Walker Cooper, .317. Again, Mort Cooper had the most effective arm (22-7) but Ted Wilks and Max Lanier each won 17 games and Harry Brecheen, 16.

The Browns hung in during the first three Series games, winning two of them, one in fact quite decisively (6-2). But after that it was all Redbirds, who won three straight and their fifth world championship.

Detroit, the team so narrowly edged out in 1944, reversed the fates in '45, inching by the Washington Senators by 1½ games. Steve O'Neill was managing the Tigers, and he relied chiefly on his pitching staff. His ace was Hal Newhouser, a superb southpaw who led the league with 25 wins against nine losses, an ERA of 1.81, and 212 strikeouts. Newhouser was also named the American League's MVP for the second year in a row. O'Neill could also count on Dizzy Trout who ended up 18-15 for the year. Not a hitter came close to the .300 mark for the Tigers, but they evinced some power in Rudy York who hit 18 homers.

In the National League, the Cardinals faded in the stretch and ended up three games behind the Chicago Cubs. Managed by Charlie Grimm, who had guided them to the World Series back in 1932 and 1935, the Cubs earned the major league Triple Crown in 1945 with a .277 batting average, 2.98 ERA, and .980 fielding average. Phil Cavarretta took the batting crown with an average of .355 and was named the league's MVP. Stan Hack batted .323 and Don Johnson, .302. Hank Wyse posted the best pitching record (22-10) while Claude Passeau won 17 games and Paul Derringer, 16. They had also acquired a very effective righthander in Hank Borowy during the season, whose cumulative record between the Yankees and Cubs that year was 21-7.

The Cubs had not won a world championship since 1908. They had come out second-best in their last six World Series appearances—only the New York Giants had failed in the postseason more often. Charlie Grimm most assuredly did not want to continue the tradition. And it looked like he might break with it when Borowy and Passeau teamed to hurl two shutouts in the first three

games. After that, however, the stars that glittered from the mound wore Tiger uniforms and bore the names Newhouser and Trout. Detroit won it in seven games, their second world title in seven Series appearances.

With the war over in 1946, baseball's big names were back. Where Tommy Holmes of the Boston Braves led the majors in home runs in 1945, Hank Greenberg led them in '46 with 44. Stan Musial was back on top of the batting order with an average of .365. And all of baseball was a little more exciting to watch.

The Red Sox fielded a wonderful team that year, spearheaded by AL MVP Ted Williams, who batted .342, clouted 38 four-baggers, and drove in 123 runs. They also had such respected baseball names in their batting order as Rudy York, Bobby Doerr, Johnny Pesky, Dom DiMaggio, and Wally Moses. On the mound was Boo Ferriss (25-6), Tex Hughson (20-11), Mickey Harris (17-9), and they had a bullpen ace in Bob Klinger. Joe Cronin was their manager and he guided the BoSox to the Al pennant, their first since 1918. And they captured it with little trouble, the Tigers a distant 12 games back when it was over. For the first time since the

World Series was inaugurated back in 1903, the season ended with two teams in a deadlock for first place. In the National League, both the St. Louis Cardinals and the Brooklyn Dodgers had identical records of 96–58. A three-game playoff was called. The Dodgers, under Leo Durocher, had a fine team, with such stellar names in the line-up as Eddie Stanky, PeeWee Reese, Cookie Lavagetto, Dixie Walker, and Carl Furillo. They had also had "Pistol" Pete Reiser, but by playoff time he was out with an injury.

"The People's Cherce," Dixie Walker hit .222 in both the 1941 and 1947 World Series for the "Bums" of Brooklyn.

St. Louis, with Eddie Dyer in his first year as pilot, hardly lacked for first-class names, and foremost was that year's MVP Stan Musial, who led in just about every batting category: average (.365), runs scored (124), hits (228), triples (20), doubles (50), slugging average (.587). Others of particular luster were Marty Marion, Red Schoendienst, Whitey Kurowski, Enos Slaughter, Harry Walker, and Joe Garagiola. Howie Pollett proved to be their top pitcher in '46 with a record of 21–10, but Murry Dickson and Harry Brecheen also won 15 games apiece for the Cards. As a team they became the first ever to win the major league Triple Crown twice when they batted .265, posted an ERA of 3.01, and fielded .980.

Although the playoff was rated a toss-up by the oddsmakers, the Cardinals made it look easy. They won the first game at home, 4–2, then went to Ebbets Field in Brooklyn and pulverized the Dodgers, 8–4. So, the Cardinals would represent the National League in the Series for the fourth time in five years.

It turned out to be one of the most exciting Series ever. The Red Sox snuck out a one-run victory in the first game, then the Cardinals countered with a shutout in the second. Boston came back and shut out the Cards in Game 3, then were decimated when St. Louis got 12 runs and 20 hits in the next game. Then it was Boston's turn, then finally St. Louis. In the seventh and final game, the Red Sox scored two runs, driven in on a clutch double by Dom DiMaggio, in the top of the eighth inning to tie the score at 3–3. But in the bottom of the inning Enos Slaughter singled for the Cards, then with two outs Harry Walker slapped another single and old "Country" raced all the way from first base to the plate on it to score the run that proved to be the game-winner.

A renewal of the rivalry that had been launched in 1941 was the menu for 1947: the Yankees and the Dodgers. Both were under new managers, New York piloted by Bucky Harris and Brooklyn under Burt Shotton.

The Yanks found little competition in the American League. The reigning pennant holders, the Red Sox, fell to third place, even though Ted Williams won the Triple Crown (average of .343, 32 home runs, 114 RBIs). The Tigers came in second behind the .320 hitting of George Kell, but they were still 12 games behind the Yankees. New York outhit and

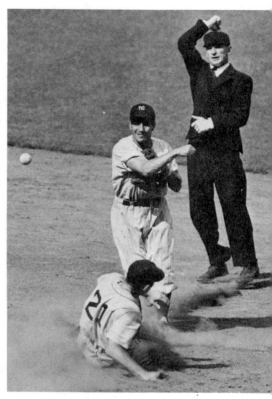

Phil "Scooter" Rizzuto, succeeding with the first half of a double play here, played in nine different World Series for the Yanks from 1941 through 1955.

outslugged all other teams in the American League in 1947, but only two hitters exceeded .300, Joe DiMaggio (.315) and George McQuinn (.304). They did not have a single 20-game winner, although Allie Reynolds came close with a record of 19–8. They did have one of the game's finest relief pitchers in "Fireman" Joe Page, who chalked up 17 saves along with 14 victories.

The Dodgers not only had a

new manager, they also had a new first baseman in Jackie Robinson, the first black to play major league baseball. And he played it well enough to win Rookie of the Year honors. The Dodgers had only two .300 hitters that year, Pete Reiser (.309) and Dixie "the People's Cherce" Walker (.306). Ralph Branca headed the mound force (21–12), Joe Hatten won another 17, and reliever Hugh Casey was credited with 18 saves. It all combined to put the Dodgers five games ahead of the St. Louis Cardinals by season's end.

For the third year in a row, the Series was a hectic, exciting, seven-game affair, keynoted by hard-hitting and some very close games. In the end, Yankee power prevailed and the bombers from the Bronx walked away wearing their eleventh world crown.

The city of New York would not see a World Series in 1948, however, as both of the '47 Series contenders fell to third place in their respective leagues. The Yanks were in the race all the way into the last week of the season but faltered there and ended up 2½ games out. It had been Joltin' Joe DiMaggio's best season since 1941. The Yankee Clipper sent 39 shots out of the park and drove in 155 runs, both

Jackie Robinson was both the first black to play in the major leagues and the first to play in a World Series in 1947. Robinson would play in six Series for the Dodgers; his best was in 1953 when he hit .320 but his overall average was only .234.

AL standards that year, and batted a neat .320.

But closer in the AL race were the Red Sox and the Indians, so close in fact that they ended up in a tie with records of 96–58. The American League flag, it was decided, would be determined by a single winner-take-all game.

Boston was now being managed by Joe McCarthy. Ted Williams was still terrorizing AL pitchers and took another batting crown with an average of .369. The Red Sox had acquired Vern Stephens and ensconced him at shortstop, added Birdie Tebbetts behind the plate, and saw a lot of promise in a southpaw named Mel Parnell.

The Indians, however, were even more impressive, winning the major league Triple Crown by logging the following collective stats: batting average .282, ERA 3.22, fielding average .982. (The Indians had won the crown once before back in 1906 when they were under Nap Lajoie). They had manager/shortstop/league-MVP Lou Boudreau, who hit .355 and drove in 106 runs; they also had fearsome hitters in Larry Doby, the first black to play in the American League, Eddie Robinson, Joe Gordon, Ken Keltner, and Dale Mitchell. Two hurlers won 20 games apiece for them, Gene Bearden and Bob Lemon, and Bob Feller recorded 19.

With the one-game playoff scheduled for Fenway Park in Boston, the Red Sox seemed to have a slight advantage, but it was nullified by the play of three Indians that autumn afternoon. First was Ken Keltner, who sent a thundering three-run homer into the seats to break a 1-1 tie; then Lou Boudreau, who collected four hits for the day, including two homers; and finally Gene Bearden who went the distance and allowed Red Sox sluggers only five hits. The final score was Cleveland 8, Boston 3. It was Cleveland's second pennant, the only one since 1920.

Despite the Red Sox loss, the city of Boston would still play host to some of the games of the 1948 World Series because the Braves triumphed in the National League, beating out the Cardinals by 6½ games. Billy Southworth was guiding the Braves that year, and he got the best hitting in the league from his ballplayers. Tops was Tommy Holmes at .325, but a close second was Rookie of the Year Alvin Dark with .322. Eddie Stanky hit .320; Jeff Heath, .319; and Mike McCormick, .303. Power was provided by Bob Elliott who clouted 23 homers and drove in 100 runs, and Heath who slugged 20 round-trippers. And pitching was also a source of gratification to manager Southworth, especially in the forms of Johnny Sain (24–15) and Warren Spahn (15–12).

For all their big-name hitters, however, neither team did very well from the batter's box in the Series. Cleveland did not even manage to hit .200 as a team, in fact were 31 percentage points below the Braves. Both teams scored 17 runs in the six games of the Series. The Indians, however, succeeded in scoring more in four of them and therefore were the champs.

After six years out of a major league dugout, Casey Stengel was back in 1949, this time wearing Yankee pinstripes. And "the Old Professor" brought the Yanks another flag, earned on the very last day of the regular season. Going into the final game, New York was tied with the Red Sox. The two teams faced each other in that game, and the Yanks prevailed.

New York had only one .300 hitter that year, Joe DiMaggio (.346), but he played in less than half their games because of an injury. But the Yanks got some power-hitting from Tommy Henrich, 24 homers, and Yogi Berra, who knocked 20 out of the ballpark. Pitching was their true source of strength in '49. Vic Raschi won 21 games while losing only 10. Allie Reynolds accounted for another 17 wins, and Tommy Byrne and Eddie Lopat got 15 apiece. Reliever Joe Page set a major league record with his 27 saves; he appeared in 60 games and posted a record of 13–8.

Brooklyn was back again, still piloted by Burt Shotton, thirsting for a little revenge for the tannings they had taken in their first two Series encounters with the Yankees. They, too, had won the pennant on the last day of the season, slipping in just a game ahead of the St. Louis Cardinals. Since their appearance in the Series in 1947, Brooklyn had added several new names to the starting line-up, most notably Duke Snider, Roy Campanella, Gil Hodges, and Billy Cox. Their brightest star that year, however, was Jackie Robinson, voted the MVP because of his league-leading average of .342. He also swiped the most bases in the majors, 37, and batted in 124 runs. Carl Furillo was the only other .300 hitter with a mark of .322, although Gene Hermanski missed by only a single percentage point. And PeeWee Reese scored the most runs in the NL, a total of 132. The staff was headed by Big Don Newcombe (17–8) and Preacher Roe (15–6).

Duke Snider played in five World Series for Brooklyn and one for Los Angeles. He is the only player in history to hit four home runs in two Series.

Four of the "Boys of Summer."

Roy Campanella was behind the plate for Brooklyn in five World Series, but never batted above .300 in any of them.

Carl Furillo played in seven World Series for the Dodgers, and had an overall average of .266.

PeeWee Reese, long the Dodgers' captain, starred in seven Series for Brooklyn and batted .272, topping the .300 mark three times.

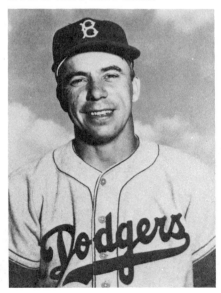

But as much as Brooklyn wanted to redirect their World Series fortunes, they didn't come close in 1949. They managed to win one game, the second, but the Yankees rebounded and took the next three. As the 1940s came to a close, the mighty Yankees could claim 12 world championships.

It had been an interesting baseball decade, marked by a war that interrupted the careers of more than 200 baseball players, just as it did to people in all other walks of life. But on either side of it, baseball fans saw some of the greatest baseball teams of all time take the field: The Yankees of 1941, the Cardinals of 1946, the Indians and Red Sox of 1948, among them. It was the age of DiMaggio, Williams, Musial, Feller, and Robinson as well as a host of other greats and near-greats who left their own individual imprints on the game of baseball.

1940

Cincinnati Reds 4
Detroit Tigers 3

Line-ups

	Cincinnati Reds		**Detroit Tigers**
1b	Frank McCormick	1b	Rudy York
2b	Eddie Joost	2b	Charlie Gehringer
3b	Bill Werber	3b	Pinky Higgins
ss	Billy Myers	ss	Dick Bartell
lf	Jimmy Ripple	lf	Hank Greenberg
cf	Mike McCormick	cf	Barney McCosky
rf	Ival Goodman	rf	Bruce Campbell
c	Jimmie Wilson	c	Billy Sullivan
mgr	Bill McKechnie	mgr	Del Baker

		R	H	E	Pitching
Game 1	Detroit	7	10	1	Bobo Newsom (W)
	Cincinnati	2	8	3	Paul Derringer, Whitey Moore (2nd), Elmer Riddle (9th)
Game 2	Detroit	3	3	1	Schoolboy Rowe, Johnny Gorsica (4th)
	Cincinnati	5	9	0	Bucky Walters (W)
Game 3	Cincinnati	4	10	1	Jim Turner, Whitey Moore (7th), Joe Beggs (8th)
	Detroit	7	13	1	Tommy Bridges (W)
Game 4	Cincinnati	5	11	1	Paul Derringer (W)
	Detroit	2	5	1	Dizzy Trout, Clay Smith (3rd), Archie McKain (7th)
Game 5	Cincinnati	0	3	0	Junior Thompson, Whitey Moore (4th), Johnny Vander Meer (5th), Johnny Hutchings (8th)
	Detroit	8	13	0	Bobo Newsom (W)

1940

Cincinnati Reds   4
Detroit Tigers   3

		R	H	E	Pitching
Game 6	Detroit	0	5	0	Schoolboy Rowe, Johnny Gorsica (1st), Fred Hutchinson (8th)
	Cincinnati	4	10	2	Bucky Walters (W)
Game 7	Detroit	1	7	0	Bobo Newsom
	Cincinnati	2	7	1	Paul Derringer (W)

Highlights

- The triumph by the Reds was the first world title taken by a National League team since the Cardinals won it in 1934.
- The Tigers exploded for five runs in the second inning of Game 1, with Pinky Higgins and Dick Bartell each driving in two runs with singles.
- Jimmy Ripple hit a two-run homer to provide the Reds' winning margin in Game 2.
- Rudy York and Pinky Higgins both hit two-run homers in the seventh inning of Game 3 to give the Tigers a win.
- Bobo Newsom hurled a three-hit shutout for Detroit in Game 5.
- Hank Greenberg drove in four runs in Game 5, three of them with a home run.
- Bucky Walters pitched a five-hit shutout for the Reds in Game 6, hit a home run, and accounted for two RBIs.
- Back-to-back doubles by Mike McCormick and Jimmy Ripple in the seventh inning of Game 7 enabled the Reds to tie the game at one apiece, then a sacrifice fly by Billy Myers sent Ripple across with the game-winning run.

Best Efforts

Batting

Average	Bill Werber	.370
Home Runs	(six players)	1 each
Triples	Rudy York	1
	Pinky Higgins	1
	Hank Greenberg	1
Doubles	Bill Werber	4
Hits	Bill Werber	10
	Hank Greenberg	10
Runs	(four players)	5 each
RBIs	Jimmy Ripple	6
	Pinky Higgins	6
	Hank Greenberg	6

Pitching

Wins	Bucky Walters	2–0
	Paul Derringer	2–1
	Bobo Newsom	2–1
ERA	Johnny Gorsica	0.79
Strikeouts	Bobo Newsom	17
Innings Pitched	Bobo Newsom	26

1941

New York Yankees 4
Brooklyn Dodgers 1

Line-ups

New York Yankees		Brooklyn Dodgers	
1b	Johnny Sturm	1b	Dolph Camilli
2b	Joe Gordon	2b	Billy Herman
3b	Red Rolfe	3b	Cookie Lavagetto
ss	Phil Rizzuto	ss	PeeWee Reese
lf	King Kong Keller	lf	Joe Medwick
cf	Joe DiMaggio	cf	Pete Reiser
rf	Tommy Henrich	rf	Dixie Walker
c	Bill Dickey	c	Mickey Owen
mgr	Joe McCarthy	mgr	Leo Durocher

		R	H	E	Pitching
Game 1	Brooklyn	2	6	0	Curt Davis, Hugh Casey (6th), Johnny Allen (7th)
	New York	3	6	1	Red Ruffing (W)
Game 2	Brooklyn	3	6	2	Whit Wyatt (W)
	New York	2	9	1	Spud Chandler, Johnny Murphy (6th)
Game 3	New York	2	8	0	Marius Russo (W)
	Brooklyn	1	4	0	Freddie Fitzsimmons, Hugh Casey (8th), Larry French (8th), Johnny Allen (9th)
Game 4	New York	7	12	0	Atley Donald, Marv Breuer (5th), Johnny Murphy (8th, W)
	Brooklyn	4	9	1	Kirby Higbe, Larry French (4th), Johnny Allen (5th), Hugh Casey (5th)
Game 5	New York	3	6	0	Ernie Bonham (W)
	Brooklyn	1	4	1	Whit Wyatt

Highlights

- The Yankees won their ninth world championship, almost twice the titles of the next most successful teams at that point, the Red Sox and the Athletics, who could claim five crowns apiece.
- Yank Red Ruffing tied the record for most career Series wins with six, sharing the record with Lefty Gomez, Waite Hoyt, and Chief Bender.
- The Dodgers batted only .187 as a team; their top hitter, Ducky Medwick, hit only .235, and the only Dodger homer came from Pete Reiser.
- Joe Gordon's average of .500 tied the record for a five-game Series set by Giant Larry McLean back in 1913. Gordon's slugging average of .929 also set a record.
- Gordon homered and drove in two runs to lead the Yanks to victory in Game 1.
- Dodger Dolph Camilli singled to send Dixie Walker home with the game-winning run in the sixth inning of Game 2.
- Back-to-back singles by Joe DiMaggio and King Kong Keller drove in two runs to provide the margin of victory in Game 3.
- Dodger catcher Mickey Owen recorded the most infamous passed ball in Series history when he let the third strike of the last out in the ninth inning of Game 4 get by him. The score had been 4–3 in favor of Brooklyn. As a result of Owen's error, Tommy Henrich got to first base and then the Yankees exploded for four runs. Instead of a Dodger win, which would have evened the Series at two games each, Brooklyn fell behind three games to one.
- In Game 4, King Kong Keller doubled in the ninth inning to drive in two runs to give the Yanks the lead. Joe Gordon followed with another double to drive in two more insurance runs.

Best Efforts

Batting

Average	Joe Gordon .500
Home Runs	Joe Gordon 1
	Tommy Henrich 1
	Pete Reiser 1
Triples	Joe Gordon 1
	Pete Reiser 1
	Mickey Owen 1
Doubles	King Kong Keller 2
	Dixie Walker 2
Hits	Joe Gordon 7
	King Kong Keller 7
Runs	King Kong Keller 5
RBIs	Joe Gordon 5
	King Kong Keller 5

Pitching

Wins	(five players) 1 game
ERA	Johnny Murphy 0.00
Strikeouts	Whit Wyatt 14
Innings Pitched	Whit Wyatt 18

1942

St. Louis Cardinals 4
New York Yankees 1

Line-ups

St. Louis Cardinals		New York Yankees	
1b	Johnny Hopp	1b	Jerry Priddy
2b	Jimmy Brown	2b	Joe Gordon
3b	Whitey Kurowski	3b	Red Rolfe
ss	Marty Marion	ss	Phil Rizzuto
lf	Stan Musial	lf	King Kong Keller
cf	Terry Moore	cf	Joe DiMaggio
rf	Enos Slaughter	rf	Roy Cullenbine
c	Walker Cooper	c	Bill Dickey
mgr	Billy Southworth	mgr	Joe McCarthy

		R	H	E	Pitching
Game 1	New York	7	11	0	Red Ruffing (W), Spud Chandler (9th)
	St. Louis	4	7	4	Mort Cooper, Harry Gumbert (8th), Max Lanier (9th)
Game 2	New York	3	10	2	Ernie Bonham
	St. Louis	4	6	0	Johnny Beazley (W)
Game 3	St. Louis	2	5	1	Ernie White (W)
	New York	0	6	1	Spud Chandler, Marv Breuer (9th), Jim Turner (9th)
Game 4	St. Louis	9	12	1	Mort Cooper, Harry Gumbert (6th), Howie Pollet (6th), Max Lanier (7th, W)
	New York	6	10	1	Hank Borowy, Atley Donald (4th), Ernie Bonham (7th)
Game 5	St. Louis	4	9	4	Johnny Beazley (W)
	New York	2	7	1	Red Ruffing

Highlights

- The Cardinals won four straight games after losing the first, at that time only the second team to rally so successfully after dropping the opener (the other, the Red Sox of 1915).
- Red Ruffing of the Yanks set a new record when he earned his seventh Series win in Game 1.
- Stan Musial singled to drive in Enos Slaughter with the game-winning run in the ninth inning of Game 2.
- Ernie White hurled a six-hit shutout for the Cards in Game 3.
- The Cardinals scored six runs in the fourth inning of Game 4, and the Yanks scored five in the sixth.
- Whitey Kurowski hit a two-run homer in the ninth inning of Game 5 to break a 2–2 tie and give St. Louis the Series crown.

Best Efforts

Batting

Average	Phil Rizzuto .381
Home Runs	King Kong Keller 2
Triples	Marty Marion 1
	Whitey Kurowski 1
Doubles	Red Rolfe 2
Hits	Phil Rizzuto 8
Runs	Red Rolfe 5
RBIs	Whitey Kurowski 5
	King Kong Keller 5

Pitching

Wins	Johnny Beazley 2–0
ERA	Ernie White 0.00
Strikeouts	Red Ruffing 11
Innings Pitched	Johnny Beazley 18

1943

New York Yankees 4
St. Louis Cardinals 1

Line-ups

New York Yankees		St. Louis Cardinals	
1b	Nick Etten	1b	Ray Sanders
2b	Joe Gordon	2b	Lou Klein
3b	Billy Johnson	3b	Whitey Kurowski
ss	Frank Crosetti	ss	Marty Marion
lf	King Kong Keller	lf	Danny Litwhiler
cf	Johnny Lindell	cf	Harry Walker
rf	Tuck Stainback	rf	Stan Musial
c	Bill Dickey	c	Walker Cooper
mgr	Joe McCarthy	mgr	Billy Southworth

		R	H	E	Pitching
Game 1	St. Louis	2	7	2	Max Lanier, Harry Brecheen (8th)
	New York	4	8	2	Spud Chandler (W)
Game 2	St. Louis	4	7	2	Mort Cooper (W)
	New York	3	6	0	Ernie Bonham, Johnny Murphy (9th)
Game 3	St. Louis	2	6	4	Al Brazie, Howie Krist (8th), Harry Brecheen (8th)
	New York	6	8	0	Hank Borowy (W), Johnny Murphy (9th)
Game 4	New York	2	6	2	Marius Russo (W)
	St. Louis	1	7	1	Max Lanier, Harry Brecheen (8th)
Game 5	New York	2	7	1	Spud Chandler (W)
	St. Louis	0	10	1	Mort Cooper, Max Lanier (8th), Murry Dickson (9th)

Highlights

- Manager Joe McCarthy chalked up his seventh World Series title, a record that would stand until Casey Stengel tied it with his seventh in 1958.
- Frank Crosetti scored what proved to be the game-winning run for the Yankees on a wild pitch by Max Lanier in the sixth inning of Game 1.
- Ray Sanders belted a two-run homer in Game 3 to provide the winning margin for the Cards in Game 2.
- The attendance for Game 3 at Yankee Stadium—69,990—set a Series record.
- Billy Johnson tripled with the bases loaded in the bottom of the eighth of Game 3 to destroy a 2–1 Cardinal lead and provide the Yanks with three of their four-run margin of victory.
- Spud Chandler pitched a shutout for the Yankees in Game 5, and Bill Dickey provided the winning runs with a two-run homer in the sixth inning.

Best Efforts

Batting

Average	Marty Marion	.357
Home Runs	Joe Gordon	1
	Ray Sanders	1
	Marty Marion	1
Triples	Billy Johnson	1
	King Kong Keller	1
Doubles	Marty Marion	2
Hits	Billy Johnson	6
Runs	Frank Crosetti	4
RBIs	Bill Dickey	4

Pitching

Wins	Spud Chandler	2–0
ERA	Marius Russo	0.00
Strikeouts	Max Lanier	13
Innings Pitched	Spud Chandler	18

1944

St. Louis Cardinals 4
St. Louis Browns 2

Line-ups

St. Louis Cardinals		St. Louis Browns	
1b	Ray Sanders	1b	George McQuinn
2b	Emil Verban	2b	Don Gutteridge
3b	Whitey Kurowski	3b	Mark Christman
ss	Marty Marion	ss	Vern Stephens
lf	Danny Litwhiler	lf	Chet Laabs
cf	Johnny Hopp	cf	Mike Kreevich
rf	Stan Musial	rf	Gene Moore
c	Walker Cooper	c	Red Hayworth
mgr	Billy Southworth	mgr	Luke Sewell

		R	H	E	Pitching
Game 1	Browns	2	2	0	Denny Galehouse (W)
	Cardinals	1	7	0	Mort Cooper, Blix Donnelly (8th)
Game 2	Browns	2	7	4	Nels Potter, Bob Muncrief (7th)
	Cardinals	3	7	0	Max Lanier, Blix Donnelly (8th, W)
Game 3	Cardinals	2	7	0	Ted Wilks, Freddie Schmidt (3rd), Al Jurisich (7th), Bud Byerly (7th)
	Browns	6	8	2	Jack Kramer (W)
Game 4	Cardinals	5	12	0	Harry Brecheen (W)
	Browns	1	9	1	Sig Jakucki, Al Hollingsworth (4th), Tex Shirley (8th)
Game 5	Cardinals	2	6	1	Mort Cooper (W)
	Browns	0	7	1	Denny Galehouse
Game 6	Browns	1	3	2	Nels Potter, Bob Muncrief (4th), Jack Kramer (7th)
	Cardinals	3	10	0	Max Lanier (W), Ted Wilks (6th)

Highlights

- St. Louis became the third locale in history to host an intracity Series (the others, Chicago and New York).
- The Cards won their fourth world title to tie the New York Giants for the most by a National League ballclub.
- Mort Cooper and Blix Donnelly collaborated to hurl a two-hitter in Game 1, but the Cards still lost.
- George McQuinn hit a two-run homer to win Game 1 for the Browns.
- Ken O'Dea hit a pinch single in the bottom of the 11th in Game 2 to send Emil Verban across with the winning run for the Cardinals.
- Stan Musial hit a two-run homer in the first inning of Game 4 to give the Cards a lead the Browns would not be able to catch.
- Cardinal Mort Cooper struck out 12 Browns batters during his shutout victory in Game 5.
- Reliever Ted Wilks came in for the Cards in the sixth inning of Game 6 and retired the next 11 consecutive Browns to save the game and give the Cardinals the Series.

Best Efforts

Batting

Average	George McQuinn	.438
Home Runs	(four players)	1
Triples	Walker Cooper	1
	Chet Laabs	1
Doubles	Marty Marion	3
	Mike Kreevich	3
Hits	(four players)	7
Runs	Ray Sanders	5
RBIs	George McQuinn	5

Pitching

Wins	(six players)	1
ERA	Jack Kramer	0.00
Strikeouts	Mort Cooper	16
Innings Pitched	Denny Galehouse	18

1945

Detroit Tigers 4
Chicago Cubs 3

Line-ups

Detroit Tigers		Chicago Cubs	
1b	Rudy York	1b	Phil Cavarretta
2b	Eddie Mayo	2b	Don Johnson
3b	Jimmy Outlaw	3b	Stan Hack
ss	Skeeter Webb	ss	Roy Hughes
lf	Hank Greenberg	lf	Peanuts Lowrey
cf	Doc Cramer	cf	Andy Pafko
rf	Roy Cullenbine	rf	Bill Nicholson
c	Paul Richards	c	Mickey Livingston
mgr	Steve O'Neill	mgr	Charlie Grimm

		R	H	E	Pitching
Game 1	Chicago	9	13	0	Hank Borowy (W)
	Detroit	0	6	0	Hal Newhouser, Al Benton (3rd), Jim Tobin (5th), Les Mueller (8th)
Game 2	Chicago	1	7	0	Hank Wyse, Paul Erickson (7th)
	Detroit	4	7	0	Virgil Trucks (W)
Game 3	Chicago	3	8	0	Claude Passeau (W)
	Detroit	0	1	2	Stubby Overmire, Al Benton (7th)
Game 4	Detroit	4	7	1	Dizzy Trout (W)
	Chicago	1	5	1	Ray Prim, Paul Derringer (4th), Hy Vandenberg (6th), Paul Erickson (8th)
Game 5	Detroit	8	11	0	Hal Newhouser (W)
	Chicago	4	7	2	Hank Borowy, Hy Vandenberg (6th), Bob Chipman (6th), Paul Derringer (7th), Paul Erickson (9th)

1945

Detroit Tigers 4
Chicago Cubs 3

		R	H	E	Pitching
Game 6	Detroit	7	13	1	Virgil Trucks, George Caster (5th), Tommy Bridges (6th), Al Benton (7th), Dizzy Trout (8th)
	Chicago	8	15	3	Claude Passeau, Hank Wyse (7th), Ray Prim (8th), Hank Borowy (9th, W)
Game 7	Detroit	9	9	1	Hal Newhouser (W)
	Chicago	3	10	0	Hank Borowy, Paul Derringer (1st), Hy Vandenberg (2nd), Paul Erickson (6th), Claude Passeau (8th), Hank Wyse (9th)

Highlights

- The Tigers won their second world crown; their first, 1935, was also gained at the Cubs' expense.
- The Cubs lost their eighth Series to equal the unprized mark held by the New York Giants.
- Hank Borowy hurled a six-hit shutout for the Cubs in Game 1.
- Hank Greenberg hit a three-run homer in Game 2 to break a 1–1 tie and provide the eventual margin of victory for Detroit.
- Claude Passeau pitched a one-hit shutout for the Cubs in Game 3, only the second one-hitter in Series history up to that time (Ed Reulbach, also of the Cubs, hurled the other back in 1906).
- Hank Greenberg hit three doubles in Game 5 and Hal Newhouser struck out nine Cubs to pace the Tigers in Game 5.
- Greenberg hit a homer in the top of the eighth of Game 6 to tie the score at 7–7 and eventually send the game into extra innings.
- In the bottom of the 12th of Game 6, Stan Hack hit a double to drive in Bill Schuster with the game-winning run. It was Hack's fourth hit and third RBI of the day.
- The Tigers blew the Cubs out with five runs in the first inning of Game 7. Three of the runs were driven in on a double by Paul Richards, who accounted for a total of four RBIs in the game.

Best Efforts

Batting

Average	Phil Cavarretta	.423
Home Runs	Hank Greenberg	2
Triples	Don Johnson	1
	Bill Nicholson	1
	Andy Pafko	1
Doubles	Hank Greenberg	3
	Stan Hack	3
	Mickey Livingston	3
Hits	Doc Cramer	11
	Phil Cavarretta	11
	Stan Hack	11
Runs	Doc Cramer	7
	Hank Greenberg	7
	Phil Cavarretta	7
RBIs	Bill Nicholson	8

Pitching

Wins	Hal Newhouser	2–1
	Hank Borowy	2–2
ERA	Dizzy Trout	0.66
Strikeouts	Hal Newhouser	22
Innings Pitched	Hal Newhouser	$20\frac{2}{3}$

1946

St. Louis Cardinals 4
Boston Red Sox 3

Line-ups

St. Louis Cardinals		Boston Red Sox	
1b	Stan Musial	1b	Rudy York
2b	Red Schoendienst	2b	Bobby Doerr
3b	Whitey Kurowski	3b	Pinky Higgins
ss	Marty Marion	ss	Johnny Pesky
lf	Harry Walker	lf	Ted Williams
cf	Terry Moore	cf	Dom DiMaggio
rf	Enos Slaughter	rf	Wally Moses
c	Joe Garagiola	c	Hal Wagner
mgr	Eddie Dyer	mgr	Joe Cronin

		R	H	E	Pitching
Game 1	Boston	3	9	2	Tex Hughson, Earl Johnson (9th, W)
	St. Louis	2	7	0	Howie Pollet
Game 2	Boston	0	4	1	Mickey Harris, Joe Dodson (8th)
	St. Louis	3	6	0	Harry Brecheen (W)
Game 3	St. Louis	0	6	1	Murry Dickson, Ted Wilks (8th)
	Boston	4	8	0	Boo Ferriss (W)
Game 4	St. Louis	12	20	1	George Munger (W)
	Boston	3	9	4	Tex Hughson, Jim Bagby (3rd), Mace Brown (8th), Mike Ryba (9th), Clem Dreisewerd (9th)
Game 5	St. Louis	3	4	1	Howie Pollet, Al Brazle (1st), Johnny Beazley (8th)
	Boston	6	11	3	Joe Dobson (W)
Game 6	Boston	1	7	0	Mickey Harris, Tex Hughson (3rd), Earl Johnson (8th)
	St. Louis	4	8	0	Harry Brecheen (W)

		R	**H**	**E**	**Pitching**
Game 7	Boston	3	8	0	Boo Ferriss, Joe Dobson (5th), Bob Klinger (8th), Earl Johnson (8th)
	St. Louis	4	9	1	Murry Dickson, Harry Brecheen (W)

Highlights

- The Cardinals extended their record of triumphs in seven-game World Series to four. Only one other team had prevailed in more than one at that time, the Pirates, who had won two of the seven-game affairs.
- The fifth world title won by the Cardinals was the most up to that time for a National League club.
- The 19 doubles slapped by Cardinal hitters set a record for a seven-game Series.
- Rudy York homered in the tenth inning to win Game 1 for the BoSox.
- Harry "the Cat" Brecheen pitched a four-hit shutout for St. Louis in Game 2.
- Boo Ferriss countered with a shutout against the Cards in Game 3, allowing only six hits.
- York hit a three-run homer in Game 3 to pace the Red Sox offense.
- The Cardinals rapped out a Series record of 20 hits in Game 4, matching the mark set by the New York Giants back in 1921. The record still stands.
- Enos Slaughter, Whitey Kurowski, and Joe Garagiola each got four hits for the Cards in Game 4, and Garagiola drove in three runs.
- The four runs scored by Slaughter in Game 4 tied a Series record.
- In Game 7, Harry Brecheen became the first pitcher to win three games in a single Series since Stan Coveleski did it for the Cleveland Indians back in 1920.
- Three batters hit over .400 in the Series: Wally Moses (.417), Harry Walker (.412), and Bobby Doerr (.409).

Best Efforts

Batting

Average	Wally Moses	.417
Home Runs	Rudy York	2
Triples	Stan Musial	1
	Enos Slaughter	1
	Rudy York	1
Doubles	Stan Musial	4
Hits	Bobby Doerr	9
Runs	Rudy York	6
RBIs	Harry Walker	6

Pitching

Wins	Harry Brecheen	3–0
ERA	Joe Dobson	0.00
Strikeouts	Harry Brecheen	11
Innings Pitched	Harry Brecheen	20

1947

New York Yankees 4
Brooklyn Dodgers 3

Line-ups

New York Yankees		Brooklyn Dodgers	
1b	George McQuinn	1b	Jackie Robinson
2b	Snuffy Stirnweiss	2b	Eddie Stanky
3b	Billy Johnson	3b	Spider Jorgensen
ss	Phil Rizzuto	ss	PeeWee Reese
lf	Johnny Lindell	lf	Gene Hermanski
cf	Joe DiMaggio	cf	Carl Furillo
rf	Tommy Henrich	rf	Dixie Walker
c	Yogi Berra	c	Bruce Edwards
mgr	Bucky Harris	mgr	Burt Shotton

		R	H	E	Pitching
Game 1	Brooklyn	3	6	0	Ralph Branca, Hank Behman (5th), Hugh Casey (7th)
	New York	5	4	0	Spec Shea (W), Joe Page (6th)
Game 2	Brooklyn	3	9	2	Vic Lombardi, Hal Gregg (5th), Hank Behman (7th), Rex Barney (7th),
	New York	10	15	1	Allie Reynolds (W)
Game 3	New York	8	13	1	Bobo Newsom, Vic Raschi (2nd), Karl Drews (3rd), Spud Chandler (4th), Joe Page (6th)
	Brooklyn	9	13	1	Joe Hatten, Ralph Branca (5th), Hugh Casey (7th, W)
Game 4	New York	2	8	1	Bill Bevens
	Brooklyn	3	1	3	Harry Taylor, Hal Gregg (1st), Hank Behman (8th), Hugh Casey (9th, W)
Game 5	New York	2	5	0	Spec Shea (W)
	Brooklyn	1	4	1	Rex Barney, Joe Hatten (5th), Hank Behman (7th), Hugh Casey (8th)

1947

New York Yankees 4
Brooklyn Dodgers 3

		R	H	E	Pitching
Game 6	Brooklyn	8	12	1	Vic Lombardi, Ralph Branca (3rd, W), Joe Hatten (6th), Hugh Casey (9th)
	New York	6	15	2	Allie Reynolds, Karl Drews (3rd), Joe Page (5th), Bobo Newsom (6th), Vic Raschi (7th), Butch Wensloff (8th)
Game 7	Brooklyn	2	7	0	Hal Gregg, Hank Behman (4th), Joe Hatten (6th), Rex Barney (6th), Hugh Casey (7th)
	New York	5	7	0	Spec Shea, Bill Bevens (2nd), Joe Page (5th, W)

Highlights

- The Yankees, appearing in their fifteenth World Series, won their eleventh world championship.
- This was the first World Series to be televised.
- Jackie Robinson, the first black to play major league baseball, became the first black to participate in a World Series.
- The eight runs scored by Billy Johnson of the Yankees tied the record for a seven-game Series. His three triples set another mark.
- Johnny Lindell's batting average of .500 tied the record for a seven-game Series.
- The Dodgers twice tied a Series record when they hit three doubles in one inning: Game 3, the second: Bruce Edwards, Eddie Stanky, and Carl Furillo; and Game 6, the third: PeeWee Reese, Jackie Robinson, and Dixie Walker.
- The attendance for Game 1 at Yankee Stadium—73,365—set a new Series standard.
- Losing 1-0, the Yankees erupted for five runs in the fifth of Game 1, with Johnny Lindell and Tommy Henrich each driving in two runs. The Yanks got only four hits all day, but still won.
- Yogi Berra hit the first pinch-hit home run in Series history in the seventh inning of Game 3.
- The Dodgers scored six runs in the second inning of Game 3, with Eddie Stanky and Carl Furillo driving in two apiece.

- Yankee hurler Bill Bevens had a no-hitter with two outs in the bottom of the ninth of Game 4 when pinch-hitter Cookie Lavagetto spoiled it with a double. Two runs scored on Lavagetto's hit, enough to win the game for the Dodgers as well.
- An RBI by Yankee pitcher Spec Shea and a home run from Joe DiMaggio provided the winning margin in Game 5. Shea went the distance, allowing the Dodgers only four hits.
- The 38 players who appeared for the Yankees and the Dodgers in Game 6 still stands as the most ever in a nine-inning game. The 21 used by the Yanks also set a mark for the most by one ballclub.
- A new Series attendance record was set at Game 6—74,065—played at Yankee Stadium.
- Reserve outfielder Al Gionfriddo saved Game 6 for the Dodgers by making a spectacular catch when he reached over the railing at the 415-foot mark to steal what would have been a three-run homer from Joe DiMaggio.

Best Efforts

Batting

Average	Johnny Lindell	.500
Home Runs	Joe DiMaggio	2
Triples	Billy Johnson	3
Doubles	Johnny Lindell	3
Hits	Tommy Henrich	10
Runs	Billy Johnson	8
RBIs	Johnny Lindell	7

Pitching

Wins	Spec Shea	2–0
	Hugh Casey	2–0
ERA	Hugh Casey	0.87
Strikeouts	Spec Shea	10
	Hal Gregg	10
Innings Pitched	Spec Shea	15⅓

1948

Cleveland Indians 4
Boston Braves 2

Line-ups

	Cleveland Indians		**Boston Braves**
1b	Eddie Robinson	1b	Earl Torgeson
2b	Joe Gordon	2b	Eddie Stanky
3b	Ken Keltner	3b	Bob Elliott
ss	Lou Boudreau	ss	Alvin Dark
lf	Dale Mitchell	lf	Marv Rickert
cf	Larry Doby	cf	Mike McCormick
rf	Walt Judnich	rf	Tommy Holmes
c	Jim Hegan	c	Bill Salkeld
mgr	Lou Boudreau	mgr	Billy Southworth

		R	H	E	Pitching
Game 1	Cleveland	0	4	0	Bob Feller
	Boston	1	2	2	Johnny Sain (W)
Game 2	Cleveland	4	8	1	Bob Lemon (W)
	Boston	1	8	3	Warren Spahn, Red Barrett (5th), Nels Potter (8th)
Game 3	Boston	0	5	1	Vern Bickford, Bill Voiselle (4th), Red Barrett (8th)
	Cleveland	2	5	0	Gene Bearden (W)
Game 4	Boston	1	7	0	Johnny Sain
	Cleveland	2	5	0	Steve Gromek (W)
Game 5	Boston	11	12	0	Nels Potter, Warren Spahn (W)
	Cleveland	5	6	2	Bob Feller, Eddie Klieman (7th), Russ Christopher (7th), Satchel Paige (7th), Bob Muncrief (8th)
Game 6	Cleveland	4	10	0	Bob Lemon (W), Gene Bearden
	Boston	3	9	0	Bill Voiselle, Warren Spahn (8th)

Highlights

- The Cleveland Indians won their second world crown (the other, 1920).
- In a classic pitching confrontation in Game 1, the Braves' Johnny Sain allowed the Indians no runs and just four hits, while Bob Feller hurled a two-hitter for Cleveland but gave up a game-losing run in the bottom of the eighth, driven in on a single by Tommy Holmes.
- Gene Bearden threw a five-hit shutout in Game 3 for the Indians.
- A run-producing double by Lou Boudreau and a home run from Larry Doby provided the margin of victory for the Indians in Game 4.
- The Braves scored six runs in the seventh to blow apart a 5–5 tie in Game 5.
- Bob Elliott hit two home runs and accounted for four RBIs for the Braves in Game 5.

Best Efforts

Batting

Average	Earl Torgeson	.389
Home Runs	Bob Elliott	2
Triples	——	
Doubles	Lou Boudreau	4
Hits	Larry Doby	7
	Earl Torgeson	7
	Bob Elliott	7
Runs	Dale Mitchell	4
	Bob Elliott	4
RBIs	Jim Hegan	5
	Bob Elliott	5

Pitching

Wins	Bob Lemon	2–0
ERA	Gene Bearden	0.00
Strikeouts	Warren Spahn	12
Innings Pitched	Johnny Sain	17

1949

New York Yankees 4
Brooklyn Dodgers 1

Line-ups

New York Yankees		Brooklyn Dodgers	
1b	Tommy Henrich	1b	Gil Hodges
2b	Jerry Coleman	2b	Jackie Robinson
3b	Bobby Brown	3b	Spider Jorgensen
ss	Phil Rizzuto	ss	PeeWee Reese
lf	Gene Woodling	lf	Luis Olmo
cf	Joe DiMaggio	cf	Duke Snider
rf	Cliff Mapes	rf	Gene Hermanski
c	Yogi Berra	c	Roy Campanella
mgr	Casey Stengel	mgr	Burt Shotton

		R	H	E	Pitching
Game 1	Brooklyn	0	2	0	Don Newcombe
	New York	1	5	1	Allie Reynolds (W)
Game 2	Brooklyn	1	7	2	Preacher Roe (W)
	New York	0	6	1	Vic Raschi, Joe Page (9th)
Game 3	New York	4	5	0	Tommy Byrne, Joe Page (4th, W)
	Brooklyn	3	5	0	Ralph Branca, Jack Banta (9th)
Game 4	New York	6	10	0	Ed Lopat, Allie Reynolds (6th, W)
	Brooklyn	4	9	1	Don Newcombe, Joe Hatten (4th), Carl Erskine (6th), Jack Banta (7th)
Game 5	New York	10	11	1	Vic Raschi (W), Joe Page (7th)
	Brooklyn	6	11	2	Rex Barney, Jack Banta (3rd), Carl Erskine (6th), Joe Hatten (6th), Erv Palica (7th), Paul Minner (9th)

Highlights

- The Yankees earned their twelfth world crown.
- Casey Stengel managed the Yankees to the first of what would prove to be seven world titles.

- The two triples hit by Yank Bobby Brown tied the Series mark for a five-game Series.
- Allie Reynolds pitched a two-hit shutout for the Yankees in Game 1, and struck out nine Dodgers in the process.
- Tommy Henrich hit a home run in the bottom of the ninth to destroy Don Newcombe's shutout and win Game 1 for the Yankees.
- Preacher Roe allowed the Yankees only six hits in his shutout for the Dodgers in Game 2.
- Gil Hodges singled to send Jackie Robinson across with the game-winning run of Game 2.
- A pinch-hit double by Johnny Mize in the ninth inning of Game 3 drove in two runs, and a single by Jerry Coleman added another to give the Yanks a one-run victory.
- The Dodgers scored their three runs in Game 3 on solo homers by PeeWee Reese, Luis Olmo, and Roy Campanella.
- Bobby Brown tripled with the bases loaded in the fifth inning of Game 4 to provide the Yanks with their winning margin.
- The Yankees tied a Series record when they hit three doubles in one inning, the fourth of Game 4 (Bobby Brown, Cliff Mapes, Eddie Lopat).

Best Efforts

Batting

Average	Bobby Brown	.500
Home Runs	(six players)	1
Triples	Bobby Brown	2
Doubles	Jerry Coleman	3
	Gene Woodling	3
Hits	Bobby Brown	6
	PeeWee Reese	6
Runs	Tommy Henrich	4
	Bobby Brown	4
RBIs	Bobby Brown	5

Pitching

Wins	(five players)	1
ERA	Allie Reynolds	0.00
	Preacher Roe	0.00
Strikeouts	Allie Reynolds	14
Innings Pitched	Vic Raschi	14$\frac{2}{3}$

THE FIFTIES

★ ★ ★   ★ ★ ★

The mid-century decade was a memorable one on many fronts. The United States went from a war in Korea to rock 'n' roll, stretched the human spectrum from the grandfatherliness of Dwight D. Eisenhower to the hip-grinding greaser-idol Elvis Presley. There was also Marlon Brando, Marilyn Monroe, James Dean, Senator Kefauver and his crime committee, Senator Joe McCarthy and his infamous congressional hearings, Davy Crockett hats, beatniks, 3-D movies, ducktail haircuts, blue suede shoes, the hula hoop, the "$64,000 Question," "Dragnet," "What's My Line?," Edward R. Murrow, Ed Sullivan, Sid Caesar, Milton Berle, and Lucy.

During that illustrious 10 years in baseball, Casey Stengel would lead the Yankees to *eight* American League pennants and *six* world championships. Ancient Connie Mack, at age 88, would finally retire after 53 years as a manager, 50 of them with the Philadelphia A's. Also leaving the field would be such superstars as Joe DiMaggio, Bob Feller, and Jackie Robinson. To replace them new legends would garner the limelight, such remarkable athletes as Duke Snider, Mickey Mantle, Whitey Ford, Willie Mays, Eddie Mathews, Hank Aaron, Frank Robinson, Ernie Banks, and Roberto Clemente. The decade would feature the Yankee-Dodger World Series rivalry, and contain such other highlights as Bobby Thomson's historic home run in the playoffs of 1951 to send the Giants to the World Series, Allie Reynold's two no-hitters in one season for the Yankees (1951), Bill Veeck sending three-foot midget Eddie Gaedel to the plate as a pinch hitter for the St. Louis Browns, and Don Larson's perfect game in the 1956 Series, among other colorful events. It was also an age of transience in the major leagues. First, the Boston Braves moved to Milwaukee, followed by the St. Louis Browns to Baltimore, then the Philadelphia A's to Kansas City, and finally the opening of the West to big-league baseball with the Dodgers going to Los Angeles and the Giants to San Francisco.

When the decade began, however, the most securely ensconced franchise was that of the New York Yankees. They had demolished the Brooklyn Dodgers in the last World Series of the '40s, four games to one, and now opened the '50s by sweeping the Series from the Philadelphia Phillies.

The Yankees, however, found a lot of competition in the Detroit Tigers, Boston Red Sox, and Cleveland Indians that year, who ran second, third, and fourth (three, four, and six games out).

The Red Sox, with a team batting average of .302 outhit the Yanks by 20 percentage points, getting better than .300 averages from Ted Williams, Dom DiMaggio, Johnny Pesky, Al Zarilla, Walt Dropo, Birdie Tebbetts, and Billy Goodman (who led the AL with .354). And the Yankees were outpitched by all three teams, at least in terms of ERA.

But the Yankees were very experienced at winning ballgames. Joe DiMaggio could still hit home runs, 32, the team's best that year, while Yogi Berra hit 28 and Johnny Mize another 25. Berra drove in the most runs, 124, and DiMaggio was only two behind. Four batters topped .300: Phil "Scooter" Rizzuto (.324, who was also the AL MVP), Berra (.322), Hank Bauer (.320), and DiMaggio (.301). Vic Raschi headed the pitching staff with a record of 21–8, and the Yanks got 18 wins from Eddie Lopat, 16 from Allie Reynolds, and 15 from Tommy Byrne. Joe Page was still their chief fireman.

In the National League, the pennant was not decided until the last day of the season. The Dodgers, a game behind the Phillies, were hosting them with a chance to tie in the standings and send the flag race into a playoff. Brooklyn, with names like Robin-

Gene Woodling consistently shined for the Yankees in the postseason. In his five World Series, he batted .318 and twice was above the .400 mark.

son, Reese, Snider, Furillo, Campanella, Hodges, Roe, and Newcombe had been the favorite to win a second consecutive pennant. But the Phillies denied it to them on that last day. The game went into extra innings but, with special heroics, Philadelphia outfielder Dick Sisler blasted a three-run, tenth inning homer to give the Phillies their first pennant since 1915.

Philadelphia was not a great hitting team in 1950. Only two batters exceeded .300, Del Ennis (.311) and Richie Ashburn (.303).

Power hitting was provided by Ennis who stroked 31 homers and drove in 126 runs, and by Willie "Puddin' Head" Jones and Andy Seminick who respectively knocked 25 and 24 over NL fences. But they had a superb mound staff with righthander Robin Roberts (20–11), southpaw Curt Simmons (17–8), and reliever Jim Konstanty (22 saves, 16 wins, and the NL MVP award).

It was Yankee pitching in the World Series, however, that determined the outcome. Five New York hurlers combined for a Se-

ries ERA of 0.73, allowing the
Phillies only five runs in four
games. Three of the games were
decided by a single run, but all
were in favor of the Yankees.

The next year it was pretty
much the same. The Indians and
the Red Sox put a little life into
the AL regular season, but when
the curtain closed it was again
the Yankees taking the bows.
They beat out Cleveland by five
and Boston by eleven.

In '51, hitting was not the Yankee strongpoint, defying what
had become almost three decades
of tradition. Rookie-of-the-Year
Gil McDougald was the only
player to bat above .300 (.306),
while Joltin' Joe DiMaggio, playing out the last year of his magnificent career, could only manage
.263 and a mere 12 home runs.
Yogi Berra, who clubbed 27 homers and drove in 88 runs—low by
exalted Yankee standards—found
that it was enough to gain for him
that year's MVP award. Pitching,
however, was very strong. Both
Eddie Lopat and Vic Raschi won
21 games while Allie Reynolds
recorded another 17.

The real baseball drama of
1951, as all baseball fans know,
came from the National League,
and involved the other two New
York teams, the longtime rivals,

Opposing pitchers in the opening
game of the 1951 Series were Dave
Koslo of the Giants and Allie Reynolds of the Yankees. It was Koslo's
only World Series, but Reynolds appeared in six for the Yankees and
posted an impressive record of 7–2.

the Giants, managed by former
Dodger pilot Leo Durocher, and
the Dodgers now under Charlie
Dressen. The season ended in a
tie, each team with a record of 96–
58. The Dodgers who had seemed
like a virtual shoo-in during Au-
gust because no team was within
13 games of them, faltered and on
came the Giants with a spectactu-
lar finish. Durocher's team won

52 of their last 63 games and sent the pennant race into a three-game playoff.

The Giants won the first game in hostile Ebbets Field, 3–1, the winning margin coming on home runs by Bobby Thomson and Monte Irvin. The next day the two teams crossed the East River to meet in the Polo Grounds, but there the high-flying Giants totally fell apart before the eyes of their home crowd. They lost 10–0. The stunned Giants, however, would have one more chance and it would be at the Polo Grounds, although after that mauling there

wasn't much evidence of a home-field advantage.

It was, of course, baseball's most fabled ending. A standing-room-filled crowd was there. The score was tied 1–1 in the top of the eighth inning when Brooklyn erupted for three runs. It appeared to be all over, the Giants again embarrassed in their home ballpark. But they had one last chance, although it was not a large one because Big Don Newcombe had been hurling strong and had only allowed the Giants five hits in eight full innings. Plus the Dodger bullpen was a very

Two memorable Yanks, pitcher Vic Raschi (left) and slugger Johnny Mize. Raschi hurled for the Yanks in six Series, winning five games and losing three. Mize appeared in five Series as a Yank and batted .286.

good one. But Newcombe's strength dissipated in the top of the ninth. Alvin Dark led off with a single, then Don Mueller got another, and when Whitey Lockman doubled to drive Dark in, Newcombe was lifted. In came Ralph Branca to face Giant slugger Bobby Thomson. He hurled a strike, then another except on the second one Thomson met it and drove the ball into the leftfield seats to give the Giants a 5-4 win and a ticket to the World Series.

Like the Yankees of '51, the Giants were not consistent hitters, in fact had hit 15 percentage points less than the Dodgers during the season. Only Monte Irvin (.312) and Alvin Dark (.303) were notable. They did have respectable power, emanating from Bobby Thomson, 32 homers and 101 RBIs, and Monte Irvin, 24 homers and 121 RBIs, as well as such other home run hitters as Wes Westrum (20), Rookie-of-the-Year Willie Mays (20), and Don Mueller (16). In the area of pitching they had two 23-game winners in Sal Maglie (23-6) and Larry Jansen (23-11) and Jim Hearn won another 17 games.

But for all the excitement of the playoffs, with its fairy-tale finish, the Giants simply could not handle the Yankees in the Series.

It took them six games to do it and they had to come back from a two-game to one deficit but the Yanks, under the "Old Professor" Casey Stengel, earned their third straight world crown.

The next year it would be extended to four straight. And the Dodgers would once again be the scapegoat. DiMaggio was gone from the Yankee line-up, but filling his patch of earth in center field was a most able 20-year-old by the name of Mickey Mantle. Once again New York had to hold off the challenge of the Cleveland Indians, who boasted a bevy of good hitters in Larry Doby, Al Rosen, Bobby Avila, Luke Easter, Dale Mitchell, and Ray Boone and a pitching staff that had three 20-game winners: Early Wynn (23-12), Mike Garcia (22-11), and Bob Lemon (22-11). But the Yankees managed to keep them a few games off the pace all the way to the finish, and when it was over, their 95 victories were two better than Cleveland's 93.

Mickey Mantle and Gene Woodling were New York's most consistent hitters, batting .311 and .309 respectively. Yogi Berra had 30 home runs (a career high), Mantle hit 23, Joe Collins had 18, and Hank Bauer, 17. Allie Reynolds, at 37 years of age, won 20 games

Hank Bauer, crossing home plate here after a home run, played in nine Series for the Yanks and hit a total of seven home runs.

against eight losses. Vic Raschi, at 33, posted a record of 16–6.

In the National League, the team most baseball pundits thought should have won the two previous pennants, Charlie Dressen's Brooklyn Dodgers, did it in '52. The Boys of Summer finally got their act in order and staved off the Giants, Cardinals, and Phillies, all of whom had a legitimate shot at the flag that year.

The Dodgers possessed a lot of power, Gil Hodges the most imposing in '52 with his 32 homers and 102 RBIs. Roy Campanella hit another 22 four-baggers, Duke Snider had 21, and Jackie Robinson and Andy Pafko stroked 19 apiece. PeeWee Reese pilfered a league-high 30 bases. Relief pitcher Joe Black was named Rookie of the Year in the NL, a

result of his 15 saves and record of 15–4, the Dodger best that year.

Neither team hit very well in the Series, and all but one of the games were very close. It went back and forth, but, at the end of seven games, as usual, the Yankees came out on top. It was Yankee pitching, especially that of Vic Raschi and Allie Reynolds, that proved to be the deciding factor. At this point in Yankee-Dodger postseason meetings, the Yankees had won all four.

The next year, 1953, it would be increased to five Dodger World Series humblings at the hands of the Yankees. It would also be an unprecedented and unequalled five straight world championships for the Yankees.

But if ever there was a year that appeared ideal for the

Dodgers to reverse the flow, this was it. They marched through the National League, winning 105 games, and ending up 13 games ahead of the second-place Braves in their first year playing out of Milwaukee. And when the season's statistics were tabulated, the Dodgers had bettered the Yankees in just about every offensive category: they outhit them by 12 percentage points, outslugged them by 57, scored 154 more runs, collected 109 more hits, and blasted 208 home runs to the Yankees' 139.

Carl Furillo of the Dodgers took the NL batting crown that year with a career high .344. Roy Campanella earned the MVP honors when he swatted 41 homers, drove in 142 runs, and hit .312. Duke Snider batted .336; Jackie Robinson, .329; and Gil Hodges, .302. Jim "Junior" Gilliam's 17 triples were the most in the majors, and he was voted NL Rookie of the Year. Duke Snider hit 42 homers, Hodges hit 31, and Furillo, 21. Carl Erskine won 20 games while losing just six, and the Dodgers got fine bullpen help from Clem Labine.

The usually intimidating bats of the Yankees, however, were quiet in '53. Only Gene Woodling and Hank Bauer hit above .300, and they did it by a mere six and

Jim "Junior" Gilliam played in seven World Series for the Dodgers, three in Brooklyn and four in Los Angeles, during the period of 1953 through 1966. He batted only .211 overall, however, far below his lifetime average of .265.

Carl Erskine, the Dodger's ever-steady righthander set a World Series record when he struck out 14 Yankees in 1953. "Oisk" took to the mound for the Dodgers in five different World Series.

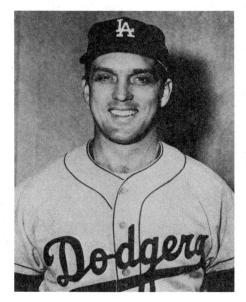

four points respectively. Yogi Berra had 27 home runs and Mickey Mantle, 21. They did not have a 20-game winner, but Whitey Ford (18–6) and Eddie Lopat (16–4) had looked very good, and Allie Reynolds, now 38, was being used effectively as a reliever.

As good as the Dodger prospects appeared on paper, they did not materialize on the field. Once again the Boys of Summer fell to the Boys of Autumn. It took the Yankees six games, but with an outstanding performance from Billy Martin and consistent pitching they did it, giving Casey Stengel his fifth world crown.

It could not, of course, go on forever. Somehow, sometime, someone had to dethrone the Yankees. And it was perhaps only appropriate that it be the Cleveland Indians, who had been runner-up in the American League for the three seasons preceding 1954. Under Al Lopez, they had given the Yankees a run each year but could never quite squeeze ahead. Now it was their turn.

Cleveland won 111 games in 1954, the most ever won by an American League team and second in major league history to the 116 victories recorded by the Chicago Cubs back in 1906. As a result, the Indians ended up eight

games in front of the hitherto unconquerable Yankees, forcing Casey Stengel to do what he must have thought he would never have to do, and that was to watch the World Series on television.

The Indians were a strong meld of good hitting and devastating pitching. In the latter area, Bob Lemon won 23 games and lost just seven, Early Wynn took another 23 against 11 losses, and Mike Garcia collected 19 wins, Art Houtteman had 15, and an aging Bob Feller, 13. Reliever Ray Narleski registered 13 saves. The team ERA of 2.78 was clearly the best in either league.

At the plate, they had the AL batting crown holder Bobby Avila (.341). Larry Doby led the league in homers (32) and RBIs (126). Al Rosen belted 24 homers and drove in 102 runs.

Like the Yankees, the Dodgers did not make it back to the Series either, although New Yorkers would still have the opportunity to attend several of the games. Leo Durocher's Giants earned the right to play in their fourteenth World Series, beating out the Dodgers by five games and the Milwaukee Braves by eight. One of the chief reasons was 23-year-old "Say Hey" Willie Mays, who fully established himself in 1954 by batting .345, best in the majors, hitting 41 home runs, 13 triples (another league high), 33 doubles, and driving in 110 runs, all of which gained for him the NL MVP honors. Also aiding the Giant cause were Don Mueller, who hit a career high .342, and Hank Thompson, who cracked 26 homers. Alvin Dark hit 20, Monte Irvin had 19, and Whitey Lockman, 16. Pinch hitter Dusty Rhodes, who would grandly display his value in the Series, batted .341. Johnny Antonelli won 21 games; Marv Grissom saved 19.

By dint of the fact that Cleveland had had such a monumental season, they were a distinct favorite, although no one was counting the Giants out. No one, however, expected Durocher's Giants to rush in and sweep the Series as decisively as they did. And no one expected the normally resourceful bats of the Indians to turn so soft and flat. With all the power from their big-name batters notwithstanding, Cleveland tapped out a dismal team average of .190 and scored only nine runs in the four games of the Series. The Giants, led by pinch hitter Dusty Rhodes, who came through just about every time he was asked to go to the plate, were not really challenged in any one of the four games. It was a great disappointment to Clevelanders,

and the Indians have yet to return to the World Series.

In 1955, it would be two old antagonists going at it again, the Yankees and the Dodgers. After their one year absence, the Bronx Bombers, whose bombardments were no longer quite as dramatic as they had been in the Ruth/Gehrig era or even the DiMaggio/Dickey/Keller period, reasserted themselves at the top of the American League ladder. Casey Stengel led them there despite a lot of pressure from the Indians, who ended up three games out, and the Chicago White Sox who came as close as five games. As a team, New York only hit .260, and Moose Skowron and Mickey Mantle were the only two to top .300 (.319 and .306 respectively). Mantle, however, led the league with 37 home runs; Yogi Berra, named MVP for the second year in succession, whacked 27, and Hank Bauer, 20, to ensure that the Yanks still had at least some power in their bats. Whitey Ford won 18 games for them, losing only seven, and Bob Turley picked up 17 wins and Tommy Byrne, 16.

But it was finally to be the year of the Dodgers. Brooklyn was now under the pilotship of Walt Alston, in his second year at the helm. No one came close to them.

Two of the biggest bats of the 1955 World Series: Hank Bauer (left) who hit .429 and Yogi Berra who batted .417.

They won 22 of their first 24 games that year and then coasted the rest of the way. Nearest at the end were the Milwaukee Braves but they were 13½ games back.

A pure powerhouse is the only way to describe the Dodgers of '55. As a team they blasted 201 home runs, second most in their entire history (they hit 208 in 1953). Duke Snider accounted for 42 of them; Roy Campanella stroked 32; Gil Hodges, 27; Carl Furillo, 26; and Don Zimmer, 15. Even PeeWee Reese and Sandy

Amoros sent 10 apiece out of the ballpark. Snider led the league in runs scored (126) and RBIs (136). Campanella hit .318 and was named MVP. Furillo batted .314 and Snider, .309. Don Newcombe had the best record (20–5) and Clem Labine came up with 11 saves and 13 wins.

Still, the Series-virgin Dodgers had failed in all seven of their previous postseason appearances, five of the defeats administered by the Yankees. Now, in '55 the taunts of "postseason choke"

Jackie Robinson steals home in the 1955 World Series. Only 12 players have ever stolen home in a Series game. The Yankee catcher is Yogi Berra; the other Dodger was pinch-hitter Frank Kellert. (Sequence continues on page 178.)

or "can't win the big one" would be laid to rest. The Dodgers finally overcame the Yankees to reap their first world championship. It took them seven games to do it, and they had to come back from a two-game to one deficit, but with consistent hitting and some fine pitching from Johnny Podres and Clem Labine, they succeeded.

The World Series of 1956 would have two things in common with the one that had just preceded it: the same two teams would face each other and the match would go the full seven games.

Walt Alston's world champion Dodgers got to the classic again after a neck-and-neck race with the Milwaukee Braves and the Cincinnati Reds, one that was not decided until the last day of the baseball season. But when it was final, the Dodgers were on top, the Braves a game behind, and the Reds trailing by two. Brooklyn's top hitter in '56 was Junior Gilliam, who only batted .300, but they still had plenty of power. Duke Snider led the league with 43 homers, Gil Hodges blasted another 32, Carl Furillo hit 21, and Roy Campanella, 20. The most luminous star that year however, was Don Newcombe, who won 27 games while losing only

Walt Alston managed world champions in Brooklyn and in Los Angeles. He managed Dodger teams in six different World Series.

seven. He was voted the league's MVP and won the Cy Young award, which was given for the first time in 1956 (it was a single major league award then, not given to a pitcher in each league until 1967). And Clem Labine racked up 19 saves, the most in either league.

The Yankees won their 22nd American League pennant in '56, and they did it with relative ease, outdistancing the second-place Cleveland Indians by nine games. Key to their success that year was Mickey Mantle, who won the

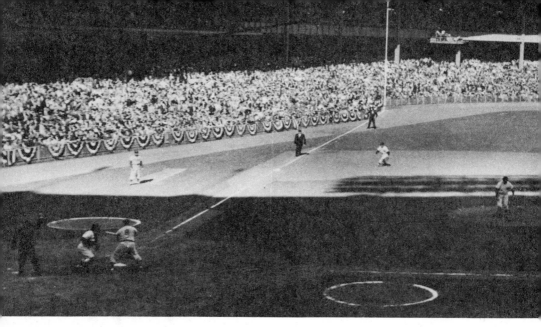

Yankee hurler Don Larsen wings the last pitch of his perfect game in the 1956 World Series here. It is the only perfect game and the only no-hitter in Series history. The victim of this strike-out is Dodger pinch hitter Dale Mitchell. The catcher is Yogi Berra.

Triple Crown with a batting average of .353, 52 home runs, and 130 RBIs. He also led the AL in runs scored with 132 and was an easy choice for MVP honors.

Also for the Yanks, Gil McDougald hit .311 and Moose Skowron, .308. Yogi Berra stroked 30 homers and drove 105 runs home, while Hank Bauer added another 26 four-baggers and Skowron, 23. Whitey Ford was still the keystone of their pitching staff (19-6), but Johnny Kucks won 18 games and Tom Sturdivant, 16.

Casey Stengel was looking for his sixth world crown and some revenge against the culprits who had deprived him of it the year before. And he got it. Whereas the previous year the Yankees won the first two games of the Series and then blew it, in '56 the Dodgers took the first two and then lost it. The highlight, without question, was Game 5 when Yankee righthander Don Larsen, who had only an 11–5 year, hurled a perfect game, retiring 27 consecutive Dodger batters. It stands as the only no-hitter ever thrown in a World Series, and it was the first perfect game since Charlie Robertson pitched one for the Chicago White Sox back in 1922.

The Braves came back to the World Series in 1957, appearing for the first time since 1948 when

Casey Stengel liked to clown but he also liked to win pennants. The Old Professor managed the Yankees in 10 World Series, the first in 1949 and the last in 1960.

they were representing the city of Boston. In the interim they had gone from beantown to beertown,

playing their baseball in Milwaukee. Under Fred Haney, in his first year as manager of the Braves, they had powered their way to the pennant behind the bats of Hank Aaron (44 home runs, 132 RBIs, both major league highs) and Eddie Mathews (32 homers, 94 RBIs). Aaron, the league MVP, also hit .322, and Red Schoendienst, acquired from the Giants during the season, batted .310 and led the majors with 200 hits. They had a superb pitching staff, highlighted by Cy Young awardee Warren Spahn (21–11, the only 20-game winner in the NL that year), Bob Buhl (18–7), and Lew Burdette (17–9).

Back again were the Yankees. Like the Braves, they too had power. Much of it was stored in Mickey Mantle's bat, which he used to pound out 34 homers, 94 RBIs, and an average of .365. For the second year in a row, he was named the American League's MVP. The Yanks also got 24 home runs from Yogi Berra, 18 from Hank Bauer, and 17 from Moose Skowron, who also hit .304. And 20-year-old Tony Kubek, who played the outfield, shortstop, and third base at various times, won AL Rookie of the Year honors. The Yankee pitching staff was not in the best of shape, however, with Whitey Ford plagued

Mickey Mantle chases a fly ball from the bat of Hank Aaron of the Milwaukee Braves in the 1957 Series. It went for a triple. Aaron hit .393 that Series.

by a bad arm. As a result, Tom Sturdivant proved to be their biggest winner (16–6), while bullpen ace Bob Grim was credited with the most saves in the league (19).

In the Series, the sluggers from Milwaukee batted only .209 as a team, 39 percentage points less than the Yankees. Only Hank Aaron, who hit .393, had an exciting Series at the plate for the Braves. But Lew Burdette was masterful from the mound, shutting out the Yankees twice and allowing them only two runs in another game. His three wins were the most in a Series since Harry Brecheen was credited with three in 1946 (one was in relief) and the most complete-game victories since Stan Coveleski of the Cleveland Indians went an equal 27 innings to win three games back in 1920. It took the Braves seven games, but they beat the Yanks, something few other teams could boast of in the 1950s.

The Braves made a return trip in 1958. So did the Yankees. And for the fourth Series in a row, it would take seven games to decide the world champion.

Neither team had much difficulty capturing its pennant. The Braves cruised in eight games ahead of the Pittsburgh Pirates,

The winningest pitcher in World Series history is Whitey Ford. In his 11 appearances from 1950 through 1964 he posted a record of 10–8. He also holds the record for most strikeouts (94).

and the Yankees ended up with 10 separating them from the Chicago White Sox. The Braves had three hitters who topped .300: Wes Covington (.330), Hank Aaron (.326), and Frank Torre (.309), and the Yankees boasted an equal number: Elston Howard (.314), Mickey Mantle (.304), and Norm Siebern (.300). Mantle again led the AL in homers with 42 as well as runs scored (127).

A Yankee line-up of World Series legends (l to r): Mickey Mantle, Yogi Berra, Whitey Ford, Joe DiMaggio, and Casey Stengel.

Eddie Mathews hit the most round-trippers for Milwaukee (31), while Aaron clouted 30; Wes Covington, 24; Joe Adcock, 19; and Del Crandall, 18. Warren Spahn won 22 games for the Braves against 11 defeats, and Lew Burdette posted a record of 20–10. The Yanks' Bob Turley, with a record of 21–7, won the Cy Young award, and Ryne Duren recorded 20 saves, the most in the American League.

The Series got underway in Milwaukee and the Braves won the first two games. Then, at Yankee Stadium, they split the next two games, and the Braves had a com-

manding three-games to one advantage. Not since 1925 had a team come back from such a deficit, but the Yankees were old pros at postseason play. They took the final in the Bronx then went back out to Milwaukee and swept the last two games. It was their eighteenth world championship, and it was Casey Stengel's seventh, tying him with Joe McCarthy for the most in baseball history.

The 1959 World Series was destined to be the largest ever attended. The reason: the Dodgers, the NL pennant winners, had moved from Brooklyn to Los An-

Highlights of the 1959 World Series.

geles and were now playing their games in a mammoth football stadium, the L.A. Coliseum. In three successive Series games out there, they would demolish all previous attendance records. For Games 3, 4, and 5, crowds of 92,394, 92,650, and 92,706 passed through the Coliseum's turnstiles. When the ticket stubs for all six games were tallied, the total was 420,784, the only time in Series history that attendance exceeded 400,000, including seven- and eight-game Series.

Facing the Dodgers were not the traditional AL flag-bearers, the Yankees. Instead they had been unseated by the Chicago White Sox who, under Al Lopez, had beaten out the Cleveland Indians by five games. Throughout baseballdom they were known as the "Go-Go" Sox, so-called because they were a team of extraor-

dinary hustle in the field and on the basepaths. In Chicago's Comiskey Park, the chant was "Go . . . go . . . go . . ." everytime a runner got on base. And they did go like no other team in the majors, stealing a total of 113 bases (the closest to them in this department were the Dodgers who pilfered 84). Luis Aparicio was the most deft at this acceptable form of thievery, snatching a major league high of 56 bases. Jim Landis stole another 20. Only Nellie Fox (.306) hit above .300, however, and only two players accounted for home runs in double figures, Sherm Lollar (22) and Al Smith (17). But the Sox had gotten some potent pitching from old vet Early Wynn, who, at 39, won 22 games and the Cy Young award that year. Bob Shaw won another 18 games and longtime Sox favorite Billy Pierce took 14.

Action from the 1959 Series. Sherm Lollar hits a long fly to center to drive in Jim Landis for the White Sox. *(Photo courtesy of the Chicago Historical Society)*

The most unorthodox stadium in which a World Series was played, the Los Angeles Coliseum. The converted football stadium held crowds of more than 92,000 in three consecutive games in the 1959 Series, the most ever to attend a Series game.

They had two strong relievers in Turk Lown (15 saves) and Gerry Staley (14 saves). The ChiSox had also acquired a certified power hitter, Ted Kluszewski, late in the season and he would certainly prove his worth in the Series. It was the first Series the Sox had earned their way to since the infamous Black Sox who threw the 1919 World Series.

The Dodgers, still piloted by Walt Alston, had just barely gotten by the Milwaukee Braves, ending up two games in front at season's end. It had been a remarkable turnaround because the Dodgers the year before, their first in Los Angeles, had languished in seventh place with a losing record of 71–83, and a distant 21 games behind the Braves.

But in '59 it was a different story. The Dodgers and the Braves battled to a tie at the end of the regular season, each team winning 86 games and losing 68. A three-game playoff was called for, the first match to be held in Milwaukee. With fine relief pitching from rookie Larry Sherry, and a clutch home run from catcher John Roseboro, the Dodgers eked out a 3–2 win. After a night flight to L.A., the Dodgers and Braves convened the next day at the Coli-

Two White Sox heroes of 1959, Nellie Fox, the AL MVP, and Early Wynn, Cy Young Award winner, pose here with AL president Will Harridge.

seum. Losing 5-2, Los Angeles rallied for three runs in the bottom of the ninth inning. Then, in the last half of the 12th, old Brooklynites, Gil Hodges (at 35 years of age) and Carl Furillo (37), teamed to produce the winning run and the NL flag.

The Dodgers had only two .300 hitters in 1959, Duke Snider (.308) and Wally Moon (.302), but they had more power than the White Sox, with such home run hitters as Hodges (25), Snider (23), Moon (19), Charlie Neal (19), and Don Demeter (18). Don Drysdale was most effective from the mound (17-13) but there was also promise from a 23-year-old southpaw named Sandy Koufax.

The Series opened in Chicago with the White Sox, never known for explosive hitting, pounding out an 11-0 victory. From that point on, however, the glory belonged to the Dodgers. The games were close, but Los Angeles managed to come out on top in four of the next five games, with much of the credit going to the work of reliever Larry Sherry, who got credit for two saves and two wins.

So ended the 1950s, the gilded age of Casey Stengel's Yankees, who were as close to being invincible as any baseball club in history. They won six world titles, and playing baseball in October had become a tradition with them. Walt Alston's Dodgers took two world crowns, one in Brooklyn and the other in Los Angeles. Leo Durocher's Giants snagged another, and Fred Haney's Milwaukee Braves grabbed one. It had been as exciting and entertaining a baseball decade as any in the history of the game.

Don Drysdale pitched two innings for the Brooklyn Dodgers in the 1956 World Series, then was a mainstay on the mound for the Los Angeles Dodgers in four other Series. His record: 3-3.

1950

New York Yankees 4
Philadelphia Phillies 0

Line-ups

New York Yankees		Philadelphia Phillies	
1b	Johnny Mize	1b	Eddie Waitkus
2b	Jerry Coleman	2b	Mike Goliat
3b	Bobby Brown	3b	Willie Jones
ss	Phil Rizzuto	ss	Granny Hamner
lf	Gene Woodling	lf	Dick Sisler
cf	Joe DiMaggio	cf	Richie Ashburn
rf	Hank Bauer	rf	Del Ennis
c	Yogi Berra	c	Andy Seminick
mgr	Casey Stengel	mgr	Eddie Sawyer

		R	H	E	Pitching
Game 1	New York	1	5	0	Vic Raschi (W)
	Philadelphia	0	2	1	Jim Konstanty, Russ Meyer (9th)
Game 2	New York	2	10	0	Allie Reynolds (W)
	Philadelphia	1	7	0	Robin Roberts
Game 3	Philadelphia	2	10	2	Ken Heintzelman, Jim Konstanty (8th), Russ Meyer (9th)
	New York	3	7	0	Ed Lopat, Tom Ferrick (9th, W)
Game 4	Philadelphia	2	7	1	Bob Miller, Jim Konstanty (1st), Robin Roberts (9th)
	New York	5	8	2	Whitey Ford (W), Allie Reynolds (9th)

Highlights

- The Yankees won their thirteenth world title and recorded their sixth Series sweep.
- The Phillies scored just five runs in the four games and batted only .203.
- Vic Raschi pitched a two-hit shutout for the Yanks in Game 1.
- Joe DiMaggio hit a home run in the top of the tenth in Game 2 to give the Yanks a win.
- With the score tied, 2–2, in Game 3, Jerry Coleman rapped a single to score Gene Woodling with the winning run in the bottom of the ninth inning. Coleman had three hits and two RBIs in the game.
- Yogi Berra homered and drove in two runs to pace the Yankees in Game 4.
- Whitey Ford got the victory in Game 4, the first of ten he would get during his Series career, the most ever compiled.

Best Efforts

Batting

Average	Gene Woodling .429
	Granny Hamner .429
Home Runs	Joe DiMaggio 1
	Yogi Berra 1
Triples	Bobby Brown 1
	Granny Hamner 1
Doubles	Granny Hamner 2
Hits	Gene Woodling 6
	Granny Hamner 6
Runs	(five players) 2
RBIs	Jerry Coleman 3

Pitching

Wins	(four players) 1
ERA	Vic Raschi 0.00
	Whitey Ford 0.00
Strikeouts	Allie Reynolds 7
Innings Pitched	Jim Konstanty 15

1951

New York Yankees 4
New York Giants 2

Line-ups

New York Yankees	New York Giants
1b Joe Collins	1b Whitey Lockman
2b Gil McDougald	2b Eddie Stanky
3b Bobby Brown	3b Bobby Thomson
ss Phil Rizzuto	ss Alvin Dark
lf Gene Woodling	lf Monte Irvin
cf Joe DiMaggio	cf Willie Mays
rf Hank Bauer	rf Hank Thompson
c Yogi Berra	c Wes Westrum
mgr Casey Stengel	mgr Leo Durocher

		R	H	E	Pitching
Game 1	Giants	5	10	1	Dave Koslo (W)
	Yankees	1	7	1	Allie Reynolds, Bobby Hogue (7th), Tom Morgan (8th)
Game 2	Giants	1	5	1	Larry Jansen, George Spencer (7th)
	Yankees	3	6	0	Eddie Lopat (W)
Game 3	Yankees	2	5	2	Vic Raschi, Bobby Hogue (5th), Joe Ostrowski (7th)
	Giants	6	7	2	Jim Hearn (W), Sheldon Jones (8th)
Game 4	Yankees	6	12	0	Allie Reynolds (W)
	Giants	2	8	2	Sal Maglie, Sheldon Jones (6th), Monte Kennedy (9th)
Game 5	Yankees	13	12	1	Eddie Lopat (W)
	Giants	1	5	3	Larry Jansen, Monte Kennedy (4th), George Spencer (6th), Al Corwin (7th), Alex Konikowski (9th)

		R	H	E	Pitching
Game 6	Giants	3	11	1	Dave Koslo, Jim Hearn (7th), George Spencer (8th)
	Yankees	4	7	0	Vic Raschi (W), Johnny Sain (7th), Bob Kuzava (9th)

Highlights

- Casey Stengel became only the second manager to win three consecutive world championships (Joe McCarthy won four for the Yankees, 1936–39).
- Monte Irvin's ten singles tied the record for a six-game Series.
- Irvin got a triple, three singles, and stole home for the Giants in Game 1.
- Alvin Dark provided the Giants with their margin of victory in Game 1 by cracking a three-run homer.
- Joe Collins slugged a homer to give the Yankees a lead in Game 2 which they would not relinquish.
- Whitey Lockman hit a three-run homer for the Giants to provide the winning runs in Game 3.
- The big hit in the Yankee win of Game 4 was Joe DiMaggio's two-run homer in the fifth inning.
- Gil McDougald of the Yankees became only the third player to hit a grand slam homer in a Series when he belted one in the third inning of Game 5. Joe DiMaggio and Phil Rizzuto drove in three runs apiece in the same game.
- Hank Bauer tripled with the bases loaded to provide the game-winning runs in Game 6 for the Yanks.

Best Efforts

Batting

Average	Monte Irvin .458
Home Runs	(seven players) 1
Triples	Hank Bauer 1
	Gene Woodling 1
	Monte Irvin 1
Doubles	Alvin Dark 3
Hits	Monte Irvin 11
Runs	Gene Woodling 6
RBIs	Gil McDougald 7

Pitching

Wins	Eddie Lopat 2–0
ERA	Eddie Lopat 0.50
Strikeouts	Allie Reynolds 8
Innings Pitched	Eddie Lopat 18

1952

New York Yankees 4
Brooklyn Dodgers 3

Line-ups

New York Yankees		Brooklyn Dodgers	
1b	Johnny Mize	1b	Gil Hodges
2b	Billy Martin	2b	Jackie Robinson
3b	Gil McDougald	3b	Billy Cox
ss	Phil Rizzuto	ss	PeeWee Reese
lf	Gene Woodling	lf	Andy Pafko
cf	Mickey Mantle	cf	Duke Snider
rf	Hank Bauer	rf	Carl Furillo
c	Yogi Berra	c	Roy Campanella
mgr	Casey Stengel	mgr	Charlie Dressen

		R	H	E	Pitching
Game 1	New York	2	6	2	Allie Reynolds, Ray Scarborough (8th)
	Brooklyn	4	6	0	Joe Black (W)
Game 2	New York	7	10	0	Vic Raschi (W)
	Brooklyn	1	3	1	Carl Erskine, Billy Loes (6th), Ken Lehman (8th)
Game 3	Brooklyn	5	11	0	Preacher Roe (W)
	New York	3	6	2	Eddie Lopat, Tom Gorman (9th)
Game 4	Brooklyn	0	4	1	Joe Black, Johnny Rutherford (8th)
	New York	2	4	1	Allie Reynolds (W)
Game 5	Brooklyn	6	10	0	Carl Erskine (W)
	New York	5	5	1	Ewell Blackwell, Johnny Sain (6th)
Game 6	New York	3	9	0	Vic Raschi (W), Allie Reynolds (8th)
	Brooklyn	2	8	1	Billy Loes, Preacher Roe (9th)

1952

New York Yankees 4
Brooklyn Dodgers 3

		R	H	E	Pitching
Game 7	New York	4	10	4	Eddie Lopat, Allie Reynolds (4th, W), Vic Raschi (7th), Bob Kuzava (7th)
	Brooklyn	2	8	1	Joe Black, Preacher Roe (6th), Carl Erskine (8th)

Highlights

- The Yankees recorded their fifteenth world championship, and their fourth in a row.
- The Dodgers lost their sixth Series in six appearances.
- Duke Snider hit four home runs to tie the record for most in a seven-game Series set by Babe Ruth back in 1926.
- Johnny Mize hit three home runs for the Yankees, one as a pinch hit.
- Dodger sluggers hit three home runs in Game 1: Jackie Robinson, Duke Snider, and PeeWee Reese.
- Vic Raschi pitched a three-hitter and Billy Martin hit a three-run homer in Game 2 to bring the Yankees a victory.
- With the score 3–2, the Dodgers ahead, in the ninth inning of Game 3, Jackie Robinson and PeeWee Reese singled, pulled off a double steal, and then both scored what proved to be the game-winning runs on Yogi Berra's passed ball.
- Allie Reynolds hurled a four-hit shutout for the Yankees in Game 4, striking out ten Dodger batters in the process.
- Johnny Mize homered and Mickey Mantle tripled and scored for the Yanks in Game 4 to provide the winning runs.
- Duke Snider hit a home run, drove in the tying run that sent Game 5 into extra innings, then batted in the winning run in the 11th inning.
- Carl Erskine pitched the entire 11 innings of Game 5, allowed only five hits, and retired the last 19 Yankees in a row.
- Duke Snider hit two homers in Game 6.
- Yogi Berra and Mickey Mantle homered for the Yanks to provide the tying and winning runs in Game 6.
- Mantle homered to break a 2–2 tie in the sixth inning of Game 7, then singled to drive in Phil Rizzuto with an insurance run the next inning.

Best Efforts

Batting

Average	Johnny Mize	.400
Home Runs	Duke Snider	4
Triples	Mickey Mantle	1
	Gene Woodling	1
Doubles	Billy Cox	2
	Carl Furillo	2
	Duke Snider	2
Hits	Mickey Mantle	10
	PeeWee Reese	10
	Duke Snider	10
Runs	Mickey Mantle	5
	Duke Snider	5
RBIs	Duke Snider	8

Pitching

Wins	Vic Raschi	2-0
	Allie Reynolds	2-1
ERA	Vic Raschi	1.59
Strikeouts	Vic Raschi	18
	Allie Reynolds	18
Innings Pitched	Joe Black	21⅓

1953

New York Yankees 4
Brooklyn Dodgers 2

Line-ups

New York Yankees		Brooklyn Dodgers	
1b	Joe Collins	1b	Gil Hodges
2b	Billy Martin	2b	Junior Gilliam
3b	Gil McDougald	3b	Billy Cox
ss	Phil Rizzuto	ss	PeeWee Reese
lf	Gene Woodling	lf	Jackie Robinson
cf	Mickey Mantle	cf	Duke Snider
rf	Hank Bauer	rf	Carl Furillo
c	Yogi Berra	c	Roy Campanella
mgr	Casey Stengel	mgr	Charlie Dressen

		R	H	E	Pitching
Game 1	Brooklyn	5	12	2	Carl Erskine, Jim Hughes (2nd), Clem Labine (6th), Ben Wade (7th)
	New York	9	12	0	Allie Reynolds, Johnny Sain (6th, W)
Game 2	Brooklyn	2	9	1	Preacher Roe
	New York	4	5	0	Eddie Lopat (W)
Game 3	New York	2	6	0	Vic Raschi
	Brooklyn	3	9	0	Carl Erskine (W)
Game 4	New York	3	9	0	Whitey Ford, Tom Gorman (2nd), Johnny Sain (5th), Art Schallock (7th)
	Brooklyn	7	12	0	Billy Loes (W), Clem Labine (9th)
Game 5	New York	11	11	1	Jim McDonald (W), Bob Kuzava (8th), Allie Reynolds (9th)
	Brooklyn	7	14	1	Johnny Podres, Russ Meyer (3rd), Ben Wade (8th), Joe Black (9th)

		R	**H**	**E**	**Pitching**
Game 6	Brooklyn	3	8	3	Carl Erskine, Bob Milliken (5th), Clem Labine (7th)
	New York	4	13	0	Whitey Ford, Allie Reynolds (8th, W)

Highlights

- The Yankees became the first and only team in World Series history to win five consecutive world championships.
- The nine Yankee home runs set a standard for a six-game Series.
- Billy Martin of the Yanks tied a record for a six-game Series when he batted .500 (12 for 24). His 12 hits are the most ever in a six-game Series.
- Five home runs were hit in Game 1: Junior Gilliam, Gil Hodges, George Shuba (pinch hit), Yogi Berra, and Joe Collins.
- Mickey Mantle hit a two-run homer to produce the winning runs in Game 2.
- In Game 3, Carl Erskine struck out 14 Yankee batters to set a new Series record.
- Roy Campanella homered in the bottom of the eighth of Game 3 to produce the game-winning run for Brooklyn.
- Duke Snider hit a home run, two doubles, and accounted for four RBIs to lead the Dodgers to victory in Game 4.
- Mickey Mantle hit the fourth grand slam home run in Series history in Game 5.
- The six home runs hit in Game 5 tied a Series record. Besides Mantle's grand slammer, four-baggers were logged by Gene Woodling, Billy Martin, Gil McDougald, Billy Cox, and Junior Gilliam.
- With the score tied, 3–3, Billy Martin singled to drive in Hank Bauer in the bottom of the ninth of Game 6 to give the Yankees the game and the Series.

Best Efforts

Batting

Average	Billy Martin	.500
Home Runs	Billy Martin	2
	Mickey Mantle	2
	Junior Gilliam	2
Triples	Billy Martin	2
Doubles	Junior Gilliam	3
	Duke Snider	3
Hits	Billy Martin	12
Runs	Hank Bauer	6
	Roy Campanella	6
RBIs	Billy Martin	8

Pitching

Wins	(six players)	1
ERA	Eddie Lopat	2.00
Strikeouts	Carl Erskine	16
Innings Pitched	Carl Erskine	14

1954

New York Giants 4
Cleveland Indians 0

Line-ups

New York Giants		**Cleveland Indians**	
1b	Whitey Lockman	1b	Vic Wertz
2b	Davey Williams	2b	Bobby Avila
3b	Hank Thompson	3b	Al Rosen
ss	Alvin Dark	ss	George Strickland
lf	Monte Irvin	lf	Al Smith
cf	Willie Mays	cf	Larry Doby
rf	Don Mueller	rf	Dave Philley
c	Wes Westrum	c	Jim Hegan
mgr	Leo Durocher	mgr	Al Lopez

		R	H	E	Pitching
Game 1	Cleveland	2	8	0	Bob Lemon
	New York	5	9	3	Sal Maglie, Don Liddle (8th), Marv Grissom (8th, W)
Game 2	Cleveland	1	8	0	Early Wynn, Don Mossi (8th)
	New York	3	4	0	Johnny Antonelli (W)
Game 3	New York	6	10	1	Ruben Gomez (W), Hoyt Wilhelm (8th)
	Cleveland	2	4	2	Mike Garcia, Art Houtteman (4th), Ray Narleski (6th), Don Mossi (9th)
Game 4	New York	7	10	3	Don Liddle (W), Hoyt Wilhelm (7th), Johnny Antonelli (8th)
	Cleveland	4	6	2	Bob Lemon, Hal Newhouser (5th), Ray Narleski (5th), Don Mossi (6th), Mike Garcia (8th)

Highlights

- The New York Giants, making their fourteenth World Series appearance, won their fifth world title.
- The six RBIs from Dusty Rhodes were the most ever by a pinch hitter.
- Hank Thompson set a four-game Series record when he collected seven bases on balls.
- Willie Mays saved Game 1 for the Giants when he made a sensational over-the-shoulder catch about 450 feet from homeplate of a towering blast from Vic Wertz with two men on base in the eighth inning.
- Dusty Rhodes won Game 1 for the Giants with a pinch-hit home run in the bottom of the tenth inning.
- Rhodes got a single and a homer in two at-bats and drove in two runs to pace the Giants in Game 2.
- Rhodes and Willie Mays batted in two runs apiece to lead the Giants in Game 3.
- Monte Irvin and Wes Westrum drove in a pair of runs each to give the Giants the edge in Game 4.

Best Efforts

Batting

Average	Vic Wertz .500
Home Runs	Dusty Rhodes 2
Triples	Vic Wertz 1
Doubles	Vic Wertz 2
Hits	Vic Wertz 8
Runs	Hank Thompson 6
RBIs	Wes Westrum 7

Pitching

Wins	(four players) 1
ERA	Johnny Antonelli 0.84
Strikeouts	Johnny Antonelli 12
Innings Pitched	Bob Lemon 13⅓

1955

Brooklyn Dodgers 4
New York Yankees 3

Line-ups

Brooklyn Dodgers		**New York Yankees**	
1b	Gil Hodges	1b	Joe Collins
2b	Junior Gilliam	2b	Billy Martin
3b	Jackie Robinson	3b	Gil McDougald
ss	PeeWee Reese	ss	Phil Rizzuto
lf	Sandy Amoros	lf	Elston Howard
cf	Duke Snider	cf	Irv Noren
rf	Carl Furillo	rf	Hank Bauer
c	Roy Campanella	c	Yogi Berra
mgr	Walt Alston	mgr	Casey Stengel

		R	H	E	Pitching
Game 1	Brooklyn	5	10	0	Don Newcombe, Don Bessent (6th), Clem Labine (8th)
	New York	6	9	1	Whitey Ford (W), Bob Grim (9th)
Game 2	Brooklyn	2	5	2	Billy Loes, Don Bessent (4th), Karl Spooner (5th), Clem Labine (8th)
	New York	4	8	0	Tommy Byrne (W)
Game 3	New York	3	7	0	Bob Turley, Tom Morgan (2nd), Johnny Kucks (5th), Tom Sturdivant (7th)
	Brooklyn	8	11	1	Johnny Podres (W)
Game 4	New York	5	9	0	Don Larsen, Johnny Kucks (5th), Rip Coleman (6th), Tom Morgan (7th), Tom Sturdivant (8th)
	Brooklyn	8	14	0	Carl Erskine, Don Bessent (4th), Clem Labine (5th, W)

1955

Brooklyn Dodgers 4
New York Yankees 3

		R	H	E	Pitching
Game 5	New York	3	6	0	Bob Grim, Bob Turley (7th)
	Brooklyn	5	9	2	Roger Craig (W), Clem Labine (7th)
Game 6	Brooklyn	1	4	1	Karl Spooner, Russ Meyer (1st), Ed Roebuck (7th)
	New York	5	8	0	Whitey Ford (W)
Game 7	Brooklyn	2	5	0	Johnny Podres (W)
	New York	0	8	1	Tommy Byrne, Bob Grim (6th), Bob Turley (8th)

Highlights

- The Brooklyn Dodgers won their first world title after failing in seven previous World Series appearances.
- Joe Gordon hit two homers and drove in three runs to lead the Yanks to victory in Game 1.
- Jackie Robinson stole home for the Dodgers in Game 1.
- Tommy Byrne held the Dodgers to five hits in nine innings and batted in two runs himself in Game 2.
- Roy Campanella hit a home run, a double, a single, and drove in three runs to spur the Dodgers to victory in Game 3.
- Duke Snider and Gil Hodges homered and drove in three runs apiece to lead the Dodger attack in Game 4.
- Snider hit two homers in Game 5, bringing his Series total to four and becoming the first and only player ever to hit that many in a Series twice (he also did it in 1952).
- Moose Skowron whacked a three-run homer for New York in Game 6, and Whitey Ford allowed the Dodgers only four hits.
- Johnny Podres hurled a shutout and Gil Hodges drove in two runs to win Game 7 and the Series for the Dodgers.

Best Efforts

Batting

Average	Hank Bauer .429
Home Runs	Duke Snider 4
Triples	Jackie Robinson 1
	Billy Martin 1
	Andy Carey 1
Doubles	Roy Campanella 3
Hits	Yogi Berra 10
Runs	Joe Collins 6
RBIs	Duke Snider 7

Pitching

Wins	Johnny Podres 2–0
	Whitey Ford 2–0
ERA	Johnny Podres 1.00
Strikeouts	Johnny Podres 10
	Whitey Ford 10
Innings Pitched	Johnny Podres 18

1956

New York Yankees   4
Brooklyn Dodgers   3

Line-ups

New York Yankees		**Brooklyn Dodgers**	
1b	Joe Collins	1b	Gil Hodges
2b	Billy Martin	2b	Junior Gilliam
3b	Andy Carey	3b	Jackie Robinson
ss	Gil McDougald	ss	PeeWee Reese
lf	Enos Slaughter	lf	Sandy Amoros
cf	Mickey Mantle	cf	Duke Snider
rf	Hank Bauer	rf	Carl Furillo
c	Yogi Berra	c	Roy Campanella
mgr	Casey Stengel	mgr	Walt Alston

		R	H	E	Pitching
Game 1	New York	3	9	1	Whitey Ford, Johnny Kucks (4th), Tom Morgan (6th), Bob Turley (8th)
	Brooklyn	6	9	0	Sal Maglie (W)
Game 2	New York	8	12	2	Don Larsen, Johnny Kucks (2nd), Tommy Byrne (2nd), Tom Sturdivant (3rd), Tom Morgan (3rd), Bob Turley (5th), Mickey McDermott (6th)
	Brooklyn	13	12	0	Don Newcombe, Ed Roebuck (2nd), Don Bessent (3rd, W)
Game 3	Brooklyn	3	8	1	Roger Craig, Clem Labine (7th)
	New York	5	8	1	Whitey Ford (W)
Game 4	Brooklyn	2	6	0	Carl Erskine, Ed Roebuck (5th), Don Drysdale (7th)
	New York	6	7	2	Tom Sturdivant (W)

		R	**H**	**E**	**Pitching**
Game 5	Brooklyn	0	0	0	Sal Maglie
	New York	2	5	0	Don Larsen (W)
Game 6	New York	0	7	0	Bob Turley
	Brooklyn	1	4	0	Clem Labine (W)
Game 7	New York	9	10	0	Johnny Kucks (W)
	Brooklyn	0	3	1	Don Newcombe, Don Bessent (4th), Roger Craig (7th), Ed Roebuck (7th), Carl Erskine (9th)

Highlights

- The Yankees laid claim to their seventeenth world title, and Casey Stengel had his sixth in eight years as their manager.
- The 12 New York home runs set a record for a seven-game Series.
- Dodger slugger Gil Hodges hit a three-run homer to provide the winning margin in Game 1.
- Game 2, which lasted three hours and 26 minutes, was the longest in terms of time up to that point in Series history.
- The seven pitchers used by the Yankees in Game 2 were the most employed in a single Series game up to that time.
- The total of 11 runs scored by the Dodgers (6) and the Yankees (5) in the second inning of Game 2 tied a single-inning Series record.
- Yogi Berra hit a grand slam homer in Game 2.
- Duke Snider hit a three-run homer and Gil Hodges drove in four runs to pace Brooklyn in Game 2.
- Enos Slaughter belted a three-run homer to provide the margin of victory for the Yankees in Game 3.
- Don Larsen pitched the World Series' first and only no-hit game for the Yankees in Game 5. It was a "perfect game," one in which he retired 27 consecutive Dodger batters, striking out seven of them.
- Both Bob Turley of the Yanks and Clem Labine of the Dodgers pitched scoreless ball through nine innings in Game 6, but Jackie Robinson ended it when he singled in the bottom of the tenth to send Junior Gilliam home with the winning run.
- Johnny Kucks pitched a three-hit shutout for New York in Game 7.
- Moose Skowron hit a grand slam home run and Yogi Berra hit two homers and batted in another four runs for the Yankees in Game 7.

Best Efforts

Batting

Average	Yogi Berra .360
Home Runs	Mickey Mantle 3
	Yogi Berra 3
Triples	PeeWee Reese 1
Doubles	(four players) 2
Hits	Yogi Berra 9
	Hank Bauer 9
Runs	Mickey Mantle 6
	Enos Slaughter 6
RBIs	Yogi Berra 10

Pitching

Wins	(seven players) 1
ERA	Don Larsen 0.00
	Clem Labine 0.00
Strikeouts	Sal Maglie 15
Innings Pitched	Sal Maglie 17

1957

Milwaukee Braves 4
New York Yankees 3

Line-ups

Milwaukee Braves		**New York Yankees**	
1b	Joe Adcock	1b	Elston Howard
2b	Red Schoendienst	2b	Jerry Coleman
3b	Eddie Mathews	3b	Jerry Lumpe
ss	Johnny Logan	ss	Gil McDougald
lf	Wes Covington	lf	Tony Kubek
cf	Hank Aaron	cf	Mickey Mantle
rf	Andy Pafko	rf	Hank Bauer
c	Del Crandall	c	Yogi Berra
mgr	Fred Haney	mgr	Casey Stengel

		R	H	E	Pitching
Game 1	Milwaukee	1	5	0	Warren Spahn, Ernie Johnson (6th), Don McMahon (7th)
	New York	3	9	1	Whitey Ford (W)
Game 2	Milwaukee	4	8	0	Lew Burdette (W)
	New York	2	7	2	Bobby Shantz, Art Ditmar (4th), Bob Grim (8th)
Game 3	New York	12	9	0	Bob Turley, Don Larsen (2nd, W)
	Milwaukee	3	8	1	Bob Buhl, Juan Pizarro (1st), Gene Conley (3rd), Ernie Johnson (5th), Bob Trowbridge (7th), Don McMahon (8th)
Game 4	New York	5	11	0	Tom Sturdivant, Bobby Shantz (5th), Johnny Kucks (8th), Tommy Byrne (8th), Bob Grim (10th)
	Milwaukee	7	7	0	Warren Spahn (W)

1957

Milwaukee Braves 4
New York Yankees 3

		R	H	E	Pitching
Game 5	New York	0	7	0	Whitey Ford, Bob Turley (8th)
	Milwaukee	1	6	1	Lew Burdette (W)
Game 6	Milwaukee	2	4	0	Bob Buhl, Ernie Johnson (3rd), Don McMahon (8th)
	New York	3	7	0	Bob Turley (W)
Game 7	Milwaukee	5	9	1	Lew Burdette (W)
	New York	0	7	3	Don Larsen, Bobby Shantz (3rd), Art Ditmar (4th), Tom Sturdivant (6th), Tommy Byrne (8th)

Highlights

- The Milwaukee Braves made their first Series appearance and won the world title.
- Lew Burdette of the Braves tied a Series record by winning three games. He went the distance in all of them, and two were shutouts.
- Tony Kubek hit two homers and drove in four runs for the Yanks in Game 3.
- Yankee slugger Frank Howard hit a three-run homer in the ninth inning of Game 4 to tie the score and send the game into extra innings.
- Hank Bauer tripled in the top of the tenth of Game 4 and drove in the lead run for the Yanks.
- In the bottom of the tenth of Game 4, Johnny Logan doubled to drive in the tying run, then Eddie Mathews hit a two-run homer to win the game for the Braves.
- Logan's ten assists in Game 4 set a Series record for a shortstop.
- Hank Bauer homered to break a 2–2 tie in Game 6 and provide the Yanks with their winning run.
- Eddie Mathews doubled to drive in two runs for the Braves in Game 7 and established a lead that would hold as Lew Burdette hurled his second Series shutout.

Best Efforts

Batting

Average	Hank Aaron	.393
Home Runs	Hank Aaron	3
Triples	Hank Aaron	1
	Hank Bauer	1
Doubles	Eddie Mathews	3
Hits	Hank Aaron	11
Runs	Hank Aaron	5
	Johnny Logan	5
	Yogi Berra	5
RBIs	Hank Aaron	7

Pitching

Wins	Lew Burdette	3–0
ERA	Lew Burdette	0.67
Strikeouts	Lew Burdette	13
Innings Pitched	Lew Burdette	27

1958

New York Yankees 4
Milwaukee Braves 3

Line-ups

New York Yankees		Milwaukee Braves	
1b	Moose Skowron	1b	Frank Torre
2b	Gil McDougald	2b	Red Schoendienst
3b	Jerry Lumpe	3b	Eddie Mathews
ss	Tony Kubek	ss	Johnny Logan
lf	Elston Howard	lf	Wes Covington
cf	Mickey Mantle	cf	Bill Bruton
rf	Hank Bauer	rf	Hank Aaron
c	Yogi Berra	c	Del Crandall
mgr	Casey Stengel	mgr	Fred Haney

		R	H	E	Pitching
Game 1	New York	3	8	1	Whitey Ford, Ryne Duren (8th)
	Milwaukee	4	10	0	Warren Spahn (W)
Game 2	New York	5	7	0	Bob Turley, Duke Maas (1st), Johnny Kucks (1st), Murry Dickson (5th), Zack Monroe (8th)
	Milwaukee	13	15	1	Lew Burdette (W)
Game 3	Milwaukee	0	6	0	Bob Rush, Don McMahon (7th)
	New York	4	4	0	Don Larsen (W), Ryne Duren (8th)
Game 4	Milwaukee	3	9	0	Warren Spahn (W)
	New York	0	2	1	Whitey Ford, Johnny Kucks (8th), Murry Dickson (9th)
Game 5	Milwaukee	0	5	0	Lew Burdette, Juan Pizarro (6th), Carl Willey (8th)
	New York	7	10	0	Bob Turley (W)

		R	H	E	Pitching
Game 6	New York	4	10	1	Whitey Ford, Art Ditmar (2nd), Ryne Duren (6th, W), Bob Turley (10th)
	Milwaukee	3	10	4	Warren Spahn, Don McMahon (10th)
Game 7	New York	6	8	0	Don Larsen, Bob Turley (3rd, W)
	Milwaukee	2	5	2	Lew Burdette, Don McMahon (9th)

Highlights

- Casey Stengel captured his seventh world title, tying him with Joe McCarthy as the Series winningest manager.
- The Yankees became only the second team in history to rally to win the Series after being behind three games to one (the Pirates did it first in 1925).
- Hank Bauer tied a six-game Series record when he clouted four home runs.
- Bill Bruton singled in the bottom of the tenth inning of Game 1 to send Joe Adcock home with the winning run for the Braves.
- Mickey Mantle whacked two home runs for New York in Game 2.
- Lew Burdette went the distance for the Braves in Game 2 and contributed to his win by homering with two men on base.
- The seven runs scored by the Braves in the first inning of Game 2 still stands as the most in any Series opening frame.
- Hank Bauer hit a home run and drove in all four Yankee runs in Game 3.
- Warren Spahn hurled a two-hit shutout for the Braves in Game 4 and drove in a run with a single as well.
- Bob Turley pitched a shutout for the Yankees in Game 5, allowing only five hits and striking out 10 Milwaukee batters.
- Gil McDougald hit a home run, a double, a single, and drove in three Yankee runs in Game 5.
- In the tenth inning of Game 6, McDougald homered and Moose Skowron drove in another run with a single to earn a victory for the Yankees.
- Skowron hit a three-run homer and accounted for four RBIs in the Yankee triumph of Game 7.

Best Efforts

Batting

Average	Bill Bruton .412
Home Runs	Hank Bauer 4
Triples	Mickey Mantle 1
	Red Schoendienst 1
Doubles	Yogi Berra 3
	Red Schoendienst 3
Hits	Hank Bauer 10
Runs	Hank Bauer 6
RBIs	Hank Bauer 8

Pitching

Wins	Bob Turley 2–1
	Warren Spahn 2–1
ERA	Don Larsen 0.96
Strikeouts	Warren Spahn 18
Innings Pitched	Warren Spahn 28$\frac{2}{3}$

1959

Los Angeles Dodgers   4
Chicago White Sox   2

Line-ups

Los Angeles Dodgers		**Chicago White Sox**	
1b	Gil Hodges	1b	Ted Kluszewski
2b	Charlie Neal	2b	Nellie Fox
3b	Junior Gilliam	3b	Billy Goodman
ss	Maury Wills	ss	Luis Aparicio
lf	Wally Moon	lf	Al Smith
cf	Don Demeter	cf	Jim Landis
rf	Norm Larker	rf	Jim Rivera
c	Johnny Roseboro	c	Sherm Lollar
mgr	Walt Alston	mgr	Al Lopez

		R	H	E	Pitching
Game 1	Los Angeles	0	8	3	Roger Craig, Chuck Churn (3rd), Clem Labine (4th), Sandy Koufax (5th), Johnny Klippstein (7th)
	Chicago	11	11	0	Early Wynn (W), Gerry Staley (8th)
Game 2	Los Angeles	4	9	1	Johnny Podres (W), Larry Sherry (7th)
	Chicago	3	8	0	Bob Shaw, Turk Lown (7th)
Game 3	Chicago	1	12	0	Dick Donovan, Gerry Staley (7th)
	Los Angeles	3	5	0	Don Drysdale (W), Larry Sherry (8th)
Game 4	Chicago	4	10	3	Early Wynn, Turk Lown (3rd), Billy Pierce (4th), Gerry Staley (7th)
	Los Angeles	5	9	0	Roger Craig, Larry Sherry (8th, W)

1959

Los Angeles Dodgers 4
Chicago White Sox 2

		R	H	E	Pitching
Game 5	Chicago	1	5	0	Bob Shaw (W), Billy Pierce (8th), Dick Donovan (8th)
	Los Angeles	0	9	0	Sandy Koufax, Stan Williams (8th)
Game 6	Los Angeles	9	13	0	Johnny Podres, Larry Sherry (4th, W)
	Chicago	3	6	1	Early Wynn, Dick Donovan (4th), Turk Lown (4th), Gerry Staley (5th), Billy Pierce (8th), Ray Moore (9th)

Highlights

- The attendance of 420,784 at the six games of the Series still stands as the largest crowd to attend any Series.
- Ted Kluszewski's 10 RBIs set a record for a six-game Series.
- Chuck Essegian of the Dodgers set a Series standard by hitting two pinch-hit home runs.
- Kluszewski hit two homers and drove in five runs for the White Sox in Game 1.
- Charlie Neal blasted two home runs (one providing the game-winning run) and collected three RBIs for the Dodgers in Game 2.
- Carl Furillo cracked a pinch-hit single to drive in two runs and provide the margin of victory for Los Angeles in Game 3.
- Gil Hodges provided the winning run for the Dodgers in Game 4 with a home run.
- The 92,706 fans who attended Game 5 at the Los Angeles Coliseum stands as the largest crowd ever to attend a World Series game.
- Three White Sox pitchers—Bob Shaw, Billy Pierce, and Dick Donovan—combined to shutout the Dodgers in Game 5.
- Charlie Neal, Duke Snider, and Wally Moon each drove in two runs to pace the Dodgers in Game 6.

Best Efforts

Batting
Average	Gil Hodges .391
	Ted Kluszewski .391
Home Runs	Ted Kluszewski 3
Triples	Gil Hodges 1
Doubles	Nellie Fox 3
	Al Smith 3
Hits	Charlie Neal 10
Runs	Jim Landis 6
RBIs	Ted Kluszewski 10

Pitching
Wins	Larry Sherry 2–0
ERA	Larry Sherry 0.71
Strikeouts	Early Wynn 10
Innings Pitched	Bob Shaw 14

THE SIXTIES

The 1960s was surely one of the most turbulent periods in American history, with more than its share of heroes and villains. The era of the Vietnam war and the civil rights movement; of protests, marches, and riots in the streets; and of assassinations, it was a far cry from the placid '50s.

In sports, it was an age of titans. Vince Lombardi's Green Bay Packers dominated pro football, Wilt Chamberlain and Bill Russell overshadowed everyone in pro basketball. In boxing there was Muhammad Ali, then known as Cassius Clay, Arnie Palmer and Jack Nicklaus in golf, Rod Laver in tennis, and Bobby Hull in hockey.

Baseball had its own history-makers. Roger Maris hit 61 home runs to break Babe Ruth's cherished record. Maury Wills stole 104 bases to demolish Ty Cobb's long-standing record of 96 thefts. Denny McLain won 31 games, the first major league pitcher to do it since Dizzy Dean back in 1934. And Sandy Koufax dazzled batters and fans alike by hurling four no-hitters in four consecutive years, the most ever by a pitcher at that time, and by establishing a new strikeout record when he fanned 382 in a single season.

Besides Koufax, the decade saw many other great pitchers reach their peak or begin to make names for themselves: his team-mate Don Drysdale, Bob Gibson, Jim Lonborg, Mickey Lolich, Juan Marichal, Jim Palmer, Gaylord Perry, Don Sutton, Steve Carlton, Tom Seaver, and Nolan Ryan among them. There were also some truly great hitters: Mickey Mantle and Willie Mays were still brilliant in the first half of the decade and there were such other memorable batsmen reaching their prime as Hank Aaron, Ernie Banks, Frank Robinson, Roberto Clemente, Harmon Killebrew, Al Kaline, Carl Yastrzemski, Tony Oliva, Willie McCovey, and Ken Boyer, and some youngsters just getting started by the names of Pete Rose, Rod Carew, Reggie Jackson, and Johnny Bench. And base-stealing became an art again with such accomplished practitioners as Luis Aparicio, Bert Campaneris, Maury Wills, and Lou Brock.

The 1960s was also a time of change in major league baseball. The Washington Senators became the Minnesota Twins. Brought into the major league fold were the California Angels, New York Mets, Houston Astros, Kansas City Royals, Montreal Expos, Seattle Pilots, and San Diego Padres. The Milwaukee Braves moved to Atlanta and the Kansas City A's relocated in Oakland. By the end of the decade, there were 24 teams in major league baseball, eight more than at the start of the '60s. And in 1969 a new system was introduced: each league was divided into two divisions of six teams with the winner of each to meet in a best-of-five playoff to determine the pennant and the right to go to the World Series.

Back in 1960, however, the Yankees were still the game's most imposing force. The powerhouse from the Bronx played in the first five World Series of the decade, although they won only two of them. The Los Angeles Dodgers under Walt Alston emerged as a team to contend with, attending three Series and triumphing in two of them. And the St. Louis Cardinals added two world crowns to their trophy case. The Pittsburgh Pirates picked up a world title, so did the San Francisco Giants, the Detroit Tigers, and the Baltimore Orioles. And to round out the decade, the long-time hapless New York Mets surprised everybody in the baseball world by not only taking the National League pennant but by winning the Series as well.

When the decade began, Casey Stengel was still directing the Yankees on the field. He had missed the previous year's post-season festival, only the second one the Yankees had been absent from in 11 years. It was rest enough. Behind the thunderous bats of Mickey Mantle, Roger Maris, Moose Skowron, and a somewhat age-weary Yogi Berra, the Yanks marched to the pennant, outdistancing the Baltimore Orioles by eight games and the previous pennant claimant, the Chicago White Sox, by 10. Mantle led the league with 40 homers, and Maris, the league's MVP, was tops with 112 RBIs, many of them the result of his 39 homers. Skowron hit another 26 round-trippers, and Berra had 15 despite the fact he was not playing much of the time. The Yanks' biggest winner that year was Art Ditmar (15–9),

and old vet Bobby Shantz served them well from the bullpen.

In the National League, the Pittsburgh Pirates were somewhat of a surprise. Under Danny Murtaugh, they had come in fourth the year before and most early-season observers ignored them and felt the NL flag would be decided among the Dodgers, Braves, and Cardinals. But when the season ended, not one of those teams was closer than seven games to the Pirates, who soared on the arms of one of the best pitching staffs in the major leagues: Vern Law won 20 games and lost only nine, Bob Friend was 18–12, and Roy Face proved to be among the best relievers around with 24 saves from his 68 game appearances. The Pirates

The catching staff of the Yankees in the Series of 1960 (l to r): Johnny Blanchard, Yogi Berra, and Elston Howard.

could also hit. Their team average of .276 was the best in the majors and was 16 percentage points above that of the Yankees. Dick Groat led the league with an average of .325 and was named MVP. Roberto Clemente hit .314, Dick Stuart whacked the most home runs, 23, while Clemente and Don Hoak clobbered 16 apiece.

The Series turned into the most striking paradox in baseball history. The Yankee hitting attack was savage, setting a plethora of Series records, most of which still stand today. In the three games they won, the New Yorkers ran up scores of 16-3, 12-0, and 10-0. When the final Series stats were toted up, the Yankees demolished the Pirates on paper, outscoring them by a whopping 28 runs and outhitting them by an incredible 82 percentage points. But statistics aside, the Pirates fared better on the field four times to give, them their first world championship in 35 years. After the disappointing Series, Casey Stengel retired as Yankee manager—he had won 10 pennants in 12 years and finished second and third in the two years he did not attend the Series. The gold-plated reins were turned over to Ralph Houk.

The following season is universally remembered as the year of Mantle and Maris. 1961 was the season when they zeroed in on Babe Ruth's revered record of 60 home runs. Maris, of course, exceeded it by one and Mantle came close with 54 and would have come closer if injuries had not sidelined him for part of the season.

The '61 Yankees proved to be the most powerful hitting team in baseball history. Their team total of 240 home runs shattered the record of 221 set by the 1947 Yankees. Besides the 61 from Maris and 54 from Mantle, Moose Skowron hit 28, Yogi Berra 22, and Elston Howard and Johnny Blanchard had 21 apiece. Howard also batted .348, second only to Tiger Norm Cash's .361, while Mantle batted .317 and Blanchard, .305. The 142 RBIs Maris accounted for were the most in the American League, and Mantle drove in a hefty 128. The MVP honors were predictably bestowed on Roger Maris. Whitey Ford was back in top form for the Yankees as well, producing by far the best record in the majors, 25-4, and winning the Cy Young award. Ralph Terry also produced well (16-3), and Luis Arroyo chalked up the most saves (29) in either league. Needless to say, the Yankees had little trouble taking the 1961 pennant. A

Yogi Berra, getting a finger on second base here, was better known for his hitting and catching than his base-running. Yogi played in 14 World Series, the most by anyone in baseball history. He batted .274 overall and cracked 12 homers.

Elston Howard is congratulated after homering in the opening game of the 1961 Series. At the left is Moose Skowron.

fine Detroit Tiger team trailed them by eight games when the season ended.

In the National League, the Pirates fell from the throne toppling all the way to sixth place, and were never in the running. Instead it was another surprise in '61, just as the Pirates had been in '60. The Cincinnati Reds, piloted by Fred Hutchinson, had risen from sixth place the year before to the number one spot, beating out a favored Los Angeles Dodgers by four games.

The Reds were a well-balanced team, although they could claim a legitimate superstar in MVP Frank Robinson, who batted .323, hit 37 homers, and drove in 124

Roger Maris slides safely into third in the 1962 Series. Maris played in seven World Series, five for the Yanks and two with the St. Louis Cardinals, but only hit .217. The Giant third baseman is Jim Davenport.

runs. Vada Pinson hit .343, second best in the National League that year. The pitching staff was especially strong with Joey Jay (21-10), Jim O'Toole (19-9), Bob Purkey (16-12), and ace reliever Jim Brosnan (16 saves, 10 wins).

In the Series, however, the Yankees continued their vanquishing ways. They were a team of great players who had gelled ever so smoothly in that memorable year. When they faced the Reds, it was no different. The Yankees hit home runs when they needed them, scored often and with apparent ease, and took the Series in five games. Whitey Ford was at his best, walking off with two shutout wins. No one was left unimpressed when the 1961 Series came to a close.

The home run production of Maris and Mantle was noticeably curtailed in 1962, although their output was still most respectable. Maris belted 33 out of the park and drove in 100 runs, while Mantle clouted 30 homers, led the

Yankee Roger Maris flips his bat away in disgust after striking out in the 1961 Series. It was the year he hit 61 home runs to break Babe Ruth's record.

The great Mickey Mantle bashes one here for the Yanks. Mantle hit 18 home runs in his 12 World Series appearances for New York.

team with an average of .321, and was named the league's MVP. The only other .300 hitter was Bobby Richardson, who topped the mark by two percentage points. Ralph Terry was the big winner for New York, his record of 23–12 the best in the league. Whitey Ford turned in a 17–8 year, and Marshall Bridges saved 18 games for the

Yanks. Young Tom Tresh, who played shortstop and in the outfield for New York, won Rookie of the Year recognition.

The National League battle took place on the West Coast in 1962. The displaced Dodgers and Giants fought all the way to the final bell and when it rang, it was a draw, 101 wins each against 61 losses. The Dodgers had looked like a sure thing in September but they faded miserably while the Giants surged and daily ate away at the Los Angeles lead. The intrastate rivals, who had formerly been intracity rivals, were forced to decide the NL flag in a three-game playoff.

The first game was held up at Candlestick Park in San Francisco, and the Giants blew the Dodgers away with as much gusto as the winds that so often raged off the nearby bay. The score was 8-0, much the result of Willie Mays' two homers, solos from Orlando Cepeda and Jim Davenport, and the three-hit pitching from former Chicago White Sox star Billy Pierce.

The second game was to be held in brand-new Dodger Stadium, the beautiful ballpark Dodger owner Walter O'Malley had built over in Chavez Ravine so that the Dodgers would not have to play in the lopsided Coliseum. But it did not seem like the new edifice held any advantage for the swooning Dodgers, who had blown the pennant and now appeared to be blowing the playoffs. After five-and-a-half innings of Game 2 they trailed 5-0. But in the bottom of the sixth inning they suddenly came alive and sent seven runs across the plate. The big hit was a bases-loaded double by pinch hitter Lee Walls, which drove in three runs. That and another run in the ninth was enough to even up the playoffs.

The third game was a classic, pitting Juan Marichal of the Giants against Johnny Podres of the Dodgers. It was a close game through eight innings. The Giants got the lead, but the Dodgers took it away when Tommy Davis banged a two-run homer in the bottom of the sixth. By the ninth inning Los Angeles had extended its lead to 4-2. Now it was the Giants' turn, erupting for four runs in the top of the inning, then bringing in old vet Billy Pierce to hold off the Dodgers in the bottom of the frame. And the Giants gave San Francisco its first pennant winner.

The Giants were as awesome a slugging team as the Yankees, in fact they had hit five more home runs than the New Yorkers. Of

Mickey Mantle makes a spectacular catch of a towering drive by Willie Mays in the 1962 Series. Also there is Roger Maris for the Yankees.

the 204 round-trippers, Willie Mays had the most, 49, which was also the most in the majors that year. Orlando Cepeda had a healthy 35; Willie McCovey, 20; Felipe Alou, 25; Tom Haller, 18; and Ed Bailey, 17. Mays also drove in 141 runs, second only to Dodger Tommy Davis' 153, and batted .304, all of which probably would have been enough to garner MVP honors for him had not Dodger speedster Maury Wills stolen 104 bases to better Ty Cobb's record which had stood since 1915. The Giants also

had .300 hitters in Felipe Alou (.316), Orlando Cepeda (.306), and former Tiger star Harvey Kuenn (.304). Jack Sanford headed the mound corps, ringing up a 24–7 record, while Billy O'Dell won 19 games, Juan Marichal won 18, and Billy Pierce, 16. Top relievers were Stu Miller with 19 saves and former Yankee Don Larsen with 11.

For all their late-season dazzle, however, the Giants could not mesmerize the postseason-seasoned veterans from New York. The Giants took the Series to

Elston Howard slides in with a Yankee run in the 1962 World Series. The San Francisco Giant catcher is Ed Bailey.

seven games, but they fell there to a masterful shutout performance by Yank hurler Ralph Terry. The Bay Area fans would have to wait until major league baseball came to Oakland before they would experience a world championship.

The year 1963 brought about a resumption of the fabled Yankee-Dodger rivalry. But for all the heat and notoriety of their intense Series confrontations, the Dodgers had won only one of the seven previous meetings.

The heart of the Dodgers of '63 was their pitching staff, and its main artery was southpaw Sandy Koufax, who won both the MVP and Cy Young awards that year, when he posted the best record in the majors (25-5), led both leagues in strikeouts (306), shut-

outs (11), and ERA (1.88), and hurled his second career no-hitter. But Koufax was not all the Dodgers had. There was also strong righthander Don Drysdale, who won 19 games, and Johnny Podres who was victorious in 14. In the bullpen they had the always dependable Ron Perranoski, who accounted for 21 saves and posted a record of 16-3.

Maury Wills was not quite the demon on the basepaths he had been the year before, but still managed to purloin 40, the most in the NL. And Tommy Davis took the NL batting crown for the second year in a row, this time with an average of .326. Wills was the only other .300 hitter (.302). A little pressure was applied by the St. Louis Cardinals, but they trailed by six games when it was all over.

Sandy Koufax, one of the game's greatest lefthanders, won four games and lost three for the Dodgers in four different World Series from 1959 through 1966.

Junior Gilliam comes across with the game-winning run in Game 3 of the 1963 Series for the Dodgers. Gilliam scored the most runs in that Series (3). Welcoming him is fellow Dodger Ron Fairly. The Yankee catcher is Elston Howard.

The Yankees had even less trouble getting to the World Series, their 28th appearance. No one came nearer to them than the White Sox and they were 19½ games back. Pitching was an overwhelming force for the Yanks in 1963. Once again it was Whitey Ford heading the roster, his record of 24–7 the best in the league. Jim Bouton also turned in a fine season, 21–7, and Ralph Terry won 17 games. Heading the relief force was Hal Reniff who saved 18 games for the Yankees.

There was still plenty of power, although not one batter ended up above the .300 mark. Elston Howard hit the most home runs (28) and was rewarded with the MVP award that year. Mantle and Maris were hampered by injuries and hit only 23 and 15 homers respectively. But Joe Pepitone got 27, Tom Tresh hit 25, and Johnny Blanchard, 16.

Despite the predominance of the Yankees in Series past, it was pure Dodgers in 1963, specifically Dodger pitchers. They swept the

Bobby Richardson steps into the box at Yankee Stadium in the 1963 Series to face the Dodgers' Johnny Podres. Richardson appeared in seven World Series with the Yanks from 1957 through 1964 and compiled an overall average of .305. The Dodger catcher is John Roseboro.

Highlights of the 1963 World Series.

Yankees, the first time the Bronx Bombers had ever experienced that particular humiliation, and the Dodgers did it by employing only three starting pitchers for 35 innings and a reliever to handle the one additional frame. Sandy Koufax went the distance twice, Don Drysdale once, and Johnny Podres got through eight innings and then let Ron Perranoski wrap it up in the ninth. The Dodger rifles allowed the Yankees only four runs and 22 hits in the four Series games.

In 1964 the Yankees had a new manager, one who had worn the pinstripes illustriously from 1946 through 1963 and become a baseball legend in himself, Yogi Berra. And just as they had so often when he was behind the plate, the Yankees won a pennant. It had been an especially close race, however, and when the season's door was finally closed New York was just a single game ahead of the Chicago White Sox and two in front of the Baltimore Orioles. Mickey Mantle, now 32 and plagued by a variety of nagging injuries, still made his presence known by hitting 35 homers, driving in 111 runs, and batting .303. Not far behind in the slugging area was Joe Pepitone, who dispatched 28 balls out of the park

and drove in 100 runs. Roger Maris counted 26 homers, and Elston Howard batted .313. Jim Bouton was the Yanks winningest pitcher, 18–13, while Whitey Ford posted a record of 17–6.

The Yankees would face the St. Louis Cardinals for the fifth time in the 1964 World Series. In the four times they had gone head-to-head before, each team had won twice.

The Cardinals, managed by Johnny Keane, had had as difficult a time getting to the Series as the Yankees, in fact had been pressed even more. Both the Cincinnati Reds and the Philadelphia Phillies were a mere game out at the end of the season, the San Francisco Giants trailed by only three, and the Milwaukee Braves were just five out.

St. Louis had the year's MVP in Ken Boyer, who hit 24 home runs and had a league-leading 119 RBIs. They had also acquired a sure-hitting, base-stealing phenomenon in Lou Brock, who batted .315 for the year (.348 in a Cardinal uniform) and stole 43 bases (33 for the Cards). Bill White hit 21 homers and batted .303, and Curt Flood hit .311. The pitching staff was very strong: Ray Sadecki had the best record with 20–11, but close behind were Bob Gibson with 19–12 and Curt Simmons, 18–9.

Curt Flood of the St. Louis Cardinals streaks into second to break up a double play in the 1964 Series. The upended Yankee is shortstop Phil Linz, the other Yank is Bobby Richardson.

The lead in the Series went back and forth through six games, but in the end it was Bob Gibson who prevailed, earning his second win of the Series in Game 7. The Cardinals now had the unique distinction of being able to claim that they had beaten the Yankees in the World Series more often than they had lost to them. And the New York Yankee dynasty was over; they would not return to a World Series until 1976.

Not only were the Yankees knocked from the American League throne in 1965, they were booted all the way into the second division. It was the first time *since 1925* that the Yankees did not finish in the first division. Replacing them at the top was the Minnesota Twins, claiming their first pennant.

Sam Mele managed the Twins and he brought them in seven games ahead of the Chicago White Sox. He had a finely tuned pitching staff with righthander Mudcat Grant (21-7), southpaw Jim Kaat (18-11), and reliever Al Worthington (21 saves, 10 wins). The Twins' Tony Oliva took the NL batting crown that year with an average of .321, and Zoilo Versalles led the league in doubles (45) and triples (12) and hit 19 homers, all of which were enough to earn him MVP honors. Other power hitters on the Twins included Bob Allison whose 23 homers were the most on the team, Don Mincher who hit 22, and Jimmy Hall, 20.

In the National League, the pennant race boiled down once again to a California affair involving the Dodgers and the Giants. San Francisco was a distinctly better hitting team, but Los Angeles had one of the most sterling pitching staffs ever to grace the game. And that is what prevailed, enabling the Dodgers to secure the flag by a two-game margin.

Walt Alston was in his 12th year as manager of the Dodgers, a career that went back to 1954 at Ebbets Field in Brooklyn. He had had some first-rate pitchers over the years, like Don Newcombe, Preacher Roe, and Carl Erskine, but he had never had as effective a staff as the one that took the mound for his Dodgers in 1965. First, there was Sandy Koufax

with a record of 26-8, who also set a major league strikeout record by fanning 382 batters. Koufax hurled his fourth no-hitter in as many consecutive years, and was a unanimous selection for the Cy Young award. Then there was Don Drysdale with a record of 23-12, who not only could blaze the ball across the plate but blast it out himself (he had seven homers that year and batted .300). And there was Claude Osteen, who won 15 games, and Ron Perranoski, who saved 17.

The Dodgers, however, were a collection of weak-sticks when it came to offense. No one batted above .300, and Maury Wills was the only full-time player who came anywhere close to that figure when he hit .286. Wills, of course, could be devastating once he got on base and proved it by stealing 94 bases. And no one hit more than the 12 home runs registered by Rookie-of-the-Year Jim Lefebvre and by Lou Johnson.

But just as the Dodgers did not need hitting to triumph in the regular season, it was also unnecessary in the Series. After surprise losses by Drysdale and Koufax in the first two games, the Dodger staff asserted itself and proceeded to systematically humble the Twins. Three of the next four Dodger victories were shutouts, two by Koufax and one by Osteen. The usually consistent-hitting Twins batted only .195 as a team, while the normally balsa-wood bats of the Dodgers hit at a clip of .274, led by a Series-revitalized Ron Fairly. The Dodgers won their third world championship since moving to Los Angeles in 1958.

The Dodgers and the Giants went at it again in 1966, a bitter campaign for the NL flag that was not decided until the last few days of the season. But once again, the Dodgers ended up on top and the Giants were left with the small consolation that they had made it an exciting pennant race. Only 1½ games separated the two teams at the close of the season.

Although it would be his last season of play because of a painfully arthritic elbow, Sandy Koufax registered his most winning season ever, victorious in 27 games while losing only nine. He led the majors in strikeouts (317), shutouts (5), ERA (1.73), innings pitched (323), completed games (27), and was for the second year in a row the unanimous selection

A day Willie Davis would rather forget. The Dodger centerfielder muffs one here in the 1966 World Series. He made two more errors in the same inning to set an all-time Series record. Davis, an otherwise splendid fielder and hitter, fared badly at World Series time, hitting only .167 in three different Series.

for the Cy Young award. Claude Osteen won another 17 games and reliever Phil Regan was credited with 21 saves and a record of 14–1.

On the other side of the game, the Dodgers were hitting a little better in 1966, having raised their puny team batting average of .245 the year before to .256. Tommy Davis broke .300 with an average of .313 but he was not a full-time player in '66. Jim Lefebvre doubled his home run output to 24, and Lou Johnson upped his to 17. Maury Wills stole 38 bases and Willie Davis pilfered another 21.

This time the Dodgers would have to face the Baltimore Orioles (formerly the St. Louis Browns), who were managed by former Yankee great Hank Bauer. It was the first trip to the Series for the Orioles, although they had had a star-studded line-up and had been a pennant contender since 1964.

Baltimore was the best-hitting team in the American League, and

Two of the game's greatest baserunners meet here in the 1966 World Series. Baltimore's Luis Aparicio tries to slide under a tag by the Dodgers' Maury Wills. Aparicio appeared in the 1959 Series for the White Sox as well. Wills wore a Dodger uniform in four World Series, from 1959 through 1966.

their cornerstone, Frank Robinson, won the Triple Crown—the first player to accomplish that since Mickey Mantle had a decade earlier. Robinson batted .316, clouted 49 homers, drove in 122 runs, and was a unanimous selection for the MVP award. He also scored a league-high 122 runs. Big Boog Powell hit another 34 homers and batted in 109 runs, Curt Blefary had 23 four-baggers, Brooks Robinson accounted for 23 home runs and 100 RBIs, and Russ Snyder hit .306.

No one shone with exceptional brilliance from the Oriole mound but there was a wealth of talent there with Jim Palmer (15–10), Dave McNally (13–6), and Wally Bunker (10–6).

Everything   deserted   the

Big Boog Powell was a key member of the Baltimore Orioles in four World Series, hitting a high .357 in 1966 and a low .111 in 1971.

Dodgers in the 1966 Series. Sandy Koufax was crippled with injury and was not effective at all. The offense set a standard of ineptitude and futility unprecedented in the Series when they scored only two runs in the four games of the Series and batted at the anemic rate of .142. They virtually rewrote the wrong side of the Series record book. And the Baltimore Orioles, with three shutouts to the credits of Jim Palmer, Wally Bunker, and Dave McNally, swept the Series with ease. The Dodgers would not return to a World Series until 1974.

Both the Dodgers and the Orioles would take deep tumbles in 1967, the Dodgers falling all the way to eighth place in the National League; the Orioles coming to rest in sixth in the American.

While Baltimore floundered about in the second division, there was a spirited fight for the flag at the top of the AL ladder. Four teams battled into the last week of the season hoping to come out of it with the pennant. And the one that did was the biggest surprise of all. The Boston Red Sox, under new manager Dick Williams, had in one year gone from ninth place (72–90, 26 games out) to first (92–70) with virtually the same line-up.

The teams that gave the BoSox so much trouble were the Detroit Tigers and the Minnesota Twins, both of whom trailed by only a game at season's end, and the Chicago White Sox who were just three games off the pace.

Key to the success of Boston was slugger Carl Yastrzemski, who won the Triple Crown and MVP honors. Yaz, as he was familiarly known, batted .326, hit 44 homers, and drove in 121 runs. The Red Sox also had a fine supporting group of home run hitters: Tony Conigliaro (20), George Scott (19), Rico Petrocelli (17), Joe Foy (16), and Reggie Smith (15). Scott also hit .303. On the mound, righthander Jim Lonborg blossomed, posting a record of 22-9 and leading the league in strikeouts with 246.

In the National League, the St. Louis Cardinals, under their one-time star second baseman, Red Schoendienst, also moved from the second division to first place in a single year, although their rise from sixth place, 12 games back was not as dramatic as that of the Red Sox. But unlike the AL race nobody came close to St. Louis as they surged upward. The second place San Francisco Giants were 10½ games back when the season ended.

The Cards were a solid hitting team, spearheaded by Curt Flood (.335) and Orlando Cepeda (.325). They also had one of the game's premier speedsters in Lou Brock, who stole 52 bases, the most in the National League. The most power was supplied by Cepeda, who hit 25 homers and drove in 111 runs. He took MVP honors, and he had the distinction of being the first National Leaguer to be a unanimous selection. Brock hit 21 homers; Tim McCarver and Julian Javier added 14 each.

Key to the pitching staff was Bob Gibson, but he had been sidelined for much of the season with a broken bone in his leg and therefore contributed only 13 wins. Picking up the slack were Dick Hughes (16-6), Nelson Briles (14-5), and a 22-year-old southpaw named Steve Carlton (14-9).

St. Louis moved out to a three-game to one lead in the Series, but the Cinderella Red Sox battled back to tie it up and bring it to a climactic seventh game showdown. But there Bob Gibson, well-recovered now, was too strong for them, just as he had been in two earlier Series games. In the final game, Gibson gave up only three hits in the nine innings he pitched, and his teammates chipped in with seven runs to give the Cardinals another world championship.

The Detroit Tigers, who had come so close in 1967, made it to the top in '68, finishing a long 12 games ahead of the Baltimore Orioles, while the defending champion Red Sox fell to fourth place. With Mayo Smith in his second year as manager, the Tigers got most of their fuel from the pitching staff, most notably Denny McLain, who won 31 games and was a unanimous selection for both MVP and the Cy Young awards. McLain lost only six games all year, led the league in innings pitched (336) and completed games (28). The Tigers also had a star-quality hurler in southpaw Mickey Lolich who won 17 games and lost just nine that year.

Detroit's bats were less than loud, the team average a scrawny .235. No one batted over .300, but there was some power. Willie Horton had 36 homers, Norm Cash and Bill Freehan had 25 each, and Jim Northrup another 21.

Pitching was also the forte of the NL pennant winners, repeats from the year before, the St. Louis Cardinals. And still heading their staff was the ever-intimidating Bob Gibson. The big righthander won 22 games while losing only nine and posted an incredible ERA of just 1.12. His 268 strikeouts and 13 shutouts were the league's best. In the twentieth century, only Grover Cleveland Alexander of the Philadelphia Phillies had thrown more shutouts in a single season when he posted 16 back in 1916. Like McLain in the AL, Gibson was the recipient of both the MVP and Cy Young awards. Nelson Briles had a fine season too (19–11) and Joe Hoerner was a trusty reliever, racking up 17 saves.

Lou Brock was still making news with his base-running skills, his 62 thefts enough to share major league honors with Bert Campaneris of the Oakland A's. Brock also led the majors in triples with 14 and doubles, 46. Curt Flood was the only .300 hitter and he exceeded it by just one percentage point.

It had been a relatively relaxing campaign for the pennant for St. Louis in 1968, almost as easy as it had been the year before. When the league's books were closed, St. Louis stood nine games ahead of San Francisco.

It did not surprise anyone when the outcome of the 1968 World Series was decided on pitching. But it was not borne by 31-game–winner McLain; in fact, he won only one Series game and lost two for the Tigers. Nor was it Gibson, who had won three Series contests the year before. The laurels instead went to Detroit's Mickey Lolich, who rose to the occasion, went the distance thrice, and chalked up three fine victories. Also contributing to the Tigers' fortunes were old pros Al Kaline and Norm Cash, who both hit consistently and in the clutch. It was the Tigers' first world championship since 1945.

If the Red Sox were a surprise commodity in the 1967 World Series, the New York Mets of 1969 would have to fetch adjectives like "astonishing," "miraculous," or "incredible." In their previous seven years as a major league team they had ended up in the cellar five times and in ninth place twice. Suddenly and startlingly, they rose to first place.

The "Amazin' Mets," as some scribes took to calling them, not only won their division, the NL East, but then defeated the NL West champion Atlanta Braves in the National League's first divisional playoff.

The Mets were piloted by former Dodger great Gil Hodges, then in his second year at the helm. They were paced by young righthander Tom Seaver, who posted the best record in the National League that year, 25-7, and won the Cy Young award. Augmenting him were Jerry Koos-

man, who won 17 games, and Gary Gentry, who chalked up 13. The bullpen was strong with Ron Taylor and Tug McGraw (13 and 12 saves respectively) and a young fastballer named Nolan Ryan. Cleon Jones batted .340, and Tommie Agee hit 26 home runs. With all that going for them, the Mets moved through the NL East with impunity and ended up eight games in front of the second-place Chicago Cubs.

The Atlanta Braves were a definite favorite in the NL playoffs, paced by such fearsome hitters as Hank Aaron, Orlando Cepeda, Felipe Alou, and Rico Carty and pitchers like Phil Niekro and Ron Reed. But the Mets disposed of them in three straight games, ringing up run totals of nine, eleven, and seven, to enact a swift and sure decimation.

Over in the American League, it was Baltimore again, this time with Earl Weaver in his first full year as manager. Many of the same players who participated in the Oriole's 1966 Series triumph were back: most notably Frank Robinson, Brooks Robinson, Boog Powell, Jim Palmer, and Dave McNally.

The Orioles had been devastating. They won 109 games against 53 losses in the AL East, enough to put them a full 19 games ahead of the second-place Detroit Tigers. Frank Robinson was the top hitter with an average of .308, and Boog Powell had both home run honors (37) and RBIs (121). Frank Robinson whacked 32 homers and drove in 100 runs. Paul Blair clouted another 26 round-trippers and Brooks Robinson, 23. Mike Cuellar won 23 games, losing only 11, and shared the Cy Young award with Denny McLain of Detroit. Dave McNally had a record of 20-7, and an injured Jim Palmer still managed to win 16 games.

The Minnesota Twins were a remarkable team as well, and they easily won the AL West. They had MVP Harmon Killebrew (49 homers, 140 RBIs), league batting crown wearer Rod Carew (.332), as well as such good hitters as Tony Oliva, Rich Reese, Cesar Tovar, and Graig Nettles. They also had two pitchers who won 20 games, Jim Perry and Dave Boswell, and the top reliever in the majors, Ron Perranoski, who had 31 saves to his credit. The Orioles got by the Twins by a single run in each of the first two playoff games, then annihilated them 11-2 in the third to sweep the AL playoffs.

Predictably the Orioles were the Series' favorite. With such abundant strength in the batter's box and on the mound, and a proven record of winning handily, it seemed the Mets' bubble would quickly be burst. The first game of the Series only added credence to that proposition, with the Orioles easily winning the game. But that was it. The Amazin' Mets responded with four straight wins and left baseball fans everywhere puzzled but delighted, surprised but greatly entertained.

If the New York Yankees had begun the decade of the '60s with their own unique traditional splendor, it was the New York Mets who gave it an incredulous, even inspirational climax.

1960

Pittsburgh Pirates   4
New York Yankees   3

Line-ups

Pittsburgh Pirates		New York Yankees	
1b	Dick Stuart	1b	Moose Skowron
2b	Bill Mazeroski	2b	Bobby Richardson
3b	Don Hoak	3b	Gil McDougald
ss	Dick Groat	ss	Tony Kubek
lf	Gino Cimoli	lf	Yogi Berra
cf	Bill Virdon	cf	Mickey Mantle
rf	Roberto Clemente	rf	Roger Maris
c	Smoky Burgess	c	Elston Howard
mgr	Danny Murtaugh	mgr	Casey Stengel

		R	H	E	Pitching
Game 1	New York	4	13	2	Art Ditmar, Jim Coates (1st), Duke Maas (5th), Ryne Duren (7th)
	Pittsburgh	6	8	0	Vern Law (W), Roy Face (8th)
Game 2	New York	16	19	1	Bob Turley (W), Bobby Shantz (9th)
	Pittsburgh	3	13	1	Bob Friend, Freddie Green (5th), Clem Labine (6th), George Witt (6th), Joe Gibbon (7th), Tom Cheney (9th)
Game 3	Pittsburgh	0	4	0	Vinegar Bend Mizell, Clem Labine (1st), Freddie Green (1st), George Witt (4th), Tom Cheney (6th), Joe Gibbon (8th)
	New York	10	16	1	Whitey Ford (W)
Game 4	Pittsburgh	3	7	0	Vern Law (W), Roy Face (7th)
	New York	2	8	0	Ralph Terry, Bobby Shantz (7th), Jim Coates (8th)

1960

Pittsburgh Pirates 4
New York Yankees 3

		R	H	E	Pitching
Game 5	Pittsburgh	5	10	2	Harvey Haddix (W), Roy Face (7th)
	New York	2	5	2	Art Ditmar, Luis Arroyo (2nd), Bill Stafford (3rd), Ryne Duren (8th)
Game 6	New York	12	17	1	Whitey Ford (W)
	Pittsburgh	0	7	1	Bob Friend, Tom Cheney (3rd), Vinegar Bend Mizell (4th), Freddie Green (6th), Clem Labine (6th), George Witt (9th)
Game 7	New York	9	13	1	Bob Turley, Bill Stafford (2nd), Bobby Shantz (3rd), Jim Coates (8th), Ralph Terry (9th)
	Pittsburgh	10	11	0	Vern Law, Roy Face (6th), Bob Friend (9th), Harvey Haddix (9th, W)

Highlights

- The Pittsburgh Pirates won their third world title, the first since 1925.
- The Yankees outscored the Pirates 55–27, outhit them 91–60, outhomered them 10–4, and posted an ERA of 3.54 to Pittsburgh's 7.11, but still lost the Series.
- New York set seven-game Series records in the following team categories: batting average (.338), slugging average (.528), runs scored (55), RBIs (54), hits (91), singles (64), total bases (142), and extra-base hits (27).
- Bobby Richardson of the Yanks drove in 12 runs, the most in any Series.
- Pirate reliever Roy Face was credited with three saves, a Series standard.
- Whitey Ford pitched two shutouts for the Yanks, giving up only four hits in one (Game 3) and seven in the other (Game 6).
- The eight runs scored by Mickey Mantle and Bobby Richardson tied the mark for a seven-game Series.
- Bill Mazeroski hit a two-run homer to provide the margin of victory for the Pirates in Game 1.

- Elston Howard belted a two-run, pinch-hit homer for the Yanks in Game 1.
- The 32 hits by both teams in Game 2 still stands as the most in a Series game.
- Mickey Mantle hit two home runs and accounted for five RBIs for the Yankees in Game 2.
- Bobby Richardson hit a grand slam home run in Game 3, and his six RBIs were the most ever in a single Series game.
- Bill Virdon provided the Pirates with their winning margin in Game 4 when he singled to drive in two runs.
- The 12–0 shutout by New York in Game 6 is the largest shutout margin in Series history.
- Richardson hit two triples, tying a Series mark, and drove in three Yankee runs in Game 6.
- Yogi Berra homered and drove in four runs for New York in Game 7.
- Reserve catcher Hal Smith hit a three-run homer to break a tie for Pittsburgh in the bottom of the eighth of Game 7.
- Mickey Mantle and Yogi Berra teamed to drive in two Yankee runs in the ninth to tie Game 7.
- Bill Mazeroski hit a homer in the bottom of the ninth of Game 7 to win the game and the Series for the Pirates.

Best Efforts

Batting

Average	Elston Howard	.462
Home Runs	Mickey Mantle	3
Triples	Bobby Richardson	2
Doubles	Bill Virdon	3
Hits	Moose Skowron	12
Runs	Mickey Mantle	8
	Bobby Richardson	8
RBIs	Bobby Richardson	12

Pitching

Wins	Vern Law	2–0
	Harvey Haddix	2–0
	Whitey Ford	2–0
ERA	Whitey Ford	0.00
Strikeouts	Vern Law	8
	Whitey Ford	8
Innings Pitched	Vern Law	18⅓

1961

New York Yankees   4
Cincinnati Reds   1

Line-ups

New York Yankees		**Cincinnati Reds**	
1b	Moose Skowron	1b	Gordy Coleman
2b	Bobby Richardson	2b	Elio Chacon
3b	Clete Boyer	3b	Gene Freese
ss	Tony Kubek	ss	Eddie Kasko
lf	Yogi Berra	lf	Wally Post
cf	Roger Maris	cf	Vada Pinson
rf	Johnny Blanchard	rf	Frank Robinson
c	Elston Howard	c	Johnny Edwards
mgr	Ralph Houk	mgr	Fred Hutchinson

		R	H	E	Pitching
Game 1	Cincinnati	0	2	0	Jim O'Toole, Jim Brosnan (8th)
	New York	2	6	0	Whitey Ford (W)
Game 2	Cincinnati	6	9	0	Joey Jay (W)
	New York	2	4	3	Ralph Terry, Luis Arroyo (8th)
Game 3	New York	3	6	1	Bill Stafford, Bud Daley (7th), Luis Arroyo (8th, W)
	Cincinnati	2	8	0	Bob Purkey
Game 4	New York	7	11	0	Whitey Ford (W), Jim Coates (6th)
	Cincinnati	0	5	1	Jim O'Toole, Jim Brosnan (6th), Bill Henry (9th)
Game 5	New York	13	15	1	Ralph Terry, Bud Daley (3rd, W)
	Cincinnati	5	11	3	Joey Jay, Jim Maloney (1st), Ken Johnson (2nd), Bill Henry (3rd), Sherman Jones (4th), Bob Purkey (5th), Jim Brosnan (7th), Ken Hunt (9th)

Highlights

- Yankee southpaw Whitey Ford extended his total of consecutive innings of scoreless pitching to 32, which broke the record set by Babe Ruth (29⅔) back in 1918 when he hurled for the Red Sox.
- Bobby Richardson's nine hits and eight singles tied records for a five-game Series.
- Ford pitched a two-hit shutout in Game 1.
- Elston Howard and Moose Skowron homered to provide the Yankee margin of victory in Game 1.
- Gordy Coleman belted a two-run homer to help the Reds take Game 2.
- In Game 3, Johnny Blanchard pinch hit a home run in the eighth inning to tie the score for the Yankees, then Roger Maris belted another in the ninth to provide the winning run.
- Whitey Ford and reliever Jim Coates combined to shutout the Reds in Game 4 and between them gave up only five hits.
- Reserve outfielder Hector Lopez drove in five runs with a home run and a triple, and Moose Skowron added another three RBIs to pace the Yankee attack in Game 5.

Best Efforts

Batting

Average	Johnny Blanchard	.400
Home Runs	Johnny Blanchard	2
Triples	Hector Lopez	1
Doubles	Elston Howard	3
Hits	Bobby Richardson	9
Runs	Elston Howard	5
RBIs	Hector Lopez	7

Pitching

Wins	Whitey Ford	2–0
ERA	Whitey Ford	0.00
Strikeouts	Whitey Ford	7
	Ralph Terry	7
Innings Pitched	Whitey Ford	14

1962

New York Yankees   4
San Francisco Giants 3

Line-ups

New York Yankees		San Francisco Giants	
1b	Moose Skowron	1b	Orlando Cepeda
2b	Bobby Richardson	2b	Chuck Hiller
3b	Clete Boyer	3b	Jim Davenport
ss	Tony Kubek	ss	Jose Pagan
lf	Tom Tresh	lf	Harvey Kuenn
cf	Mickey Mantle	cf	Willie Mays
rf	Roger Maris	rf	Felipe Alou
c	Elston Howard	c	Tom Haller
mgr	Ralph Houk	mgr	Alvin Dark

		R	H	E	Pitching
Game 1	New York	6	11	0	Whitey Ford (W)
	San Francisco	2	10	0	Billy O'Dell, Don Larsen (8th), Stu Miller (9th)
Game 2	New York	0	3	1	Ralph Terry, Bud Daley (8th)
	San Francisco	2	6	0	Jack Sanford (W)
Game 3	San Francisco	2	4	3	Billy Pierce, Don Larsen (7th), Bobby Bolin (8th)
	New York	3	5	1	Bill Stafford (W)
Game 4	San Francisco	7	9	1	Juan Marichal, Bobby Bolin (5th), Don Larsen (6th, W), Billy O'Dell (7th)
	New York	3	9	1	Whitey Ford, Jim Coates (7th), Marshall Bridges (7th)
Game 5	San Francisco	3	8	2	Jack Sanford, Stu Miller (8th)
	New York	5	6	0	Ralph Terry (W)
Game 6	New York	2	3	2	Whitey Ford, Jim Coates (5th), Marshall Bridges (8th)
	San Francisco	5	10	1	Billy Pierce (W)
Game 7	New York	1	7	0	Ralph Terry (W)
	San Francisco	0	4	1	Jack Sanford, Billy O'Dell (8th)

Highlights

- The Yankees recorded their twentieth world championship, 14 more than the second winningest team at that point in Series history, the St. Louis Cardinals.
- In Game 1, Whitey Ford continued his string of scoreless innings pitched to 33⅔, a record that still stands.
- Jack Sanford hurled a three-hit shutout for the Giants in Game 2.
- Chuck Hiller hit a grand slam homer to help the Giants to victory in Game 4.
- Tom Tresh broke a 2–2 tie in Game 5 with a three-run homer for the Yanks in the bottom of the eighth, which proved to be the game-winning runs.
- Billy Pierce allowed Yankee batters only three hits to lead the Giants to triumph in Game 6.
- Ralph Terry pitched a four-hit shutout for New York in Game 7.

Best Efforts

Batting

Average	Jose Pagan	.368
Home Runs	(five players)	1
Triples	Moose Skowron	1
	Felipe Alou	1
	Willie McCovey	1
Doubles	Chuck Hiller	3
Hits	Tom Tresh	9
Runs	Tom Tresh	5
RBIs	Roger Maris	5
	Chuck Hiller	5

Pitching

Wins	Ralph Terry	2–1
ERA	Ralph Terry	1.80
Strikeouts	Jack Sanford	19
Innings Pitched	Ralph Terry	25

1963

Los Angeles Dodgers 4
New York Yankees 0

Line-ups

Los Angeles Dodgers		New York Yankees	
1b	Moose Skowron	1b	Joe Pepitone
2b	Dick Tracewski	2b	Bobby Richardson
3b	Junior Gilliam	3b	Clete Boyer
ss	Maury Wills	ss	Tony Kubek
lf	Tommy Davis	lf	Tom Tresh
cf	Willie Davis	cf	Mickey Mantle
rf	Frank Howard	rf	Hector Lopez
c	John Roseboro	c	Elston Howard
mgr	Walt Alston	mgr	Ralph Houk

		R	H	E	Pitching
Game 1	Los Angeles	5	9	0	Sandy Koufax (W)
	New York	2	6	0	Whitey Ford, Stan Williams (6th), Steve Hamilton (9th)
Game 2	Los Angeles	4	10	1	Johnny Podres (W), Ron Perranoski (9th)
	New York	1	7	0	Al Downing, Ralph Terry (6th), Hal Reniff (9th)
Game 3	New York	0	3	0	Jim Bouton, Hal Reniff (8th)
	Los Angeles	1	4	1	Don Drysdale (W)
Game 4	New York	1	6	1	Whitey Ford, Hal Reniff (8th)
	Los Angeles	2	2	1	Sandy Koufax (W)

Highlights

- The Dodgers won their third world title and became the first team to sweep a Series from the Yankees.
- New York scored just four runs in the Series four games and, as a team, batted a meager .171.
- The 23 strikeouts by Dodger southpaw Sandy Koufax set a Series record for a four-game Series.
- Koufax fanned 15 Yankee batters in Game 1 to break the record set by another Dodger, Carl Erskine, back in 1953.
- The margin of victory in Game 1 was provided by Dodger John Roseboro with a three-run homer.
- A double by Willie Davis drove in two Dodger runs and gave them a lead in Game 2 they would not relinquish.
- Don Drysdale hurled a three-hit shutout for the Dodgers in Game 3.
- Yank hurlers Whitey Ford and Hal Reniff allowed only two Dodger hits in Game 4, but still lost (one was a homer by Frank Howard).

Best Efforts

Batting

Average	Tommy Davis	.400
Home Runs	(five players)	1
Triples	Tommy Davis	2
Doubles	Willie Davis	2
	Hector Lopez	2
Hits	Tommy Davis	6
Runs	Junior Gilliam	3
RBIs	Moose Skowron	3
	Willie Davis	3
	John Roseboro	3

Pitching

Wins	Sandy Koufax	2–0
ERA	Don Drysdale	0.00
Strikeouts	Sandy Koufax	23
Innings Pitched	Sandy Koufax	18

1964

St. Louis Cardinals 4
New York Yankees 3

Line-ups

St. Louis Cardinals		New York Yankees	
1b	Bill White	1b	Joe Pepitone
2b	Dal Maxvill	2b	Bobby Richardson
3b	Ken Boyer	3b	Clete Boyer
ss	Dick Groat	ss	Phil Linz
lf	Lou Brock	lf	Tom Tresh
cf	Curt Flood	cf	Roger Maris
rf	Mike Shannon	rf	Mickey Mantle
c	Tim McCarver	c	Elston Howard
mgr	Johnny Keane	mgr	Yogi Berra

		R	H	E	Pitching
Game 1	New York	5	12	2	Whitey Ford, Al Downing (6th), Rollie Sheldon (8th), Pete Mikkelson (8th)
	St. Louis	9	12	0	Ray Sadecki (W), Barney Schultz (7th)
Game 2	New York	8	12	0	Mel Stottlemyre (W)
	St. Louis	3	7	0	Bob Gibson, Barney Schultz (9th), Gordie Richardson (9th), Roger Craig (9th)
Game 3	St. Louis	1	6	0	Curt Simmons, Barney Schultz (9th)
	New York	2	5	2	Jim Bouton (W)
Game 4	St. Louis	4	6	1	Ray Sadecki, Roger Craig (1st, W), Ron Taylor (6th)
	New York	3	6	1	Al Downing, Pete Mikkelson (7th), Ralph Terry (8th)
Game 5	St. Louis	5	10	1	Bob Gibson (W)
	New York	2	6	2	Mel Stottlemyre, Hal Reniff (8th), Pete Mikkelson (8th)

		R	H	E	Pitching
Game 6	New York	8	10	0	Jim Bouton (W), Steve Hamilton (9th)
	St. Louis	3	10	1	Curt Simmons, Ron Taylor (7th), Barney Schultz (8th), Gordie Richardson (8th), Bob Humphreys (9th)
Game 7	New York	5	9	2	Mel Stottlemyre, Al Downing (5th), Rollie Sheldon (5th), Steve Hamilton (7th), Pete Mikkelson (8th)
	St. Louis	7	10	1	Bob Gibson (W)

Highlights

- The Cardinals gained their seventh world title, and it was their third triumph over the Yankees in five postseason encounters.
- Bobby Richardson of the Yanks set a record for a seven-game Series with his 13 hits.
- Cardinal righthander Bob Gibson set a seven-game Series mark with 31 strikeouts.
- Mickey Mantle tied the seven-game Series standard with his eight runs scored.
- Mike Shannon hit a two-run homer for the Cards in Game 1.
- Mickey Mantle clouted a homer in the ninth to provide the Yanks with their winning run in Game 3.
- Ken Boyer hit a grand slam home run which also provided the margin of victory for New York in Game 4.
- Tom Tresh connected on a two-run homer in the bottom of the ninth of Game 5 to tie the game and send it into extra innings.
- Tim McCarver clobbered a three-run homer in the tenth inning of Game 5, providing what turned out to be the game-winning runs.
- Bob Gibson struck out 13 Yankee batters in Game 5.
- Joe Pepitone hit a grand slam home run for the Yanks in Game 6.
- Mickey Mantle hit a three-run homer for New York in Game 7.
- Tim McCarver stole home for the Cards in Game 7.

Best Efforts

Batting

Average	Tim McCarver	.478
Home Runs	Mickey Mantle	3
Triples	Tim McCarver	1
	Dick Groat	1
	Curt Flood	1
Doubles	(four players)	2
Hits	Bobby Richardson	13
Runs	Mickey Mantle	8
RBIs	Mickey Mantle	6
	Tom Tresh	6

Pitching

Wins	Jim Bouton	2–0
	Bob Gibson	2–1
ERA	Jim Bouton	1.56
Strikeouts	Bob Gibson	31
Innings Pitched	Bob·Gibson	27

1965

Los Angeles Dodgers   4
Minnesota Twins   3

Line-ups

Los Angeles Dodgers		**Minnesota Twins**	
1b	Wes Parker	1b	Don Mincher
2b	Dick Tracewski	2b	Frank Quilici
3b	Junior Gilliam	3b	Harmon Killebrew
ss	Maury Wills	ss	Zoilo Versalles
lf	Lou Johnson	lf	Bob Allison
cf	Willie Davis	cf	Joe Nossek
rf	Ron Fairly	rf	Tony Oliva
c	John Roseboro	c	Earl Battey
mgr	Walt Alston	mgr	Sam Mele

		R	H	E	Pitching
Game 1	Los Angeles	2	10	1	Don Drysdale, Howie Reed (3rd), Jim Brewer (5th), Ron Perranoski (7th)
	Minnesota	8	10	0	Mudcat Grant (W)
Game 2	Los Angeles	1	7	3	Sandy Koufax, Ron Perranoski (7th), Bob Miller (8th)
	Minnesota	5	9	0	Jim Kaat (W)
Game 3	Minnesota	0	5	0	Camilio Pascual, Jim Merritt (6th), Johnny Klippstein (8th)
	Los Angeles	4	10	1	Claude Osteen (W)
Game 4	Minnesota	2	5	2	Mudcat Grant, Al Worthington (6th), Bill Pleis (8th)
	Los Angeles	7	10	0	Don Drysdale (W)
Game 5	Minnesota	0	4	1	Jim Kaat, Dave Boswell (3rd), Jim Perry (6th)
	Los Angeles	7	14	0	Sandy Koufax (W)

1965

Los Angeles Dodgers 4
Minnesota Twins 3

		R	H	E	Pitching
Game 6	Los Angeles	1	6	1	Claude Osteen, Howie Reed (6th), Bob Miller (8th)
	Minnesota	5	6	1	Mudcat Grant (W)
Game 7	Los Angeles	2	7	0	Sandy Koufax (W)
	Minnesota	0	3	1	Jim Kaat, Al Worthington (4th), Johnny Klippstein (6th), Jim Merritt (7th), Jim Perry (9th)

Highlights

- The Dodgers won their third world championship since moving to Los Angeles seven years earlier.
- Walt Alston became the first National League manager to win four world titles (he also piloted the 1955 champs from Brooklyn).
- Dodger pitchers shutout the Twins in three games.
- The Twins scored six runs in the third inning of Game 1, three of them on a home run by Zoilo Versalles.
- Jim Kaat went the distance in Game 2 for the Twins and drove in two runs to help his cause.
- Claude Osteen hurled a five-hit shutout for the Dodgers in Game 3.
- Don Drysdale went the distance in Game 4, allowing the Twins only five hits and striking out 11.
- Sandy Koufax blanked the Twins in Game 5, giving up just four hits and fanning 10 Twin batters.
- Maury Wills of the Dodgers got two doubles and two singles in five at-bats in Game 5.
- Dodger Willie Davis stole three bases in Game 5 to tie the Series record set by Honus Wagner of the Pirates back in 1909.
- Mudcat Grant gave up only one run and six hits in nine innings of Game 6 for the Twins and belted a three-run homer as well.
- Sandy Koufax pitched his second shutout of the Series for the Dodgers in Game 7, this time allowing only three hits and striking out 10.

Best Efforts

Batting

Average	Ron Fairly .379
Home Runs	Ron Fairly 2
	Lou Johnson 2
Triples	Wes Parker 1
	Zoilo Versalles 1
	Earl Battey 1
Doubles	Ron Fairly 3
	Maury Wills 3
Hits	Ron Fairly 11
	Maury Wills 11
Runs	Ron Fairly 7
RBIs	Ron Fairly 6

Pitching

Wins	Sandy Koufax 2–1
	Mudcat Grant 2–1
ERA	Sandy Koufax 0.38
Strikeouts	Sandy Koufax 29
Innings Pitched	Sandy Koufax 24

1966

Baltimore Orioles 4
Los Angeles Dodgers 0

Line-ups

Baltimore Orioles		Los Angeles Dodgers	
1b	Boog Powell	1b	Wes Parker
2b	Dave Johnson	2b	Jim Lefebvre
3b	Brooks Robinson	3b	Junior Gilliam
ss	Luis Aparicio	ss	Maury Wills
lf	Curt Blefary	lf	Tommy Davis
cf	Paul Blair	cf	Willie Davis
rf	Frank Robinson	rf	Lou Johnson
c	Andy Etchebarren	c	John Roseboro
mgr	Hank Bauer	mgr	Walt Alston

		R	H	E	Pitching
Game 1	Baltimore	5	9	0	Dave McNally, Moe Drabowski (3rd, W)
	Los Angeles	2	3	0	Don Drysdale, Joe Moeller (3rd), Bob Miller (5th), Ron Perranoski (8th)
Game 2	Baltimore	6	8	0	Jim Palmer (W)
	Los Angeles	0	4	6	Sandy Koufax, Ron Perranoski (7th), Phil Regan (8th), Jim Brewer (9th)
Game 3	Los Angeles	0	6	0	Claude Osteen, Phil Regan (8th)
	Baltimore	1	3	0	Wally Bunker (W)
Game 4	Los Angeles	0	4	0	Don Drysdale
	Baltimore	1	4	0	Dave McNally (W)

Highlights

- The Baltimore Orioles captured their first world title, charting three shutouts in their four game sweep of the Series.
- The Dodgers set (or tied) nine ignominious Series records: fewest runs (2), fewest hits (17), fewest singles (13), fewest doubles (3), fewest total bases (23), fewest extra-base hits (4), lowest team batting average (.142), lowest team slugging average (.192), and most consecutive scoreless innings (33).
- Frank Robinson and Brooks Robinson hit back-to-back home runs for the Orioles in Game 1 off Don Drysdale.
- Reliever Moe Drabowsky of Baltimore did not allow a hit and struck out 11 Dodgers in 6⅔ innings during Game 1.
- Jim Palmer hurled a four-hit shutout for the Orioles in Game 2.
- Dodger centerfielder Willie Davis set an unprized record when he made three errors in one inning (the fifth) of Game 2. It also stands as the most by an outfielder in a single Series game and the most in a four-game Series.
- Wally Bunker shutout the Dodgers in Game 3, giving up only six hits.
- Dave McNally threw a four-hit shutout for the Orioles in Game 4.

Best Efforts

Batting

Average	Boog Powell	.357
Home Runs	Frank Robinson	2
Triples	Frank Robinson	1
Doubles	Wes Parker	2
Hits	Boog Powell	5
Runs	Frank Robinson	4
RBIs	Frank Robinson	3

Pitching

Wins	(four players)	1
ERA	Jim Palmer	0.00
	Wally Bunker	0.00
	Moe Drabowsky	0.00
Strikeouts	Moe Drabowsky	11
Innings Pitched	Dave McNally	11⅓

1967

St. Louis Cardinals 4
Boston Red Sox 3

Line-ups

St. Louis Cardinals		Boston Red Sox	
1b	Orlando Cepeda	1b	George Scott
2b	Julian Javier	2b	Jerry Adair
3b	Mike Shannon	3b	Dalton Jones
ss	Dal Maxvill	ss	Rico Petrocelli
lf	Lou Brock	lf	Carl Yastrzemski
cf	Curt Flood	cf	Reggie Smith
rf	Roger Maris	rf	Jose Tartabull
c	Tim McCarver	c	Elston Howard
mgr	Red Schoendienst	mgr	Dick Williams

		R	H	E	Pitching
Game 1	St. Louis	2	10	0	Bob Gibson (W)
	Boston	1	6	0	Jose Santiago, John Wyatt (8th)
Game 2	St. Louis	0	1	1	Dick Hughes, Ron Willis (6th), Joe Hoerner (7th), Jack Lamabe (7th)
	Boston	5	9	0	Jim Lonborg (W)
Game 3	Boston	2	7	1	Gary Bell, Gary Waslewski (3rd), Lee Stange (6th), Dan Osinski (8th)
	St. Louis	5	10	0	Nelson Briles (W)
Game 4	Boston	0	5	0	Jose Santiago, Gary Bell (1st), Jerry Stephenson (3rd), Dave Morehead (5th), Ken Brett (8th)
	St. Louis	6	9	0	Bob Gibson (W)
Game 5	Boston	3	6	1	Jim Lonborg (W)
	St. Louis	1	3	2	Steve Carlton, Ray Washburn (7th), Ron Willis (9th), Jack Lamabe (9th)

		R	H	E	Pitching
Game 6	St. Louis	4	8	0	Dick Hughes, Ron Willis (4th), Nelson Briles (5th), Jack Lamabe (7th), Joe Hoerner (7th), Larry Jaster (7th), Ray Washburn (7th), Hal Woodeshick (8th)
	Boston	8	12	1	Gary Waslewski, John Wyatt (6th, W), Gary Bell (8th)
Game 7	St. Louis	7	10	1	Bob Gibson (W)
	Boston	2	3	1	Jim Lonborg, Jose Santiago (7th), Dave Morehead (9th), Dan Osinski (9th), Ken Brett (9th)

Highlights

- The Cardinals were credited with their eighth world title, second only to the New York Yankees in total Series crowns.
- Bob Gibson became the seventh pitcher in history to win three games in a Series without suffering a defeat.
- Lou Brock stole seven bases to top the World Series record of six set by Jimmy Slagle of the Chicago Cubs back in 1907.
- Brock's eight runs scored tied the record for a seven-game Series.
- Roger Maris drove in both Cardinal runs in Game 1 to account for their victory.
- Jim Lonborg of the Red Sox hurled a one-hit shutout in Game 2. It was only the fourth one-hitter in Series history, the hit coming from Julian Javier in the top of the eighth.
- Carl Yastrzemski hit two homers and drove in four runs in Game 2.
- Bob Gibson pitched a five-hit shutout for the Cards in Game 4.
- Elston Howard's ninth inning single brought in the winning runs for the BoSox in Game 5.
- For the first and only time in Series history, one team, the Red Sox, collected three home runs in a single inning. In the fourth of Game 6, Carl Yastrzemski, Reggie Smith, and Rico Petrocelli each knocked one out of Fenway Park. (Petrocelli had two homers in the game.)
- The 11 pitchers used by both teams in Game 6 and the eight by St. Louis set Series records.

- Gibson allowed only three hits in Game 7, struck out 10 Red Sox batters, and hit a home run.
- Lou Brock stole three bases for the Cards in Game 7 to tie the Series mark.

Best Efforts

Batting

Average	Lou Brock .414
Home Runs	Carl Yastrzemski 3
Triples	Lou Brock 1
	Dal Maxvill 1
	George Scott 1
Doubles	Julian Javier 3
Hits	Lou Brock 12
Runs	Lou Brock 8
RBIs	Roger Maris 7

Pitching

Wins	Bob Gibson 3–0
ERA	Bob Gibson 1.00
Strikeouts	Bob Gibson 26
Innings Pitched	Bob Gibson 27

1968

Detroit Tigers   4
St. Louis Cardinals 3

Line-ups

Detroit Tigers		**St. Louis Cardinals**	
1b	Norm Cash	1b	Orlando Cepeda
2b	Dick McAuliffe	2b	Julian Javier
3b	Don Wert	3b	Mike Shannon
ss	Mickey Stanley	ss	Dal Maxvill
lf	Willie Horton	lf	Lou Brock
cf	Jim Northrup	cf	Curt Flood
rf	Al Kaline	rf	Roger Maris
c	Bill Freehan	c	Tim McCarver
mgr	Mayo Smith	mgr	Red Schoendienst

		R	H	E	Pitching
Game 1	Detroit	0	5	3	Denny McLain, Pat Dobson (6th), Don McMahon (8th)
	St. Louis	4	6	0	Bob Gibson (W)
Game 2	Detroit	8	13	1	Mickey Lolich (W)
	St. Louis	1	6	1	Nelson Briles, Steve Carlton (6th), Ron Willis (7th), Joe Hoerner (9th)
Game 3	St. Louis	7	13	0	Ray Washburn (W), Joe Hoerner (6th)
	Detroit	3	4	0	Earl Wilson, Pat Dobson (5th), Don McMahon (6th), Daryl Patterson (7th), John Hiller (8th)
Game 4	St. Louis	10	13	0	Bob Gibson (W)
	Detroit	1	5	4	Denny McLain, Joe Sparma (3rd), Daryl Patterson (4th), Fred Lasher (6th), John Hiller (8th), Pat Dobson (8th)
Game 5	St. Louis	3	9	0	Nelson Briles, Joe Hoerner (7th), Ron Willis (7th)
	Detroit	5	9	1	Mickey Lolich (W)

1968

Detroit Tigers   4
St. Louis Cardinals   3

		R	H	E	Pitching
Game 6	Detroit	13	12	1	Denny McLain (W)
	St. Louis	1	9	1	Ray Washburn, Larry Jaster (3rd), Ron Willis (3rd), Dick Hughes (3rd), Steve Carlton (4th), Wayne Granger (7th), Mel Nelson (9th)
Game 7	Detroit	4	8	1	Mickey Lolich (W)
	St. Louis	1	5	0	Bob Gibson

Highlights

- The Tigers won their third world championship, the first since 1945.
- Mickey Lolich won three games and lost none for the Tigers, only the eighth pitcher in Series history to post such a record.
- Lou Brock of the Cards stole seven bases to tie the Series record he set the year before.
- Brock's 13 hits tied the mark for a seven-game Series.
- Bob Gibson's 35 strikeouts broke the record of 31 he set in 1964.
- Gibson extended his streak of consecutive Series wins to seven, a record that still stands.
- Gibson set a single-game strikeout record in Game 1 by fanning 17 Tiger batters, which remains the most ever in any Series game.
- Gibson was credited with a five-hit shutout in Game 1.
- Mickey Lolich allowed the Cards only one run and six hits in Game 2, struck out 10, hit a home run and a single, and drove in two runs.
- Tim McCarver and Orlando Cepeda each hit three-run homers for the Cardinals in Game 3.
- Lou Brock stole three bases in Game 3 to tie the Series record (he had also tied it the year before).
- Gibson allowed the Tigers only one run and five hits in Game 4, scored two runs himself, and drove in another pair for the Cardinals.
- Al Kaline batted in two runs and Norm Cash another in the seventh inning of Game 5 to provide the victory margin for the Tigers.
- The Tigers scored 10 runs in the third inning of Game 6 to tie the Series mark set by the Philadelphia A's in 1929. The runs were the result of seven hits (two were by Kaline), four bases on balls, a hit-batsman, and a sacrifice.
- Jim Northrup hit a grand slam home run for the Tigers in Game 6.
- Northrup drove in two runs with a triple in Game 7 to provide the winning margin for the Tigers.

Best Efforts

Batting

Average	Lou Brock .464
Home Runs	(four players) 2
Triples	Tim McCarver 2
Doubles	Lou Brock 3
Hits	Lou Brock 13
Runs	Lou Brock 6
	Al Kaline 6
	Willie Horton 6
RBIs	Al Kaline 8
	Jim Northrup 8

Pitching

Wins	Mickey Lolich 3–0
ERA	Mickey Lolich 1.67
	Bob Gibson 1.67
Strikeouts	Bob Gibson 35
Innings Pitched	Mickey Lolich 27
	Bob Gibson 27

1969

New York Mets 4
Baltimore Orioles 1

Line-ups

New York Mets		Baltimore Orioles	
1b	Donn Clendenon	1b	Boog Powell
2b	Al Weis	2b	Dave Johnson
3b	Ed Charles	3b	Brooks Robinson
ss	Bud Harrelson	ss	Mark Belanger
lf	Cleon Jones	lf	Don Buford
cf	Tommie Agee	cf	Paul Blair
rf	Ron Swododa	rf	Frank Robinson
c	Jerry Grote	c	Ellie Hendricks
mgr	Gil Hodges	mgr	Earl Weaver

		R	H	E	Pitching
Game 1	New York	1	6	1	Tom Seaver, Don Cardwell (6th), Ron Taylor (7th)
	Baltimore	4	6	0	Mike Cuellar (W)
Game 2	New York	2	6	0	Jerry Koosman (W), Ron Taylor (9th)
	Baltimore	1	2	0	Dave McNally
Game 3	Baltimore	0	4	1	Jim Palmer, Dave Leonhard (7th)
	New York	5	6	0	Gary Gentry (W), Nolan Ryan (7th)
Game 4	Baltimore	1	6	1	Mike Cuellar, Eddie Watt (8th), Dick Hall (10th), Pete Richert (10th)
	New York	2	10	1	Tom Seaver (W)
Game 5	Baltimore	3	5	2	Dave McNally, Eddie Watt (8th)
	New York	5	7	0	Jerry Koosman (W)

Highlights

- The New York Mets won their first and so far only world title.
- Donn Clendenon of the Mets clouted three home runs to set the standard for a five-game Series.
- Mike Cuellar allowed the Mets only one run and six hits in Game 1 and batted in a run himself.
- Jerry Koosman pitched a two-hitter through 8⅔ innings for the Mets in Game 2.
- Al Weis drove Ed Charles home with the game-winning run for the Mets in the ninth inning of Game 2.
- Gary Gentry and Nolan Ryan teamed to hurl a four-hit shutout for the Mets in Game 3. Gentry also drove in two runs with a double.
- Tom Seaver pitched all 10 innings for the Mets in Game 4, giving up only one run and six hits.
- A two-run homer by Donn Clendenon and a solo from Al Weis enabled the Mets to tie the score in Game 5, then a double by Ron Swoboda sent Cleon Jones across with what proved to be the game-winning run.

Best Efforts

Batting

Average	Al Weis .455
Home Runs	Donn Clendenon 3
Triples	——
Doubles	Jerry Grote 2
Hits	Ron Swoboda 6
Runs	Donn Clendenon 4
RBIs	Donn Clendenon 4

Pitching

Wins	Jerry Koosman 2–0
ERA	Mike Cuellar 1.13
Strikeouts	Mike Cuellar 13
	Dave McNally 13
Innings Pitched	Jerry Koosman 17⅔

The ten years that extended from 1970 through 1979 contained a wealth of great sports performances and many legends in the making. Pro football gave us the Dallas Cowboys and the Pittsburgh Steelers, O. J. Simpson and Roger Staubach; in boxing there was Muhammad Ali and Joe Frazier and their classic, bouts; basketball had Kareem Abdul Jabbar, Julius "Dr. Dunk" Erving, Earvin "Magic" Johnson, and Larry Bird; hockey, Bobby Orr and Phil Esposito; tennis, Jimmy Connors and Bjorn Borg; horse racing, Secretariat and Seattle Slew; and such Olympic titans as Mark Spitz, Frank Shorter, Bruce Jenner, and Sugar Ray Leonard.

In the baseball world it was the time of controversial owners, like Charley Finley, George Steinbrenner, and Ted Turner; flamboyant managers, such as Billy Martin, Earl Weaver, Tommy Lasorda, and (still) Leo Durocher; and colorful ballplayers who left their marks in a variety of ways and via various personalities, among them Dick Allen, Reggie Jackson, Pete Rose, Mark "The Bird" Fidrych, and Al Hrabosky.

Baseball experienced its first baseball strike in 1972; got the designated hitter in 1973 (at least in the American League); and the first black manager, Frank Robinson, at Cleveland in 1975. There was Nolan Ryan's four no-hitters, two in the same year; Hank Aaron breaking Babe Ruth's career home run record; Lou Brock racing away with the all-time record for base thefts in a season; and Reggie "Mr. October" Jackson's phenomenal performances in the World Series.

And pervading all of that was the transformation of baseball into a very big business. Within the '70s it moved from Curt Flood's challenge of baseball's exemption from the federal antitrust laws, to the practice of arbitration, to free agency, to multi-million-dollar player contracts.

The decade began with the Baltimore Orioles winning their second American League pennant in a row, and the Cincinnati Reds their first NL flag since 1961. Earl Weaver got the Orioles there by steering them through very easy waters in the AL East where no team got nearer them at the end of the regular season than the New York Yankees, who were 15 out.

The Orioles had *three* 20-game winners in 1970: Mike Cuellar (24–8), Dave McNally (24–9), and Jim Palmer (20–10). They also had strong bullpen help from Pete Richert and Eddie Watt. Their only .300 hitter was Frank Robinson (.306), who also hit 25 home runs. Baltimore's biggest power

hitter, however, was Boog Powell, who hammered 35 home runs, accounted for 114 RBIs, and was named the league's MVP. Brooks Robinson dispatched another 18 out of the ballpark as did Merv Rettenmund; Don Buford hit 17.

Baltimore marched through the playoffs just as they had the regular season, eliminating the AL West champion Minnesota Twins in three games, none of which was even close (the nearest the Twins got was the 10–6 loss in the first game.)

Sparky Anderson was in his first year as manager of the Cincinnati Reds in 1970 and he made a most impressive debut. The Reds won 102 games and finished 14½ ahead of the Los Angeles Dodgers to take the NL West. They were blessed both with consistent hitting and the most power in the entire National League. Johnny Bench led the league in two categories, home runs (45) and RBIs (148) and took MVP honors. Tony Perez whacked 40 home runs and drove in 129 runs, while Lee May clouted 34, Bernie Carbo, 21; Bobby Tolan, 16; and Pete Rose, 15. Perez hit .317, Rose and Tolan, .316; and Carbo, .310. Tolan also led the majors with 57 stolen bases. Jim Merritt was Cincinnati's only 20-game winner (20–12) but Gary Nolan had a fine record (18–7), and Wayne Granger was credited with 35 saves, the most in either league.

The Pittsburgh Pirates won the NL East, principally on the bats of Roberto Clemente (.352) and Manny Sanguillen (.325) and the power of Willie Stargell (31 homers). But the Reds disposed of them in three straight. Gary Nolan hurled a shutout in the first game, and Bobby Tolan homered and scored all three of Cincinnati's runs in the second, then drove in the winning run in the third game.

In the Series itself, however, Baltimore was clearly the champ, winning the first three games handily, then, after a setback, taking it all in the fifth game.

Baltimore roared back in 1971, with the second-place Detroit Tigers trailing by 12 games when the AL East season closed. The Orioles had four 20-game winners that year: Dave McNally (21–5), Pat Dobson (20–8), and Mike Cuellar and Jim Palmer (20–9 each). Only one other time in baseball history had a major league team produced four 20-game winners in the same season, the Chicago White Sox back in 1920 (Red Faber, Lefty Williams, Dickie Kerr, and Eddie Cicotte). Baltimore power was also still

there. Frank Robinson banged out 28 homers, Boog Powell, 22; Brooks Robinson, 20; and Don Buford, 19. Merv Rettenmund, however, was the only Baltimore batter to exceed .300, and he did it with an average of .318.

In the AL West, a new powerhouse was developing, one that still needed another year before it would indelibly inscribe its name in baseball lore. Under the tutelage of Dick Williams, the Oakland A's had blitzed the rest of its division, finishing 16 games ahead of the Kansas City Royals. The A's got strong hitting from Reggie Jackson, Sal Bando, and Joe Rudi, and they had one of the game's finest shortstops and base-stealers in Bert Campaneris. They also possessed a mound staff which consisted of Vida Blue, that year's MVP and Cy Young award winner, and Catfish Hunter, Blue Moon Odom, Chuck Dobson, and reliever Rollie Fingers.

But Baltimore zapped them in three straight, scoring five runs in each game and getting some fine pitching from Jim Palmer, Mike Cuellar, and Dave McNally.

Pittsburgh, who had won its last world championship 11 years earlier, was the team the Orioles would have to face in the 1971 World Series. A runner-up the year before, Danny Murtaugh's Pirates had gotten everything together and had little trouble triumphing in the NL East. The Cardinals exerted some pressure but trailed by seven games when the season ended.

Pirate slugger Willie Stargell led both leagues with 48 home runs, he also drove in 125 and scored 104 runs. Roberto Clemente batted .341 and Manny Sanguillen, .319. Dock Ellis was their winningest pitcher (19–9), but Steve Blass accounted for 15 wins and Dave Giusti was credited with a league-high 30 saves.

To get to the Series, however, they had to get by a very fine San Francisco Giant team, who just barely inched by the Los Angeles Dodgers to take the NL West crown. Willie Mays, now 40, still swung a bat for them and no one took him lightly even in the twilight of his career. The Giants also had such fine hitters as Willie McCovey and Bobby Bonds and a pitching staff that boasted Juan Marichal and Gaylord Perry.

The Giants looked like they might waltz away with the pennant after they opened in Candlestick Park and romped with Gaylord Perry's fine nine innings of pitching and a pair of home runs from Willie McCovey and Tito

Fuentes. But the next day they were brought back to reality by Bob Robertson of the Pirates, who clouted three home runs, a double, and drove in five runs. At home in Pittsburgh, the Pirates then won two straight for the pennant.

The Pirates stepped off in the wrong direction in the Series, just as they had in the NL playoffs, this time losing the first two games, both played in hostile Baltimore. In the friendlier confines of Pittsburgh, however, they won three straight. They lost a true nailbiter in extra innings in Baltimore to set the stage for a dramatic seventh-game decider. And, with brilliant pitching from Steve Blass and clutch hits by Roberto Clemente and Jose Pagan, they edged out the Orioles by a single run to take their fourth world championship.

After that, however, the team to watch was the Oakland Athletics. Despite a chaotic relationship between owner Charley Finley and his managers and players, the A's would still manage to win three consecutive world titles.

Oakland was pressed by the Chicago White Sox in the AL West in 1972 but survived and won the divisional title by five-and-a-half games. Pitching was

Oakland's foremost tool that year, with Catfish Hunter winning 21 games and losing just seven, Ken Holtzman registering 19 wins, and Blue Moon Odom, 15. Rollie Fingers saved 21 games. There was also an abundance of power. Mike Epstein hit 26 homers, Reggie Jackson had 25, and Joe Rudi and Dave Duncan, 19 apiece. Bert Campaneris stole 52 bases, the most in the American League. But only Rudi managed to bat above .300 (.305).

The American League playoffs were the most exciting since the divisional format had been adopted. The Detroit Tigers, directed by the ever-volatile Billy Martin, won the East behind the bats of aging Al Kaline and Norm Cash and the pitching of Mickey Lolich and Joe Coleman. The first game went 11 innings, with the A's sneaking by to score the game-winner on an error. The second game was all Blue Moon Odom, who hurled a three-hit shutout for the A's. But back in Detroit, the Tigers turned the momentum when first Joe Coleman shutout the A's, and the next day Detroit batters staged a remarkable three-run rally in the bottom of the tenth to rescue the fourth game. But Oakland slipped by the next day by a single run and earned the AL pennant.

Sparky Anderson's Reds were back to represent the National League in 1972. They had glided through the NL West, no team closer than 10½ games. Most of the same stars of the 1970 pennant-winners were still there. Johnny Bench again took the NL home run crown, this time with 40, and the RBI crown with 125, and was named MVP for the second time. Tony Perez accounted for another 21 round-trippers and Joe Morgan hit 16. Pete Rose batted .307 and collected a league-high 198 hits. Gary Nolan won 15 games and Ross Grimsley took 14, and Clay Carroll's 37 saves were the major league tops that year.

Awaiting them were the reigning flag-holders from Pittsburgh and it, too, would be an exciting playoff series. In the fifth game, the decider at Cincinnati, the Pirates had a one-run lead in the ninth, but then saw the pennant flutter away. First, Johnny Bench smashed a homer to tie the game, then a few batters later Pirate reliever Bob Moose threw a wild pitch which enabled George Foster to score from third the game-winning run.

The Series also went the distance, as nip-and-tuck as any ever played. Six of the games were decided by a single run, including the decisive seventh. Oakland's four one-run victories were enough, however, to bring Charley Finley his first world crown.

In 1973, the designated hitter came to the American League. Oakland found theirs in Deron Johnson but neither he nor any of the other eight batters in the A's line-up hit above .300. Still Oakland prevailed in the AL West, beating out the Kansas City Royals by six games. They did it chiefly on their pitching, three 20-game winners: Catfish Hunter (21-5), Ken Holtzman (21-13), and Vida Blue (20-9), complemented by a superb reliever Rollie Fingers (22 saves). The biggest gun in their offensive attack was Reggie Jackson, who led the league in homers (32), RBIs (117), and runs scored (99). He was honored as the league's MVP. Sal Bando contributed 29 four-baggers; other sluggers: Gene Tenace (24), Deron Johnson (19), and Joe Rudi (12). On the basepaths Billy North pilfered 53; Bert Campaneris, 34; and Reggie Jackson, 22.

It was the Orioles that Oakland would have to face in the '73 playoffs. They also had excellent pitching, especially from Jim Palmer (that year's Cy Young award winner), Mike Cuellar, and Dave McNally. They got good hitting from Rich Coggins, Boog Powell, Paul Blair, Tommy Davis, and Rookie of the Year Al Bumbry.

Palmer lived up to his Cy Young status in the first playoff game and scorched Oakland with a five-hit shutout. But the A's rebounded to take the next two. Baltimore turned it into a five-game affair by winning the fourth game, but then Catfish Hunter gilded Oakland's fortunes by shutting the Orioles out in the fifth game.

The National League race in 1973 was much closer than that in the American. In the East, four teams had a shot at the divisional title during the last week of the season: the New York Mets, Pittsburgh Pirates, St. Louis Cardinals, and Montreal Expos. As it turned out, the Mets, managed by Yogi Berra, got the prize; the Cardinals were second, one-and-a-half games behind; and the Pirates trailed by two-and-a-half and the Expos three-and-a-half.

The Mets, amazingly enough, were the second worst-hitting team in the entire National League, their average of .246 and home run total of 85 were exceeded by 10 other clubs. No batter approached the .300 mark by less than 10 percentage points. John Milner led the team in home runs with 23, Wayne Garret added 16, and Rusty Staub, 15. They had a fine pitching staff, however, headed by Cy Young award-winner Tom Seaver (19-10): Both Jerry Koosman and Jon Matlack won 14 games, and Tug McGraw was the cornerstone of the bullpen, logging 25 saves.

In the NL West, Cincinnati had a brawl on its hands with the Los Angeles Dodgers, but Sparky Anderson's Reds managed to get by them by three-and-a-half games. Cincinnati was a better hitting team than the Mets. They had the batting crown champ and MVP, Pete Rose, who hit .338 and his 230 hits were the most in the majors. Tony Perez batted .314 and slugged a team-high 27 home runs. Joe Morgan clouted 26 homers and Johnny Bench, 25. Bench drove in the most runs, 104, three more than Perez. Their pitching staff also compared well. Jack Billingham posted the best record (19–10), Don Gullett won another 18 games, and Ross Grimsley, 13. The bullpen was consistent with Clay Carroll and Pedro Borbon getting the most calls.

The NL playoff also went five games that year. Among the highlights, Jon Matlack's two-hit shutout in one game for the Mets and Pete Rose's 12th inning, game-winning homer for the Reds in

another. But when it was over the Mets were the winners and were off to attend their third World Series.

Once again, the Series, like the two playoffs that preceded it, went the distance. Oakland was the favorite from the start and they proved the oddsmakers correct, although it was close all the way and Oakland had to come back from a three-game to two deficit to win the world title.

One casualty of the '73 Series was Oakland manager Dick Williams, who quit after it because of major disagreements with owner Charley Finley. Replacing him was veteran manager Alvin Dark, and he brought the A's in again to capture their third successive AL pennant. Oakland had little trouble getting through the AL West. Billy Martin's Texas Rangers gave them a run for awhile but finished five games back. Catfish Hunter earned the Cy Young award, his prize for winning 25 games and posting a league-leading ERA of 2.49. Ken Holtzman won 19 and Vida Blue took 17. Rollie Fingers was still the bullpen mainstay, chalking up 18 saves. The A's had four sluggers who hit more than 20 home runs: Reggie Jackson (29), Gene Tenace (26), and Sal Bando and Joe Rudi

The famous Dodger infield of the 1970s (l to r); Ron Cey, Bill Russell, Davey Lopes, and Steve Garvey. The four played together in the World Series of 1974, 1977, 1978, and 1981.

(22 apiece). Rudi also led the league in doubles with 34. And Billy North was the NL's most accomplished base thief, copping 54. But no one hit .300 or better.

Baltimore was also a repeat winner, barely edging the New York Yankees by two games. The Orioles did not have a single .300 hitter either, nor did any Baltimore batter swat 20 home runs, although Bobby Grich was close with 19. Pitching is what made the difference in the AL East, and performing best for the Orioles was Mike ·Cuellar (22–10), Ross Grimsley (18–13), and Dave McNally (16–10).

Baltimore stepped out smartly in the playoffs, winning the first

game with ease. But then back-to-back shutouts by Ken Holtzman and Vida Blue and a one-run performance by Catfish Hunter, aided by Rollie Fingers, in the fourth game gave the pennant to the A's.

The Los Angeles Dodgers finally made it back to the World Series, from which they had been absent since 1966. Still under Walt Alston, then in his 21st year as pilot of the Dodgers, LA claimed both the MVP, Steve Garvey, and the Cy Young award winner, Mike Marshall, the first relief pitcher to be so honored. The Dodgers hit more home runs than any other team in the majors in 1974, led by Jim Wynn, who clouted 32. Steve Garvey hit 21, Ron Cey, 18, and Joe Ferguson, 16. Bill Buckner batted .314 and Garvey hit .312. Andy Messersmith had the best record in the league, 20–5, Don Sutton won 19 games, and Mike Marshall took 15 and was credited with 21 saves.

Don Sutton hurled for the Dodgers in three World Series in the 1970s, winning two games and losing two.

The Dodgers came in four games ahead of the Cincinnati Reds, who had been after their third straight divisional title. Then LA took on the Pittsburgh Pirates, whose destinies rode on the bats of Willie Stargell, Al Oliver, Richie Zisk, Mannie Sanguillen, and Reggie Stennett. But the Dodgers blew them away in four games, with Don Sutton capturing two of the Dodger wins.

The all-California Series, the first of its kind in the Golden State, was decided in five games. All were close, but Oakland succeeded in four of them, although three were determined by just a single run.

Oakland would not make it four straight world titles, however, even though they gave it quite a try. The A's did win the AL West for the fifth consecutive year, with no one closer than the Kansas City Royals, who were seven games behind. But they ran into a hard-hitting Boston Red Sox team in the playoffs, one that had surprised most baseball observers when they overcame a favored Baltimore Orioles in the AL East race.

The Red Sox were managed by Darrell Johnson, and still got a lot of clutch hitting and team leadership from 35-year-old Carl Yastrzemski. They also had five batters above the .300 mark: Fred Lynn, the AL MVP, and Carlton Fisk (both .311), Cecil Cooper (.311), Denny Doyle (.310), and Jim Rice (.309). Rice and Lynn were the most productive home run hitters with 22 and 21 respectively. Lynn drove in 105 runs and Rice, 102. Rick Wise posted the best record (19–12) and Luis Tiant was close behind (18–14) as was Bill Lee (17–9). Top reliever was Dick Drago, who saved 15 games.

Oakland certainly had a lot more experience in the playoffs but it was not evident when the two teams met. The Red Sox destroyed them in three straight, none of which were even close.

Cincinnati wreaked its revenge on the Dodgers and did it brutally in 1975, winning a total of 108 games in the NL West and finishing a lengthy 20 games ahead of the second-place Dodgers. Like the Red Sox, the Reds were a fine hitting team. MVP of the year Joe Morgan topped the club with an average of .327, following were Pete Rose (.317), Ken Griffey (.305), and George Foster (.300). Rose led the league with 47 doubles. Homers were in relative abundance: Johnny Bench (28), George Foster (23), Tony Perez (20), and Joe Morgan (17). The Reds had three 15-game winners in Don Gullett, Gary Nolan, and Jack Billingham, and an especially good bullpen with Rawly Eastwick (22 saves) and Will McEnaney (15 saves).

Moment of triumph. Reliever Will McEnaney (37) signals the ultimate victory of the Cincinnati Reds in Game 7 of the 1975 World Series. He was credited with a save that day. The other Red is first baseman Tony Perez.

The Reds continued their winning ways in the NL playoffs, quickly and decisively disposing of the Pittsburgh Pirates in three straight games.

Sparky Anderson's Reds did not have as easy a time in the Series, however. The Red Sox stayed with them all the way through six games and eight innings of the deciding seventh game. It was there in that last frame where Joe Morgan drove in the winning run and destroyed Boston's dream of an upset championship. It was the Reds' first world title since 1940.

They would add another title the following year. Once again, they would put the Dodgers in their place in the NL West, although this time the margin would only be 10 games at the season's close. Five players hit better than .300 for Cincinnati: Ken Griffey (.336), Pete Rose (.323), Joe Morgan (.320), Cesar Geronimo (.307), and George Foster (.306). Rawly Eastwick again was the most effective reliever in the league, recording 26 saves. For the second year in a row, Joe Morgan was named MVP, the first time a player was so honored in two successive years since "Mr. Cub" Ernie Banks back in 1958 and 1959.

In the NL East, the Philadelphia Phillies won their first divisional title. With Danny Ozark holding the reins, the Phils beat out the Pirates by nine full games. They had some notorious power in the bats wielded by Mike Schmidt, who led the league with 38 homers, and Greg Luzinski, and they got consistent hitting from Gary Maddox and Jay Johnstone. Toiling well from the mound for them were Steve Carlton and Jim Lonborg. But when they faced the seasoned Cincinnati nine, they fell apart. The Reds demolished them in the first two games, then made it a sweep when they came from behind with three runs in the bottom of the ninth of the third game for a one-run victory.

The New York Yankees had not been to a World Series since the glory days of the early '60s when Mickey Mantle was swinging a bat for them and Whitey Ford was sending enemy batters back to the dugout. But in 1976 they made it under Billy Martin in his first tour of duty as manager in New York. Owner George Steinbrenner had begun to buy a host of stars, a practice he would continue over the next few years, and

Thurman Munson was the Yankee catcher in 1976–78 World Series, batting a hefty .373.

the talent that turned out in Yankee pinstripes was good enough to take the AL East by 10½ games over the Baltimore Orioles.

One of the keys to New York's success, Thurman Munson, however, had always been a Yankee, ever since the day he made his major league debut in 1969. Now, eight years later, Munson was the AL's MVP. He hit .302, clouted 17 homers, and drove in a team-high 105 runs. Graig Nettles led the league in homers with 32, and Mickey Rivers batted .312. On the mound the Yanks relied on Ed Figueroa (19–10), Catfish Hunter (17–15), Dock Ellis (17–8), and when they faltered Billy Martin could call on ace reliever Sparky Lyle, who saved a league-high 23 games.

The Yanks had to get by a very strong Kansas City Royals, however, before they could come home to the Series. Whitey Herzog led the Royals to a title by edging another powerhouse, the Oakland A's, by two-and-a-half games. With hitters like batting crown wearer George Brett (.333), Hal McRae, and Amos Otis, they were a team to contend with. It took the Yankees five games to overcome them, and that was accomplished only by a game-winning run scored in the bottom of the ninth of the fifth game.

The Yankees did not fare anywhere near as well in the Series, however. With the bats of Johnny Bench and George Foster ringing loudest and those of most of the other Cincinnati hitters adding a profound chorus they swept it in four games.

Disappointed, George Steinbrenner went shopping. This time he picked up superstar Reggie Jackson as well as an excellent lefthander in Don Gullett and one of the game's finer shortstops, Bucky Dent. It would prove to be enough.

The Yankees won the AL East by two-and-a-half games, but it had been a very close race. Both the Baltimore Orioles and the Boston Red Sox had pressured the Yanks all the way to the finish line and both trailed by only that small margin.

Reggie Jackson had come through for them, batting in a team-high 110 runs and clobbering 32 homers. Graig Nettles hit the most home runs, however, 37, and he drove in another 107 runs. And Thurman Munson, who batted .308, also had 100 RBIs. Mickey Rivers took the team batting crown with an average of .326. Both Ron Guidry and Ed Figueroa won 16 games for the Yankees, and Sparky Lyle, cred-

Graig Nettles was the fielding ace of the Yankees in four World Series from 1976 through 1981, but batted only .221 overall.

ited with 26 rescues, earned the Cy Young award.

Again, it was Kansas City who prevailed in the West, and again it took the Yankees five games to dispose of them in the AL playoffs. The Royals actually led most of the time through the first four games. And it took another ninth inning, come-from-behind effort in the fifth game for the Yankees to win it.

The Dodgers were more than happy to resume their classic postseason rivalry with the Yankees. With Tommy Lasorda in his first year as pilot, having replaced the Dodger legend Walt Alston who had guided them ever since 1954, the Dodgers had staggering power. Besides finishing 10 games ahead of the world title-holder, the Cincinnati Reds, they became the first team in major league history to have four batters hit 30 or more home runs in a single season: Steve Garvey (33), Reggie Smith (32), and Ron Cey and Dusty Baker (30 each). On the mound, they could count on Tommy John (20-7) as well as Rick Rhoden (16 wins) and Don

Two stars of the 1978 World Series pose together, the Yanks' Reggie Jackson and the Dodgers' Steve Garvey. Jackson batted .391 in that Series but Garvey hit only .208.

Sutton and Doug Rau (14 victories apiece). Charlie Hough was also one of the most consistently effective relievers in the league and was credited with 22 saves.

Their opponent in the NL playoffs was no less fearsome a ballclub than the Philadelphia Phillies, who triumphed in 101 games in 1977 and still had the booming bats of Mike Schmidt, Greg Luzinski, and Gary Maddox as well as the gifted arm of Steve Carlton and the very promising one of Larry Christenson.

The Phillies jumped to the front in the first game played out in Los Angeles, but the Dodgers came back the next day and won easily on the fine pitching of Don Sutton. A dramatic come-from-behind win for the Dodgers in the third game (three runs in the ninth to win by a run) destroyed the Phillies in their own hometown. The next day the Dodgers, with masterful hurling by Tommy John, made easy work of them.

The Series was another tale altogether. The Yankees moved ahead three games to one, but then the Dodgers exploded in LA and it looked as if they were on the way back. In New York, however, "Mr. October" engraved his nickname forever in Yankee Stadium; Reggie Jackson hit three home runs in three straight at-bats and led the Yanks in a definitive decimation of the Dodgers. The Dodgers simply could not shake free of the postseason hold the Yankees exerted over them. They would, however, have another chance the following year.

One of the most noticeable figures not to make it back to the 1978 World Series was Yankee manager Billy Martin, who was fired in midseason by George Steinbrenner and replaced by Bob Lemon. But the rest of the Yankees were there. They had barely survived in the East by a single game over a very strong Boston Red Sox team. When the season ended, New York and Boston had identical records of 99–63. A one-game playoff was called to decide the East title with the Red Sox getting the home field advantage. But Yankee Bucky Dent nullified that with a three-run homer and New York went on to pull out a one-run

The Yankee managers of 1978. Billy Martin (right) was fired during the season and Bob Lemon successfully piloted them through the World Series.

victory and the right to meet the Kansas City Royals in a repeat of the previous two AL playoffs.

The only major difference between this playoff and those of 1976 and 1977 was that it took the Yankees only four games to win it instead of five. The last two Yankee wins were due to the magnificent relief pitching of Goose Gossage.

The National League playoffs were a repeat of the previous year, too. The Dodgers again beat out the Cincinnati Reds in the West, although this time it was only by two-and-a-half games.

Their home run production was down from the year before, but was still the most in the NL. Reggie Smith was tops with 29, Ron Cey had 23, and Steve Garvey pitched in with 21. Burt Hooton turned in the best Dodger record (19–10), and Terry Forster had been converted to a most effective reliever (22 saves).

The Phillies had an even closer race in the NL East but managed to end up one-and-a-half games ahead of the Pirates. But Danny Ozark's Philadelphians did not have it when they met up with the Dodgers. In the City of Broth-

Reggie Smith connects here for a home run for the Dodgers in the 1978 World Series. Smith hit only .200, however, in that Series. The Yankee battery is pitcher Ed Figueroa and catcher Thurman Munson.

erly Love, the Dodgers won the first two games with ease. Then, after dropping one in sunny LA, they came back and capped the divisional title with a one-run victory in the fourth game.

The Dodgers had been favored to win the Series the year before, but they had fallen. They were not the favorites in '78. But they certainly looked like they should be after the first two games, both played in LA, which they won handily. Back in New York, however, their world caved in. With .great hitting from Brian Doyle, Bucky Dent, and, of course, Reggie Jackson, and some astounding fielding plays by third baseman Graig Nettles, they defeated the Dodgers three straight, then went back to the West Coast and demolished the Dodgers in Game 6. In their 10 postseason meetings to date, the Yankees had come out on top eight times.

Neither team would be back in 1979. The Yankees fell to fourth place in the AL East and the Dodgers dropped to third in the NL West. Instead it would be the Baltimore Orioles representing the American League, their first Series since 1971, and the fourth to which Earl Weaver had led them. In the National League, it would be the Pittsburgh Pirates,

Mr. October, Reggie Jackson, poses here before a 1978 Series game. In Jackson's three World Series as a Yank and two as an Oakland A, he posted an average of .357 and pounded 10 home runs.

who had not been to the Series since 1971 either. In that Series, eight years earlier, the Pirates had triumphed four games to three. They were managed by Danny Murtaugh then, now they were in the hands of Chuck Tanner, and they would do it to the Orioles in the same fashion.

Pittsburgh had some real trouble in the NL East with the Montreal Expos. But they survived to win that division by two games, much the result of their power hitting and their excellent bullpen. Willie Stargell hit 32 home runs and shared the MVP award as a result (with Keith Hernandez of the Cardinals). Dave Parker hit another 25 homers and Bill Robinson connected on 24. Bill Madlock hit .328 and Parker batted at a clip of .310. Kent Tekulve was the chief fireman, garnering 31 saves while appearing in 94 games. Grant Jackson was also effective in relief, and added another 14 saves to the Pirates' stats.

Cincinnati survived in the NL West, ending up one-and-a-half games ahead of the Houston Astros. The Reds were now piloted by John McNamara, but most of their luminaries from the triumphal days earlier in the decade had aged or were gone. They fell in three straight games to the Pirates.

Baltimore was not pressed in the AL East. The Milwaukee Brewers came the closest but they were a distant eight games back. The Orioles did not have one .300 hitter, but they did have power. Ken Singleton hit 35 homers, Eddie Murray and Gary Roenicke connected on 25 each, and Lee May, 19. Mike Flanagan, with the league's best record of 23–9,

won the Cy Young award, while Dennis Martinez and Scott McGregor were also effective from the mound.

In the West, it was the California Angels who finally prevailed over the Kansas City Royals. But for the fifth year in a row the East in the American League routed the West. With clutch hitting by Eddie Murray and Pat Kelly, and a playoff-clinching shutout from Scott McGregor, the Orioles took the pennant.

Just as in their previous meeting in '71, the Pirates and the Orioles went seven games to decide the world championship. And again the Pirates soundly outhit the Orioles. The bats that did it before were those of Roberto Clemente and Mannie Sanguillen; this time they belonged to Willie Stargell and Phil Garner. But it was not easy. Baltimore had a three to one game edge, but the Pirates managed to eliminate the deficit with three straight routs.

And with it closed the 1970s, a decade that was highlighted by some truly marvelous baseball teams, like Earl Weaver's Baltimore Orioles, Dick Williams' Oakland A's, Sparky Anderson's Cincinnati Reds, Tommy Lasorda's Los Angeles Dodgers, Whitey Herzog's Kansas City Royals, and Billy Martin's New York Yankees. It had been one of the most competitive decades in baseball history, involving a wide-ranging array of teams battling for division titles, pennants, and world championships. It bode well for the ever-expanding game of major league baseball.

1970

Baltimore Orioles 4
Cincinnati Reds 1

Line-ups

Baltimore Orioles		**Cincinnati Reds**	
1b	Boog Powell	1b	Lee May
2b	Dave Johnson	2b	Tommy Helms
3b	Brooks Robinson	3b	Tony Perez
ss	Mark Belanger	ss	Dave Concepcion
lf	Don Buford	lf	Hal McRae
cf	Paul Blair	cf	Bobby Tolan
rf	Frank Robinson	rf	Pete Rose
c	Ellie Hendricks	c	Johnny Bench
mgr	Earl Weaver	mgr	Sparky Anderson

		R	H	E	Pitching
Game 1	Baltimore	4	7	2	Jim Palmer (W), Pete Richert (9th)
	Cincinnati	3	5	0	Gary Nolan, Clay Carroll (7th)
Game 2	Baltimore	6	10	2	Mike Cuellar, Tom Phoebus (3rd, W), Moe Drabowsky (5th), Marcelino Lopez (7th), Dick Hall (7th)
	Cincinnati	5	7	0	Jim McGlothlin, Milt Wilcox (5th), Clay Carroll (5th), Don Gullett (8th)
Game 3	Cincinnati	3	9	0	Tony Cloninger, Wayne Granger (6th), Don Gullett (7th)
	Baltimore	9	10	1	Dave McNally (W)
Game 4	Cincinnati	6	8	3	Gary Nolan, Don Gullett (3rd), Clay Carroll (6th, W)
	Baltimore	5	8	0	Jim Palmer, Eddie Watt (8th), Moe Drabowsky (9th)

1970

Baltimore Orioles 4
Cincinnati Reds 1

		R	H	E	Pitching
Game 5	Cincinnati	3	6	0	Jim Merritt, Wayne Granger (2nd), Milt Wilcox (3rd), Tony Cloninger (5th), Ray Washburn (7th), Clay Carroll (8th)
	Baltimore	9	15	0	Mike Cuellar (W)

Highlights

- The Orioles, making their third appearance in the last five World Series, took their second world crown.
- The six runs scored by Lee May and by Boog Powell tied the mark for a five-game Series.
- The nine hits by Brooks Robinson and by Paul Blair tied the record for a five-game Series.
- Brooks Robinson's 17 total bases set a new five-game Series mark.
- The 10 home runs by Baltimore sluggers set a new standard for a five-game Series.
- Game 1, played at Cincinnati's Riverfront Stadium, was the first Series game to be played on an artificial surface.
- Home runs by Boog Powell, Ellie Hendricks, and Brooks Robinson provided the winning runs for the Orioles in Game 1.
- The Orioles exploded for five runs in the 5th inning of Game 2, the result of five singles and an Ellie Hendrick's double (which drove in two runs), for the winning edge.
- Dave McNally went the distance for the Orioles in Game 3 and hit a grand slam homer, the only one ever hit in a Series by a pitcher.
- Pete Rose's solo home run and Lee May's with two on base provided the winning runs for the Reds in Game 4.
- Frank Robinson, Dave Johnson, and reserve outfielder Merv Rettenmund each drove in two runs to lead the Orioles to victory in Game 5.

Best Efforts

Batting

Average	Paul Blair .474
Home Runs	(four players) 2
Triples	Dave Concepcion 1
Doubles	(four players) 2
Hits	Paul Blair 9
	Brooks Robinson 9
Runs	Boog Powell 6
	Lee May 6
RBIs	Lee May 8

Pitching

Wins	(five players) 1
ERA	Clay Carroll 0.00
Strikeouts	Clay Carroll 11
Innings Pitched	Jim Palmer 15$\frac{2}{3}$

1971

Pittsburgh Pirates 4
Baltimore Orioles 3

Line-ups

Pittsburgh Pirates		**Baltimore Orioles**	
1b	Bob Robertson	1b	Boog Powell
2b	Dave Cash	2b	Dave Johnson
3b	Jose Pagan	3b	Brooks Robinson
ss	Jackie Hernandez	ss	Mark Belanger
lf	Willie Stargell	lf	Don Buford
cf	Al Oliver	cf	Merv Rettenmund
rf	Roberto Clemente	rf	Frank Robinson
c	Manny Sanguillen	c	Ellie Hendricks
mgr	Danny Murtaugh	mgr	Earl Weaver

		R	H	E	Pitching
Game 1	Pittsburgh	3	3	0	Dock Ellis, Bob Moose (3rd), Bob Miller (7th)
	Baltimore	5	10	3	Dave McNally (W)
Game 2	Pittsburgh	3	8	1	Bob Johnson, Bruce Kison (4th), Bob Moose (4th), Bob Veale (5th), Bob Miller (6th), Dave Guisti (8th)
	Baltimore	11	14	1	Jim Palmer (W), Dick Hall (9th)
Game 3	Baltimore	1	3	3	Mike Cuellar, Tom Dukes (7th), Eddie Watt (8th)
	Pittsburgh	5	7	0	Steve Blass (W)
Game 4	Baltimore	3	4	1	Pat Dobson, Grant Jackson (6th), Eddie Watt (7th), Pete Richert (8th)
	Pittsburgh	4	14	0	Luke Walker, Bruce Kison (1st, W), Dave Giusti (8th)

		R	H	E	Pitching
Game 5	Baltimore	0	2	1	Dave McNally, Dave Leonhard (5th), Tom Dukes (6th)
	Pittsburgh	4	9	0	Nelson Briles (W)
Game 6	Pittsburgh	2	9	1	Bob Moose, Bob Johnson (6th), Dave Giusti (7th), Bob Miller (10th)
	Baltimore	3	8	0	Jim Palmer, Pat Dobson (10th), Dave McNally (10th, W)
Game 7	Pittsburgh	2	6	1	Steve Blass (W)
	Baltimore	1	4	0	Mike Cuellar, Pat Dobson (9th), Dave McNally (9th)

Highlights

- The Pittsburgh Pirates collected their fourth world championship.
- Dave McNally of the Orioles gave up only three hits in Game 1 and teammate Frank Robinson and Merv Rettenmund belted homers to provide the winning runs.
- Steve Blass of the Pirates allowed only one run and three hits in Game 3, and his win was ensured by Bob Robertson's three-run homer.
- Game 4 was the first night game in World Series history.
- Pinch hitter Milt May singled to drive in the winning run for Pittsburgh in Game 4.
- Nelson Briles hurled a two-hit shutout for Pittsburgh in Game 5.
- Brooks Robinson drove in Frank Robinson with the game-winning run for the Orioles in the bottom of the tenth of Game 6.
- Roberto Clemente's homer, Jose Pagan's run-producing double, and the four-hit pitching of Steve Blass provided the victory edge for the Pirates in Game 7.

Best Efforts

Batting

Average	Roberto Clemente	.414
Home Runs	(four players)	2
Triples	Roberto Clemente	1
	Gene Clines	1
	Mark Belanger	1
Doubles	Roberto Clemente	2
	Jose Pagan	2
	Al Oliver	2
Hits	Roberto Clemente	12
Runs	Frank Robinson	5
RBIs	Bob Robertson	5
	Brooks Robinson	5

Pitching

Wins	Steve Blass	2-0
	Dave McNally	2-1
ERA	Nelson Briles	0.00
Strikeouts	Jim Palmer	15
Innings Pitched	Steve Blass	18

1972

Oakland Athletics 4
Cincinnati Reds   3

Line-ups

Oakland Athletics		Cincinnati Reds	
1b	Mike Epstein	1b	Tony Perez
2b	Dick Green	2b	Joe Morgan
3b	Sal Bando	3b	Denis Menke
ss	Bert Campaneris	ss	Dave Concepcion
lf	Joe Rudi	lf	Pete Rose
cf	George Hendrick	cf	Bobby Tolan
rf	Matty Alou	rf	Cesar Geronimo
c	Gene Tenace	c	Johnny Bench
mgr	Dick Williams	mgr	Sparky Anderson

		R	H	E	Pitching
Game 1	Oakland	3	4	0	Ken Holtzman (W), Rollie Fingers (6th), Vida Blue (7th)
	Cincinnati	2	7	0	Gary Nolan, Pedro Borbon (7th), Clay Carroll (8th)
Game 2	Oakland	2	9	2	Catfish Hunter (W), Rollie Fingers (9th)
	Cincinnati	1	6	0	Ross Grimsley, Pedro Borbon (6th), Tom Hall (8th)
Game 3	Cincinnati	1	4	2	Jack Billingham (W), Clay Carroll (9th)
	Oakland	0	3	2	Blue Moon Odom, Vida Blue (8th), Rollie Fingers (8th)
Game 4	Cincinnati	2	7	1	Don Gullett, Pedro Borbon (8th), Clay Carroll (9th)
	Oakland	3	10	1	Ken Holtzman, Vida Blue (8th), Rollie Fingers (9th, W)

1972

Oakland Athletics 4
Cincinnati Reds 3

		R	H	E	Pitching
Game 5	Cincinnati	5	8	0	Jim McGlothlin, Pedro Borbon (4th), Tom Hall (5th), Clay Carroll (7th), Ross Grimsley (8th, W), Jack Billingham (9th)
	Oakland	4	7	2	Catfish Hunter, Rollie Fingers (5th), Dave Hamilton (9th)
Game 6	Oakland	1	7	1	Vida Blue, Bob Locker (6th), Dave Hamilton (7th), Joe Horlen (7th)
	Cincinnati	8	10	0	Gary Nolan, Ross Grimsley (5th, W), Pedro Borbon (6th), Tom Hall (7th)
Game 7	Oakland	3	6	1	Blue Moon Odom, Catfish Hunter (5th, W), Ken Holtzman (8th), Rollie Fingers (8th)
	Cincinnati	2	4	2	Jack Billingham, Pedro Borbon (6th), Clay Carroll (6th), Ross Grimsley (7th), Tom Hall (8th)

Highlights

- For the first time in history, six of seven Series games were decided by a single run.
- Gene Tenace's four home runs and slugging average of .913 set records for a seven-game Series.
- Tenace hit a home run in each of his first two at-bats for the A's in Game 1, the only player in Series history to accomplish that feat.
- Joe Rudi hit a home run to provide the margin of victory for the A's in Game 2.
- Jack Billingham and reliever Clay Carroll teamed to hurl a three-hit shutout for the Reds in Game 3.
- Blue Moon Odom struck out 11 Cincinnati batters in seven innings during Game 3.

- Don Mincher, pinch hitting in the bottom of the ninth of Game 4, singled to drive in the game-tying run. Then pinch hitter Angel Mangual singled to bring in the game-winning run.
- Pete Rose, with a homer, two singles, and two RBIs, paced the Reds to victory in Game 5.
- Gene Tenace drove in two runs and Sal Bando one to lead the A's to victory in Game 7.

Best Efforts

Batting

Average	Tony Perez .435
Home Runs	Gene Tenace 4
Triples	Dave Concepcion 1.
Doubles	Tony Perez 2
	Joe Morgan 2
	Dick Green 2
Hits	Tony Perez 10
Runs	Gene Tenace 5
RBIs	Gene Tenace 9

Pitching

Wins	Catfish Hunter 2–0
	Ross Grimsley 2–1
ERA	Jack Billingham 0.00
	Tom Hall 0.00
Strikeouts	Blue Moon Odom 13
Innings Pitched	Catfish Hunter 16

1973

Oakland Athletics 4
New York Mets 3

Line-ups

Oakland Athletics		**New York Mets**	
1b	Gene Tenace	1b	John Milner
2b	Dick Green	2b	Felix Millan
3b	Sal Bando	3b	Wayne Garrett
ss	Bert Campaneris	ss	Bud Harrelson
lf	Joe Rudi	lf	Cleon Jones
cf	Reggie Jackson	cf	Don Hahn
rf	Jesus Alou	rf	Rusty Staub
c	Ray Fosse	c	Jerry Grote
mgr	Dick Williams	mgr	Yogi Berra

		R	H	E	Pitching
Game 1	New York	1	7	2	Jon Matlack, Tug McGraw (7th)
	Oakland	2	4	0	Ken Holtzman (W), Rollie Fingers (6th), Darold Knowles (9th)
Game 2	New York	10	15	1	Jerry Koosman, Ray Sadecki (3rd), Harry Parker (5th), Tug McGraw (6th, W), George Stone (12th)
	Oakland	7	13	5	Vida Blue, Horacio Pina (6th), Darold Knowles (6th), Blue Moon Odom (8th), Rollie Fingers (10th), Paul Lindblad (12th)
Game 3	Oakland	3	10	1	Catfish Hunter, Darold Knowles (7th), Paul Lindblad (9th, W), Rollie Fingers (11th)
	New York	2	10	2	Tom Seaver, Ray Sadecki (9th), Tug McGraw (9th), Harry Parker (11th)

		R	H	E	Pitching
Game 4	Oakland	1	5	1	Ken Holtzman, Blue Moon Odom (1st), Darold Knowles (4th), Horacio Pina (5th), Paul Lindblad (8th)
	New York	6	13	1	Jon Matlack (W), Ray Sadecki (9th)
Game 5	Oakland	0	3	1	Vida Blue, Darold Knowles (6th), Rollie Fingers (7th)
	New York	2	7	1	Jerry Koosman (W), Tug McGraw (7th)
Game 6	New York	1	6	2	Tom Seaver, Tug McGraw (8th)
	Oakland	3	7	0	Catfish Hunter (W), Darold Knowles (8th), Rollie Fingers (8th)
Game 7	New York	2	8	1	Jon Matlack, Harry Parker (3rd), Ray Sadecki (5th), George Stone (7th)
	Oakland	5	9	1	Ken Holtzman (W), Rollie Fingers (6th), Darold Knowles (9th)

Highlights

- The Oakland A's became the first team to take back-to-back world titles since the New York Yankees did it in 1961 and 1962.
- Game 2, which lasted four hours and 13 minutes, stands as the longest game in terms of time in any Series.
- The 11 pitchers used by both teams in Game 2 tied the Series mark.
- Reggie Jackson got four hits and drove in two runs for the A's in Game 2.
- Bert Campaneris got three hits and drove in the winning run in the tenth inning of Game 3 for the A's.
- Tom Seaver struck out 11 Oakland batters in eight innings of Game 3.

- Rusty Staub cracked a home run and three singles in four-at-bats and drove in five runs for the Mets in Game 4.
- Jerry Koosman and reliever Tug McGraw combined to pitch a three-hit shutout for the Mets in Game 5.
- Reggie Jackson collected two doubles and a single, drove in two runs, and scored the game-winner for the A's in Game 6.
- Bert Campaneris hit a homer and two singles and drove in two runs while Reggie Jackson homered and brought in another two to lead the A's to victory in Game 7.

Best Efforts

Batting

Average	Rusty Staub	.423
Home Runs	Wayne Garrett	2
Triples	(five players)	1
Doubles	Reggie Jackson	3
Hits	Rusty Staub	11
Runs	Bert Campaneris	6
RBIs	Rusty Staub	6
	Reggie Jackson	6

Pitching

Wins	Ken Holtzman	2–1
ERA	Rollie Fingers	0.66
Strikeouts	Tom Seaver	18
Innings Pitched	Jon Matlack	16⅔

1974

Oakland Athletics   4
Los Angeles Dodgers   1

Line-ups

Oakland Athletics		**Los Angeles Dodgers**	
1b	Gene Tenace	1b	Steve Garvey
2b	Dick Green	2b	Davey Lopes
3b	Sal Bando	3b	Ron Cey
ss	Bert Campaneris	ss	Bill Russell
lf	Joe Rudi	lf	Bill Buckner
cf	Bill North	cf	Jim Wynn
rf	Reggie Jackson	rf	Joe Ferguson
c	Ray Fosse	c	Steve Yeager
mgr	Dick Williams	mgr	Walt Alston

		R	H	E	Pitching
Game 1	Oakland	3	6	2	Ken Holtzman, Rollie Fingers (5th, W), Catfish Hunter (9th)
	Los Angeles	2	11	1	Andy Messersmith, Mike Marshall (9th)
Game 2	Oakland	2	6	0	Vida Blue, Blue Moon Odom (8th)
	Los Angeles	3	6	1	Don Sutton (W), Mike Marshall (9th)
Game 3	Los Angeles	2	7	2	Al Downing, Jim Brewer (4th), Charlie Hough (5th), Mike Marshall (7th)
	Oakland	3	5	2	Catfish Hunter (W), Rollie Fingers (8th)
Game 4	Los Angeles	2	7	1	Andy Messersmith, Mike Marshall (7th)
	Oakland	5	7	0	Ken Holtzman (W), Rollie Fingers (8th)
Game 5	Los Angeles	2	5	1	Don Sutton, Mike Marshall (6th)
	Oakland	3	6	1	Vida Blue, Blue Moon Odom (7th, W), Rollie Fingers (8th)

Highlights

- The Oakland A's became only the second major league team in history to win three consecutive world titles (the Yankees exceeded it twice, 1936–39 and 1949–53).
- Four of the five games of the Series were decided by identical scores, 3–2.
- Joe Ferguson hit a two-run homer for the Dodgers in Game 2 to provide what proved to be the game-winning runs.
- Oakland pitcher Ken Holtzman hit a home run in Game 4.
- Jim Holt got a pinch-hit single to drive in two runs for the A's in Game 4.
- Joe Rudi hit a homer in Game 5 which proved to be the run that won the game and the Series for the A's.

Best Efforts

Batting

Average	Reggie Jackson .571
Home Runs	(eight players) 1
Triples	Bill Russell 1
Doubles	Bert Campaneris 2
Hits	Steve Garvey 8
Runs	Reggie Jackson 3
	Sal Bando 3
	Bill North 3
RBIs	Joe Rudi 4

Pitching

Wins	(five players) 1
ERA	Mike Marshall 1.00
Strikeouts	Andy Messersmith 10
	Don Sutton 10
Innings Pitched	Andy Messersmith 14

1975

Cincinnati Reds 4
Boston Red Sox 3

Line-ups

Cincinnati Reds	Boston Red Sox
1b Tony Perez	1b Cecil Cooper
2b Joe Morgan	2b Denny Doyle
3b Pete Rose	3b Rico Petrocelli
ss Dave Concepcion	ss Rick Burleson
lf George Foster	lf Carl Yastrzemski
cf Cesar Geronimo	cf Fred Lynn
rf Ken Griffey	rf Dwight Evans
c Johnny Bench	c Carlton Fisk
mgr Sparky Anderson	mgr Darrell Johnson

		R	H	E	Pitching
Game 1	Cincinnati	0	5	0	Don Gullett, Clay Carroll (7th), Will McEnaney
	Boston	6	12	0	Luis Tiant (W)
Game 2	Cincinnati	3	7	1	Jack Billingham, Pedro Borbon (6th), Will McEnaney (7th), Rawly Eastwick (8th, W)
	Boston	2	7	0	Bill Lee, Dick Drago (9th)
Game 3	Boston	5	10	2	Rick Wise, Jim Burton (5th), Reggie Cleveland (5th), Jim Willoughby (7th), Roger Moret (9th)
	Cincinnati	6	7	0	Gary Nolan, Pat Darcy (5th), Clay Carroll (7th), Will McEnaney (7th), Rawly Eastwick (9th, W)
Game 4	Boston	5	11	1	Luis Tiant (W)
	Cincinnati	4	9	1	Gary Nolan, Pedro Borbon (4th), Clay Carroll (5th), Rawly Eastwick (7th)

1975

Cincinnati Reds 4
Boston Red Sox 3

		R	H	E	Pitching
Game 5	Boston	2	5	0	Reggie Cleveland, Jim Willoughby (6th), Dick Pole (8th), Diego Segui (8th)
	Cincinnati	6	8	0	Don Gullett (W), Rawly Eastwick (9th)
Game 6	Cincinnati	6	14	0	Gary Nolan, Fred Norman (3rd), Jack Billingham (3rd), Clay Carroll (5th), Pedro Borbon (6th), Rawly Eastwick (8th), Will McEnaney (9th), Pat Darcy (10th)
	Boston	7	10	1	Luis Tiant, Roger Moret (8th), Dick Drago (9th), Rick Wise (12th, W)
Game 7	Cincinnati	4	9	0	Don Gullett, Jack Billingham (5th), Clay Carroll (7th, W), Will McEnaney (9th)
	Boston	3	5	2	Bill Lee, Roger Moret (7th), Jim Willoughby (7th), Jim Burton (9th), Reggie Cleveland (9th)

Highlights

- The Cincinnati Reds won their third world championship, the first since 1940.
- Luis Tiant hurled a shutout for the Red Sox in Game 1, allowing only five hits.
- Dave Concepcion singled to drive in the tying run for the Reds in the ninth inning of Game 2, and Ken Griffey doubled to bring in the winning run.
- The six home runs hit in Game 3 tied the Series mark: one each by Johnny Bench, Dave Concepcion, Cesar Geronimo, Carlton Fisk, Bernie Carbo, and Dwight Evans.

- The two-run homer hit by Dwight Evans in the ninth inning for the Red Sox sent Game 3 into extra innings.
- Joe Morgan singled to drive in Cesar Geronimo with the game-winning run for the Reds in the bottom of the tenth of Game 3.
- The Red Sox erupted for five runs in the fourth inning of Game 4, two scoring on Dwight Evans' triple, which secured the win for Boston.
- Tony Perez hit two home runs and accounted for four RBIs in leading the Reds to triumph in Game 5.
- The eight pitchers employed by the Reds in Game 6 tied the Series mark.
- Both Fred Lynn and Bernie Carbo hit three-run homers for the BoSox in Game 6. (Carbo's was a pinch hit which tied the score in the eighth and eventually sent the game into extra innings.)
- Carlton Fisk hit a home run in the bottom of the 12th of Game 6 to win it for the Red Sox.
- Pete Rose singled to drive in Ken Griffey with the game-tying run in the seventh inning of Game 7 for the Reds. Joe Morgan singled to score Griffey in the ninth inning with what proved to be the game-winning run.

Best Efforts

Batting

Average	Pete Rose	.370
Home Runs	Tony Perez	3
Triples	(five players)	1
Doubles	Ken Griffey	3
Hits	Pete Rose	10
Runs	Carl Yastrzemski	7
RBIs	Tony Perez	7

Pitching

Wins	Luis Tiant	2–0
	Rawley Eastwick	2–0
ERA	Jack Billingham	1.00
Strikeouts	Don Gullett	15
Innings Pitched	Luis Tiant	25

1976

Cincinnati Reds 4
New York Yankees 0

Line-ups

Cincinnati Reds		**New York Yankees**	
1b	Tony Perez	1b	Chris Chambliss
2b	Joe Morgan	2b	Willie Randolph
3b	Pete Rose	3b	Graig Nettles
ss	Dave Concepcion	ss	Fred Stanley
lf	George Foster	lf	Roy White
cf	Cesar Geronimo	cf	Mickey Rivers
rf	Ken Griffey	rf	Oscar Gamble
c	Johnny Bench	c	Thurman Munson
dh	Dan Driessen	dh	Lou Piniella
mgr	Sparky Anderson	mgr	Billy Martin

		R	H	E	Pitching
Game 1	New York	1	5	1	Doyle Alexander, Sparky Lyle (7th)
	Cincinnati	5	10	1	Don Gullett (W), Pedro Borbon (8th)
Game 2	New York	3	9	1	Catfish Hunter
	Cincinnati	4	10	0	Fred Norman, Jack Billingham (7th, W)
Game 3	Cincinnati	6	13	2	Pat Zachry (W), Will McEnaney (7th)
	New York	2	8	0	Dock Ellis, Grant Jackson (4th), Dick Tidrow (8th)
Game 4	Cincinnati	7	9	2	Gary Nolan (W), Will McEnaney (7th)
	New York	2	8	0	Ed Figueroa, Dick Tidrow (9th), Sparky Lyle (9th)

Highlights

- The Reds made it back-to-back world titles when they swept the Series from the Yankees.
- This was the first Series in which a designated hitter was used.
- Joe Morgan homered and Tony Perez collected a double and two singles to lead the Reds in Game 1.
- Tony Perez singled in the bottom of the ninth of Game 2 to send Ken Griffey across with the winning run.
- George Foster drove in two runs and Dan Driessen hit a homer, a double, and a single to pace the Reds in Game 3.
- Johnny Bench hit two home runs and drove in five runs to lead the Reds to victory in Game 4.

Best Efforts

Batting

Average	Johnny Bench	.533
Home Runs	Johnny Bench	2
Triples	(four players)	1
Doubles	Cesar Geronimo	2
	Dan Driessen	2
Hits	Thurman Munson	9
Runs	Johnny Bench	4
	Dan Driessen	4
RBIs	Johnny Bench	6

Pitching

Wins	(four players)	1
ERA	Don Gullett	1.23
Strikeouts	Pat Zachry	6
Innings Pitched	Catfish Hunter	8⅔

1977

New York Yankees   4
Los Angeles Dodgers   2

Line-ups

New York Yankees		**Los Angeles Dodgers**	
1b	Chris Chambliss	1b	Steve Garvey
2b	Willie Randolph	2b	Davey Lopes
3b	Graig Nettles	3b	Ron Cey
ss	Bucky Dent	ss	Bill Russell
lf	Lou Piniella	lf	Dusty Baker
cf	Mickey Rivers	cf	Rick Monday
rf	Reggie Jackson	rf	Reggie Smith
c	Thurman Munson	c	Steve Yeager
mgr	Billy Martin	mgr	Tommy Lasorda

		R	H	E	Pitching
Game 1	Los Angeles	3	6	0	Don Sutton, Lance Rautzhan (8th), Elias Sosa (8th), Mike Garman (9th), Rick Rhoden (12th)
	New York	4	11	0	Don Gullett, Sparky Lyle (9th, W)
Game 2	Los Angeles	6	9	0	Burt Hooton (W)
	New York	1	5	0	Catfish Hunter, Dick Tidrow (3rd), Ken Clay (6th), Sparky Lyle (9th)
Game 3	New York	5	10	0	Mike Torrez (W)
	Los Angeles	3	7	1	Tommy John, Charlie Hough (7th)
Game 4	New York	4	7	0	Ron Guidry (W)
	Los Angeles	2	4	0	Doug Rau, Rick Rhoden (2nd), Mike Garman (9th)

		R	H	E	Pitching
Game 5	New York	4	9	2	Don Gullett, Ken Clay (5th), Dick Tidrow (6th), Catfish Hunter (7th)
	Los Angeles	10	13	0	Don Sutton (W)
Game 6	Los Angeles	4	9	0	Burt Hooton, Elias Sosa (4th), Doug Rau (5th), Charlie Hough (7th)
	New York	8	8	1	Mike Torrez (W)

Highlights

- The Yankees won their first world title since 1962, and defeated the Dodgers for the seventh time in their nine Series encounters.
- Reggie Jackson's five home runs, 10 runs scored, 25 total bases, and slugging average of 1.250 set new marks for a six-game Series.
- The nine home runs hit by Dodger batters tied the six-game Series mark.
- Lee Lacy got a pinch-hit single in the ninth inning of Game 1 to send Dusty Baker across with the game-tying run for the Dodgers.
- Reserve outfielder Paul Blair cracked a single in the bottom of the 12th of Game 1, scoring Willie Randolph to win it for the Yanks.
- Dodger sluggers hit four home runs in Game 2: one each from Ron Cey, Steve Yeager, Reggie Smith, and Steve Garvey.
- Burt Hooton allowed only one Yankee run and five hits in Game 2.
- Dusty Baker homered and drove in all three Dodger runs in Game 3.
- Ron Guidry hurled a four-hitter for the Yankees in Game 4.
- Steve Yeager hit a homer and accounted for four Dodger RBIs in Game 5.
- Reggie Jackson, in Game 6, became the only player in World Series history to hit three consecutive home runs in one game. The only other player to hit three in a single game was Babe Ruth, who did it twice (1926 and 1928), but in each case only two were consecutive. Jackson also accounted for five RBIs, and his four runs scored tied the Series record.

Best Efforts

Batting

Average	Reggie Jackson	.450
Home Runs	Reggie Jackson	5
Triples	Steve Garvey	1
	Davey Lopes	1
	Bill Russell	1
Doubles	(four players)	2
Hits	Reggie Jackson	9
	Steve Garvey	9
Runs	Reggie Jackson	10
RBIs	Reggie Jackson	8

Pitching

Wins	Mike Torrez	2–0
ERA	Ron Guidry	2.00
Strikeouts	Mike Torrez	15
Innings Pitched	Mike Torrez	18

1978

New York Yankees 4
Los Angeles Dodgers 2

Line-ups

New York Yankees		Los Angeles Dodgers	
1b	Chris Chambliss	1b	Steve Garvey
2b	Brian Doyle	2b	Davey Lopes
3b	Graig Nettles	3b	Ron Cey
ss	Bucky Dent	ss	Bill Russell
lf	Roy White	lf	Dusty Baker
cf	Mickey Rivers	cf	Rick Monday
rf	Lou Piniella	rf	Reggie Smith
c	Thurman Munson	c	Steve Yeager
dh	Reggie Jackson	dh	Lee Lacy
mgr	Bob Lemon	mgr	Tommy Lasorda

		R	H	E	Pitching
Game 1	New York	5	9	1	Ed Figueroa, Ken Clay (2nd), Paul Lindblad (5th), Dick Tidrow (7th)
	Los Angeles	11	15	2	Tommy John (W), Terry Forster (8th)
Game 2	New York	3	11	0	Catfish Hunter, Goose Gossage (7th)
	Los Angeles	4	7	0	Burt Hooton (W), Terry Forster (7th), Bob Welch (9th)
Game 3	Los Angeles	1	8	0	Don Sutton, Lance Rautzhan (7th), Charlie Hough (8th)
	New York	5	10	1	Ron Guidry (W)
Game 4	Los Angeles	3	6	1	Tommy John, Terry Forster (8th), Bob Welch (8th)
	New York	4	9	0	Ed Figueroa, Dick Tidrow (6th), Goose Gossage (9th, W)

1978

New York Yankees   4
Los Angeles Dodgers   2

		R	H	E	Pitching
Game 5	Los Angeles	2	9	3	Burt Hooton, Lance Rautzhan (3rd), Charlie Hough (4th)
	New York	12	18	0	Jim Beattie (W)
Game 6	New York	7	11	0	Catfish Hunter (W), Goose Gossage (8th)
	Los Angeles	2	7	1	Don Sutton, Bob Welch (6th), Doug Rau (8th)

Highlights

- The Yankees won their 22nd world championship in what was their 32nd Series appearance.
- Davey Lopes clouted two homers and drove in five runs for the Dodgers in Game 1.
- Ron Cey hit a three-run homer and drove in another run with a single to lead the Dodgers to victory in Game 2.
- Yank Mickey Rivers collected three hits in Game 3.
- Thurman Munson drove in the tying run in Game 4 for the Yankees in the eighth inning, and Lou Piniella batted in the winner in the tenth.
- The Yankees got 18 hits in Game 5, only two short of the all-time record for a single game. Their 16 singles constituted a new Series record.
- Munson drove in five runs and collected three hits in Game 5.
- Bucky Dent got three hits and drove in three Yankee runs in Game 6. Reggie Jackson and Brian Doyle drove in two runs apiece.
- Three players hit over .400 in the Series: Brian Doyle (.438), Bill Russell (.423), and Bucky Dent (.417).

Best Efforts

Batting

Average	Brian Doyle .438
Home Runs	Davey Lopes 3
Triples	——
Doubles	Thurman Munson 3
Hits	Bill Russell 11
Runs	Roy White 9
RBIs	Reggie Jackson 8

Pitching

Wins	(six players) 1
ERA	Ron Guidry 1.00
Strikeouts	Jim Beattie 8
	Don Sutton 8
Innings Pitched	Tommy John 14$\frac{2}{3}$

1979

Pittsburgh Pirates 4
Baltimore Orioles 3.

Line-ups

Pittsburgh Pirates		Baltimore Orioles	
1b	Willie Stargell	1b	Eddie Murray
2b	Phil Garner	2b	Rich Dauer
3b	Bill Madlock	3b	Doug DeCinces
ss	Tim Foli	ss	Kiko Garcia
lf	Bill Robinson	lf	John Lowenstein
cf	Omar Moreno	cf	Al Bumbry
rf	Dave Parker	rf	Ken Singleton
c	Ed Ott	c	Rick Dempsey
mgr	Chuck Tanner	mgr	Earl Weaver

		R	H	E	Pitching
Game 1	Pittsburgh	4	11	3	Bruce Kison, Jim Rooker (1st) Enrique Romo (5th), Don Robinson (6th), Grant Jackson (8th)
	Baltimore	5	6	3	Mike Flanagan (W)
Game 2	Pittsburgh	3	11	2	Bert Blyleven (W), Don Robinson (7th), Kent Tekulve (9th)
	Baltimore	2	6	1	Jim Palmer, Don Stanhouse (8th), Tippy Martinez (9th)
Game 3	Baltimore	8	13	0	Scott McGregor (W)
	Pittsburgh	4	9	2	John Candelaria, Enrique Romo (4th), Grant Jackson (7th), Kent Tekulve (8th)
Game 4	Baltimore	9	12	0	Dennis Martinez, Sam Stewart (2nd), Steve Stone (5th), Tim Stoddard (7th, W)
	Pittsburgh	6	17	1	Jim Bibby, Grant Jackson (6th), Don Robinson (8th), Kent Tekulve (8th)

		R	H	E	Pitching
Game 5	Baltimore	1	6	2	Mike Flanagan, Tim Stoddard (7th), Tippy Martinez (7th), Don Stanhouse (8th)
	Pittsburgh	7	13	1	Jim Rooker, Bert Blyleven (6th, W)
Game 6	Pittsburgh	4	10	0	John Candelaria (W), Kent Tekulve (7th)
	Baltimore	0	7	1	Jim Palmer, Tim Stoddard (9th)
Game 7	Pittsburgh	4	10	0	Jim Bibby, Don Robinson (5th), Grant Jackson (5th, W), Kent Tekulve (8th)
	Baltimore	1	4	2	Scott McGregor, Tim Stoddard (9th), Mike Flanagan (9th), Don Stanhouse (9th), Tippy Martinez (9th), Dennis Martinez (9th)

Highlights

- The Pittsburgh Pirates won their fifth world crown, tying them with the New York Giants for second among National League world champs (the St. Louis Cardinals are first with nine titles).
- Phil Garner's batting average of .500 (12 for 24) tied the seven-game Series record.
- Willie Stargell's 25 total bases set a new seven-game Series standard.
- Dave Parker got four hits in five at-bats for the Pirates in Game 1.
- Manny Sanguillen got a pinch-hit single for the Pirates in the ninth inning of Game 2 to score Ed Ott with the game-winning run.
- Eddie Murray got three hits and drove in two runs for the Orioles in Game 2.
- Kiko Garcia hit a bases-loaded triple, a double, two singles, and accounted for four RBIs in Game 3 for the Orioles.
- Oriole pinch hitters John Lowenstein and Terry Crowley each doubled, driving in two runs apiece in the eighth inning of Game 4 to provide the winning edge for Baltimore.
- Tim Foli had a triple and two singles and drove in three runs for the Pirates in Game 5.

1979

Pittsburgh Pirates 4
Baltimore Orioles 3

- Bill Madlock cracked four singles in four at-bats for the Pirates in Game 5.
- John Candelaria and reliever Kent Tekulve teamed to hurl a seven-hit shutout for the Pirates in Game 6.
- Willie Stargell provided the winning margin for the Pirates in Game 7 with a two-run homer. Stargell also hit two doubles and a single in that game.

Best Efforts

Batting

Average	Phil Garner	.500
Home Runs	Willie Stargell	3
Triples	Tim Foli	1
	Kiko Garcia	1
Doubles	Phil Garner	4
	Willie Stargell	4
Hits	Phil Garner	12
	Willie Stargell	12
Runs	Willie Stargell	7
RBIs	Willie Stargell	7

Pitching

Wins	(seven players)	1
ERA	Jim Rooker	1.04
Strikeouts	Mike Flanagan	13
Innings Pitched	Scott McGregor	17

THE EIGHTIES

★ ★ ★   ★ ★ ★

By the time the 1980s arrived, a treasure trove of baseball legends had passed through the eight decades of World Series play. Such luminous names as Mack, McGraw, Cobb, Mathewson, Johnson, Ruth, Speaker, Gehrig, Hornsby, Hubbell, Frisch, Foxx, Greenberg, DiMaggio, Musial, Stengel, Mays, Mantle, Berra, Koufax, and the Baltimore Robinsons all had left their imprint on the postseason classic.

The 1980s also possessed a fair share of baseball greats, some somewhat aged but still strong forces to be reckoned with on a baseball diamond. And most are destined to one day see their names and faces sculpted on plaques in the Hall of Fame at Cooperstown, New York. Still hitting the ball were such accomplished batsmen as Carl Yastrzemski, Rod Carew, Pete Rose, Reggie Jackson, Johnny Bench, Joe Morgan, Steve Garvey, Mike Schmidt, and George Brett. Still overwhelming batters were such master hurlers as Steve Carlton, Nolan Ryan, Tom Seaver, Gaylord Perry, Jim Palmer, Don Sutton, Tommy John, and Ferguson Jenkins.

When the 1980 World Series opened in Philadelphia, several of those illustrious names were in uniform, and they would contribute substantially to the excitement of it all.

For Philadelphia, it was the

first time the city had hosted a World Series since the Phillies were embarrassed by a Yankee sweep back in 1950. For Kansas City, it was the very first time that midwestern metropolis had the pleasure of entertaining World Series crowds.

The Royals, under the managerial guidance of Jim Frey, had gotten to the championship fest in impressive fashion. Behind the hitting of major league batting champ and MVP George Brett (.390, the best any major league batter had posted since Ted Williams' .409 back in 1941), Kansas City virtually devastated the rest of the league taking the AL West crown with a 14-game margin separating them from the second-place Oakland A's. The Royals had another superb hitter in Willie Wilson (.326), who led the

league in hits (230), runs scored (133), and triples (15). They had fine pitching from righthander Dennis Leonard (20–11) and southpaw Larry Gura (18–10), not to mention the relief performances of Dan Quisenberry who registered a major league high 33 saves (more than the total recorded by nine other American League *teams* that year).

Taking the division crown enabled the Royals to face the New York Yankees, no small consideration in 1980. The Yankees' offensive attack was keynoted by Reggie Jackson, who had sent a league-high 41 home runs out of AL ballparks, batted a crisp .300, and drove in 111 runs. Mr. October was always a postseason threat. Bob Watson also batted a nifty .307. For the second year in a row, 37-year-old Tommy John

George Brett, American League MVP who batted .390 in 1980, made his World Series debut that year. He hit .375 in the Series despite being plagued with one of the world's most widely publicized cases of hemorrhoids.

Amos Otis batted .478 for the Kansas City Royals in the 1980 Series.

had exceeded the 20-game mark for the Yanks, the strong left-hander posting a record of 22–9. Ron Guidry was also impressive at 17–10, and Rudy May (15–5) had the NL's best ERA (2.47). Fast-balling fireman Goose Gossage racked up 33 saves to equal Quisenberry's total.

But the Royals found no more trouble in the playoffs than they had encountered in the regular season. They took three straight behind the smoldering bats of

Frank White (.545), who collected six hits in the short series, and George Brett who walloped two homers, including a three-run shot that provided the winning margin in the Royals' 4–2 victory in the third and final game.

The Phillies, with Dallas Green at the helm, had a much tougher time of it. They just barely edged the Montreal Expos by a single game in the NL East. But they had great talent. Steve Carlton, the league's premier lefthander, won 24 games against nine losses and led the majors with 286 strike-outs and 304 innings pitched. He was a cinch to win his third Cy Young award. Also gracing Phila-

Mike Schmidt, perennial power-hitter for the Philadelphia Phillies, made his World Series debut in 1980. He batted .381, clouted two home runs, and accounted for seven RBIs.

delphia's mound was Dick Ruthven (17–10) and reliever Tug McGraw (20 saves and an ERA of 1.47). From the plate, MVP Mike Schmidt stroked 48 homers, the most in the majors, and drove in 121 runs. Bake McBride hit .309, and firebrand Pete Rose led the majors with 42 doubles.

On paper, the Houston Astros, winners of the AL West by dint of defeating the Los Angeles Dodgers in a special one-game playoff (both had ended the season with records of 92–70), were a lot less impressive than the Phils. Managed by Bill Virdon, they had Joe Niekro on the mound (20–12) and Nolan Ryan who struck out 200 batters but posted only an 11–10 record. Power was hardly their forte; Terry Puhl led the club in homers with 13 and the team total of 75 was the third worst in the majors. Cesar Cedeno hit .309 and Jose Cruz, .302.

But on the baseball diamonds in Philadelphia and Houston, it was close all the way. The Phillies came from behind to win the first game for Steve Carlton. The Astros, however, turned around and won the next two. The Phillies managed to stay alive by scoring two runs in the tenth of Game 4. Then in the decider, the Phillies came back again. Losing 5–2, they

Steve Carlton, who has struck out more batters than any pitcher in baseball history, won two games for the Phillies in the 1980 Series. Carlton also appeared in the 1967 and 1968 World Series in a St. Louis Cardinal uniform but he did not record a win in either.

scored five runs in the top of the eighth to take the lead. The Astros, however, tied it in the bottom of the inning. But in the tenth the Phillies again took command and the one run they scored gave them the NL pennant.

It took the Phillies only six games, however, to dispose of the favored Royals in the World Series. With George Brett hobbled by what is now perhaps the

Tug McGraw was the Phillie fireman in 1980, making appearances in four games. He was credited with one win and two saves and sported an ERA of 1.17. McGraw also pitched in five games of the 1973 Series for the New York Mets and chalked up a win and a save that year.

world's most publicized case of hemorrhoids and Dan Quisenberry less than effective in relief, Kansas City just could not get itself going. The Phils, paced by a superlative offensive attack, had five hitters above the .300 mark in the Series: Bob Boone (.412), Mike Schmidt (.381), Larry Bowa (.375), Keith Moreland (.333), and Bake McBride (.304). Steve Carlton, predictably, was masterful and was credited with two wins.

The 1981 season was different altogether, fractured by a players strike that lasted two months. As a result, baseball commissioner Bowie Kuhn and the team owners got together and decided to alter

the traditional scenario. The season would be divided into two parts—the team on top in each division when the strike began in June was declared winner of that segment and would face the winner of the second segment in a special five-game "mini-playoff" series to determine the divisional champ.

For sheer dramatics, the arena was the National League. It was there that the Los Angeles Dodgers put on a display that would forever define what constitutes true come-from-behind miraculousness.

Tommy Lasorda in his fifth year as the Dodgers' pilot had his eye set on his third NL pennant.

The Dodgers had much the same batting order in '81 as that which went to the plate for them in the 1977 and 1978 World Series. The only notable newcomer was Pedro Guerrero, who batted .300 and clouted 12 homers in 1981. The only other .300 hitters that year were Dusty Baker (.320) and reserve outfielder/pinch hitter Rick Monday (.315). The pitching department was almost totally different. Gone were Don Sutton, Tommy John, and Doug Rau. In their places in the rotation were rookie sensation Fernando Valenzuela (13–7) who led the majors in both shutouts (8) and strikeouts (180), Jerry Reuss (10–4), and Bob Welch (9–5). Burt Hooton (11–6) was the only holdover still starting on a regular basis.

When the players walked out on strike, the Dodgers were ahead in the NL West by a half-game, enough, however, to ensure them a berth in the mini-playoffs. They muddled through the second part of the season, ending up second to the Houston Astros. So the two were forced to do battle for the division title. The Astros, thirsting for another trip to the divisional playoffs, won the first two games in Houston and looked like a sure-thing. But in Dodger Stadium, that palm tree encircled edifice that annually attracts more

Fernando Valenzuela, pitching star of the 1981 world champion L.A. Dodgers.

fans than any other stadium in the major leagues, the tide was turned. The Dodgers took three straight and sent the mortified Astros back to Houston a loser.

In the divisional playoffs, the Dodgers were matched against the Montreal Expos, who had polished off the reigning champion Philadelphia Phillies in their mini-series for the NL East crown. The Expos were a fine team and were more than anxious to bring the first World Series ever to Canada. They had good hitters in Warren Cromarte (.304), Andre Dawson (.302 and 24 homers), and rookie Tim Raines (.304), a speedster who also led the majors with 71 stolen bases. On the mound they relied on right-handers Steve Rogers (12–8), Ray Burris (9–7), and Scott Sanderson (9–7).

The Dodgers and the Expos split the first two games of the playoffs at Dodger Stadium, then headed up to the much colder climes of Montreal to finish it up. The Expos won the first game at home and needed only one more for the coveted pennant. But the Dodgers would not let them have it. With thundering bats and the pitching of Burt Hooton, the Dodgers decimated the Expos in Game 4 by a score of 7–1. Then, in Game 5, behind the dazzling pitching of Fernando Valenzuela and a ninth inning home run by Rick Monday, the Dodgers eked out a 2–1 victory and the NL title for 1981.

Just as in 1978, 1977, and eight other years in fact, they would face the New York Yankees. The postseason veterans from the Bronx, managed by Bob Lemon, got there by virtue of securing a playoff berth when they ended up ahead in the AL East at the onset

Steve Garvey, pulled off the bag, tries to put the tag on Yank Bob Watson in the 1981 World Series. Garvey hit .417 in that Series and Watson .318.

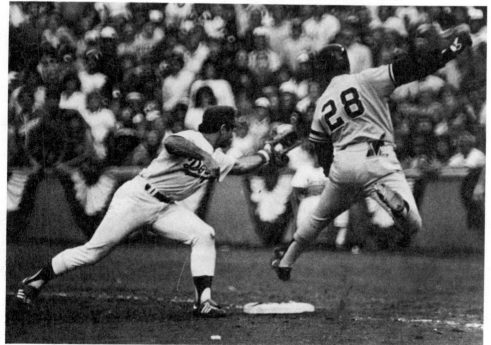

of the strike. They then eliminated the Milwaukee Brewers, who had triumphed in the second half of the ruptured season, in their mini-series. The Yankees virtually destroyed the Oakland A's in the divisional playoffs, a clean sweep without even a threat in any of the three games.

The Yankees were allegedly the best team money could buy. Owner George Steinbrenner had built a roster that glittered with gilded names whose contracts overflowed with dollar signs: Reggie Jackson, Dave Winfield, Lou Piniella, Oscar Gamble, Graig Nettles, Willie Randolph, Bucky Dent, Rick Cerone, Ron Guidry, Tommy John, and Goose Gossage, among them. And they were more than accustomed to winning in the postseason. All Tommy Lasorda and his Dodgers had to do was to look back at the '78 and '77 World Series to understand that. To reinforce the notion of New York supremacy, the Yankees handily won the first two games at home.

But the "Back-to-the-Wall Boys," as the Dodgers had come to be called, did not look back. They looked ahead to the friendly confines of Dodger Stadium in Los Angeles. There they took three straight, then came back and knocked off the Yanks in the Bronx to win the world championship.

The Dodgers had gotten some great hitting in the Series from Steve Garvey (.417), Steve Yeager (.364, 2 homers, 4 RBIs), Ron Cey (.350, 1 homer, 6 RBIs), Pedro Guerrero (.333, 2 homers, 7 RBIs), and Jay Johnsone's pinch hitting (1 homer, 3 RBIs). There was also the superb pitching of Valenzuela, Hooton, and Reuss, and the clutch relief performances of Steve Howe.

There were no mini-playoffs in 1982. Life was back to normal in the big leagues and the season went just like any other, save the previous one. But neither the high-priced Yankees nor the miracle-working Dodgers were back to battle for the world title. When the season came to a close, the Yankees languished in fifth place in the AL East, 16 games behind the Milwaukee Brewers. And the Dodgers were edged by a single game in the NL West by the Atlanta Braves.

For the AL pennant, Milwaukee had to face the very sound bats of the California Angels, who had with relative ease taken the AL West crown. And that appeared to be an overwhelming task when the Angels won the first two games easily in front of the Brew-

Tommy Lasorda erupts after the last out of the 1981 World Series, his first world championship.

Tommy Lasorda with the world championship trophy: 1981.

ers' hometown fans. They needed only one win in Anaheim to clinch what would be their first pennant. But the Brewers, taking their cue from the Dodgers of '81, rallied and pounded the Angels three straight times under the sunny California sky.

It was the Brewers' first pennant, although it would not be Milwaukee's first time to host a World Series—the NL Braves had staged a pair of them there back in 1957 and 1958. And this Brewer team, under the tutelage of Harvey Kuenn, the one-time great shortstop for the Detroit Tigers and other teams, was unique in its own way. It was a splended hitting team. MVP Robin Yount batted .331 (only a percentage point behind AL leader Willie Wilson of the Kansas City Royals), led the majors in hits (210) and doubles (46), drove in 114 runs, and won the AL Gold Glove for fielding. Gordon Thomas led both leagues with a total of 39 home runs and accounted for 112 RBIs. Then there was Cecil Cooper, who batted .313, fifth best in the AL, and drove in 121 runs. Ben Oglivie blasted another 34 home runs for the Brewers, and Paul Molitor led the league with 136 runs scored.

From the mound, the most effective hurler was Pete Vuckovich,

Shortstop Robin Yount was American League MVP and the Milwaukee Brewers most reliable hitter during the 1982 regular season and World Series.

whose record of 18–6 was the best won-lost percentage (.750) in the AL that year. There was also the highly respected veteran right-hander Don Sutton and southpaw Mike Caldwell, but ace reliever Rollie Fingers would be lost to them because of an injury.

Unlike the Brewers, their opponents, the St. Louis Cardinals were hardly neophytes to World Series play. The Redbirds were participating in their thirteenth World Series, and only the New York Yankees and the New York Giants had won more than the eight world titles collected by the Cards.

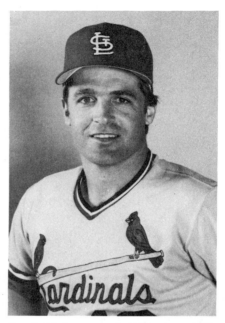

Cardinal heroes of 1982: (top left) Darrell Porter, Series MVP, batted .286, drove in five runs, and was a fielding genius; (above) Dane Iorg, designated hitter who batted .529; and (left) Joaquin Andujar who won two games and had an ERA of 1.35.

St. Louis had won the NL East, beating out the Phillies by three games. They faced a tough opponent in the Atlanta Braves, champs from the NL West who boasted power hitters like Dale Murphy and Bob Horner and such accomplished pitchers as Phil Niekro and Pasqual Perez. But when they took the field, it was all St. Louis. The Cards romped 7-0 in the first game at St. Louis, came from behind to win the second, then overwhelmed the Braves down in Atlanta to sweep the divisional playoffs.

Whitey Herzog was the Cardinal manager in 1982 and this was his first World Series. He had a fine all-around team, although they had not torn up the league from the batter's box. Lonnie Smith was the team's best hitter with an average of .307, and he was second in the NL in stolen bases (68), and Keith Hernandez was just a percentage point shy of .300. Ozzie Smith was considered among the best fielding shortstops in either league, and Willie McGee was in the running for Rookie of the Year. From the mound there was veteran Bob Forsch (15-9) and Joaquin Andujar (15-10) and, of course, one of the game's most effective relievers, Bruce Sutter.

The 1982 World Series was rated a toss-up by most observers and oddsmakers. And it proved to be that, going the full seven games, although the first and last were far from close. The Brewers annihilated the Cardinals in the opener, 10-0, but the Cards wrought vengeance in Game 6, 13-1. Stellar pitching by Andujar and Sutter in the final game gave them the Series, four games to three.

There were standout performances on both sides in the 1982 Series. For the Brewers, Robin Yount batted .414 and drove in six runs, Paul Molitor hit .355, Charlie Moore went .346, and Jim Gantner, .333, with Cecil Cooper batting in six runs. Besides the noteworthy batting of Cardinal designated hitter Dane Iorg (.529), George Hendrick and Lonnie Smith both hit .321 for St. Louis and Keith Hernandez drove in eight runs. Joaquin Andujar was credited with two Cardinal wins and Bruce Sutter chalked up a win and a save in relief.

It was the ninth World Series crown for the St. Louis Cardinals, tying them for second with the New York Giants in total world titles. And it was the 34th world championship won by the National League against the 45 taken by American League teams.

1980

Philadelphia Phillies 4
Kansas City Royals 2

Line-ups

Philadelphia Phillies		Kansas City Royals	
1b	Pete Rose	1b	Willie Aikens
2b	Manny Trillo	2b	Frank White
3b	Mike Schmidt	3b	George Brett
ss	Larry Bowa	ss	U. L. Washington
lf	Lonnie Smith	lf	Willie Wilson
cf	Garry Maddox	cf	Amos Otis
rf	Bake McBride	rf	Clint Hurdle
c	Bob Boone	c	Darrell Porter
dh	Greg Luzinski	dh	Hal McRae
mgr	Dallas Green	mgr	Jim Frey

		R	H	E	Pitching
Game 1	Kansas City	6	9	1	Dennis Leonard, Renie Martin (4th), Dan Quisenberry (8th)
	Philadelphia	7	11	0	Bob Walk (W), Tug McGraw (8th)
Game 2	Kansas City	4	11	0	Larry Gura, Dan Quisenberry (7th)
	Philadelphia	6	8	1	Steve Carlton (W), Ron Reed (9th)
Game 3	Philadelphia	3	14	0	Dick Ruthven, Tug McGraw (10th)
	Kansas City	4	11	0	Rich Gale, Renie Martin (5th), Dan Quisenberry (8th, W)
Game 4	Philadelphia	3	10	1	Larry Christenson, Dickie Noles (1st), Kevin Saucier (6th), Warren Brusstar (6th)
	Kansas City	5	10	2	Dennis Leonard (W), Dan Quisenberry (8th)

1980

Philadelphia Phillies 4
Kansas City Royals 2

		R	H	E	Pitching
Game 5	Philadelphia	4	7	0	Marty Bystrom, Ron Reed (6th), Tug McGraw (7th, W)
	Kansas City	3	12	2	Larry Gura, Dan Quisenberry (7th)
Game 6	Kansas City	1	7	2	Rich Gale, Renie Martin (3rd), Paul Splittorff (5th), Marty Pattin (7th), Dan Quisenberry (8th)
	Philadelphia	4	9	0	Steve Carlton (W), Tug McGraw (8th)

Highlights

- The Philadelphia Phillies won their very first world title in their third Series appearance.
- Willie Aikens hit two home runs and drove in four runs for the Royals in Game 1.
- Bake McBride belted a three-run homer, hit two singles, and accounted for Philadelphia's winning margin in Game 1.
- Mike Schmidt and Keith Moreland drove in the winning runs in Game 2 for the Phils.
- Steve Carlton struck out 10 Kansas City batters in eight innings during Game 2.
- Pete Rose drove in a run for Philadelphia in Game 3 to send it into extra innings.
- Willie Aikens tripled to drive in the winning run for Kansas City in the bottom of the tenth of Game 3.
- Aikens hit two homers and batted in three runs to lead the Royals to victory in Game 4. He also became the first player in history to swat two home runs twice in the same Series.
- Pinch hitter Del Unser doubled to drive in the game-tying run in the ninth inning of Game 5 for the Phillies and scored the winner when Manny Trillo singled.
- Mike Schmidt drove in two runs for the Phils in Game 6 to provide the margin of victory.

Best Efforts

Batting

Average	Amos Otis	.478
Home Runs	Willie Aikens	4
Triples	Willie Aikens	1
	George Brett	1
Doubles	Hal McRae	3
Hits	Amos Otis	11
Runs	Mike Schmidt	6
RBIs	Willie Aikens	8

Pitching

Wins	Steve Carlton	2–0
ERA	Steve Carlton	2.40
Strikeouts	Steve Carlton	17
Innings Pitched	Steve Carlton	15

1981

Los Angeles Dodgers 4
New York Yankees 2

Line-ups

Los Angeles Dodgers		New York Yankees	
1b	Steve Garvey	1b	Bob Watson
2b	Davey Lopes	2b	Willie Randolph
3b	Ron Cey	3b	Graig Nettles
ss	Bill Russell	ss	Larry Milbourne
lf	Dusty Baker	lf	Dave Winfield
cf	Pedro Guerrero	cf	Jerry Mumphrey
rf	Rick Monday	rf	Reggie Jackson
c	Steve Yeager	c	Rick Cerone
mgr	Tommy Lasorda	mgr	Bob Lemon

		R	H	E	Pitching
Game 1	Los Angeles	3	5	0	Jerry Reuss, Bobby Castillo (3rd), Dave Goltz (4th), Tom Niedenfuer (5th), Dave Stewart (8th)
	New York	5	6	0	Ron Guidry (W), Ron Davis (8th), Goose Gossage (8th)
Game 2	Los Angeles	0	4	2	Burt Hooton, Terry Forster (7th), Steve Howe (8th), Dave Stewart (8th)
	New York	3	6	1	Tommy John (W), Goose Gossage (8th)
Game 3	New York	4	9	0	Dave Righetti, George Frazier (3rd), Rudy May (5th), Ron Davis (8th)
	Los Angeles	5	11	1	Fernando Valenzuela (W)
Game 4	New York	7	13	1	Rick Reuschel, Rudy May (4th), Ron Davis (6th), George Frazier (7th), Tommy John (7th)

		R	H	E	Pitching
Game 4	Los Angeles	8	14	2	Bob Welch, Dave Goltz (1st), Terry Forster (4th), Tom Niedenfuer (5th), Steve Howe (7th, W)
Game 5	New York	1	5	0	Ron Guidry, Goose Gossage (8th)
	Los Angeles	2	4	3	Jerry Reuss (W)
Game 6	Los Angeles	9	13	1	Burt Hooton (W), Steve Howe (6th)
	New York	2	7	2	Tommy John, George Frazier (5th), Ron Davis (6th), Rick Reuschel (6th), Rudy May (7th), Dave LaRoche (9th)

Highlights

- The Dodgers won their fifth world title, their fourth since moving to Los Angeles in 1958.
- Dodger second baseman Davey Lopes set an unprized record by making six errors in the Series, but he also set a six-game Series mark by stealing four bases.
- George Frazier, Yankee relief pitcher, became only the second hurler in history to be charged with three losses in a single Series (the other, Lefty Williams, was one of the conspirators in the Black Sox scandal of 1919).
- Bob Watson hit a three-run homer for the Yankees in Game 1.
- Tommy John and Goose Gossage teamed to hurl a four-hit shutout for New York in Game 2.
- Ron Cey hit a three-run homer for the Dodgers in Game 3.
- Jay Johnstone contributed a two-run, pinch hit home run for the Dodgers in Game 4.
- Jerry Reuss went the distance for Los Angeles in Game 5, allowing the Yankees only one run and five hits.
- Pedro Guerrero and Steve Yeager hit back-to-back home runs in the bottom of the seventh of Game 5 to provide Los Angeles with their winning runs.
- Guerrero homered, tripled, singled, and drove in five runs for the Dodgers in Game 6.

Best Efforts

Batting

Average	Lou Piniella	.438
Home Runs	(four players)	2
Triples	Pedro Guerrero	1
	Willie Randolph	1
Doubles	Larry Milbourne	2
Hits	Steve Garvey	10
Runs	Davey Lopes	6
RBIs	Pedro Guerrero	7
	Bob Watson	7

Pitching

Wins	(six players)	1
ERA	Burt Hooton	1.59
Strikeouts	Burt Hooton	9
Innings Pitched	Ron Guidry	14

1982

St. Louis Cardinals 4
Milwaukee Brewers 3

Line-ups

St. Louis Cardinals		Milwaukee Brewers	
1b	Keith Hernandez	1b	Cecil Cooper
2b	Tommy Herr	2b	Jim Gantner
3b	Ken Oberkfell	3b	Paul Molitor
ss	Ozzie Smith	ss	Robin Yount
lf	Lonnie Smith	lf	Ben Oglivie
cf	Willie McGee	cf	Gorman Thomas
rf	George Hendrick	rf	Charlie Moore
c	Darrell Porter	c	Ted Simmons
dh	Dane Iorg	dh	Don Money
mgr	Whitey Herzog	mgr	Harvey Kuenn

		R	H	E	Pitching
Game 1	Milwaukee	10	17	0	Mike Caldwell (W)
	St. Louis	0	3	1	Bob Forsch, Jim Kaat (6th), Dave LaPoint (8th), Jeff Lahti (9th)
Game 2	Milwaukee	4	10	1	Don Sutton, Bob McClure (7th), Pete Ladd (8th)
	St. Louis	5	8	0	John Stuper, Jim Kaat (5th), Doug Bair (6th), Bruce Sutter (7th, W)
Game 3	St. Louis	6	6	1	Joaquin Andujar (W), Jim Kaat (7th), Doug Bair (7th), Bruce Sutter (7th)
	Milwaukee	2	5	3	Pete Vuckovich, Bob McClure (9th)
Game 4	St. Louis	5	8	1	Dave LaPoint, Doug Bair (7th), Jim Kaat (7th), Jeff Lahti (7th)
	Milwaukee	7	10	2	Moose Haas, Jim Slaton (6th, W), Bob McClure (7th)

1982

St. Louis Cardinals 4
Milwaukee Brewers 3

		R	H	E	Pitching
Game 5	St. Louis	4	15	2	Bob Forsch, Bruce Sutter (8th)
	Milwaukee	6	11	1	Mike Caldwell (W), Bob McClure (9th)
Game 6	Milwaukee	1	4	4	Don Sutton, Jim Slaton (5th), Doc Medich (6th), Dwight Bernard (8th)
	St. Louis	13	12	1	John Stuper (W)
Game 7	Milwaukee	3	7	0	Pete Vuckovich, Bob McClure (6th), Moose Haas (7th), Mike Caldwell (9th)
	St. Louis	6	15	1	Joaquin Andujar (W), Bruce Sutter (8th)

Highlights

- The St. Louis Cardinals took their ninth world championship, exceeded only by the 22 won by the New York Yankees.
- Robin Yount of Milwaukee became the first player in history to collect four hits in a single game twice in World Series play.
- Milwaukee second baseman Jim Gantner set a seven-game Series record when he committed five errors.
- Mike Caldwell hurled a shutout for Milwaukee in Game 1, allowing only three hits.
- Paul Molitor got five hits in six at-bats for the Brewers in Game 1, the most hits in any single Series game in history. Robin Yount went four for six in the same game.
- Darrell Porter cracked a double to drive in two runs and tie Game 2 for the Cardinals.
- Rookie reliever Peter Ladd of Milwaukee walked Steve Braun to force in the winning run in Game 2.
- Willie McGee hit a three-run homer and a solo round-tripper to account for four RBIs in Game 3 for the Cards.
- The Brewers scored six runs in the bottom of the seventh of Game 4 to change a 5–1 deficit to a 7–5 victory.

- Robin Yount homered, doubled, and singled twice in four at-bats in Game 5 for the Brewers.
- Keith Hernandez homered and accounted for four RBIs for the Cardinals in Game 6.
- John Stuper went the distance for St. Louis in Game 6, giving up only four hits.
- Keith Hernandez drove in two runs with a single to tie the score for the Cards in Game 7, then George Hendrick singled in the go-ahead run.

Best Efforts

Batting
Average	Robin Yount	.414
Home Runs	Willie McGee	2
	Ted Simmons	2
Triples	(five players)	1
Doubles	Jim Gantner	4
	Dane Iorg	4
	Lonnie Smith	4
Hits	Robin Yount	12
Runs	Robin Yount	6
	Lonnie Smith	6
	Willie McGee	6
RBIs	Keith Hernandez	8

Pitching
Wins	Joaquin Andujar	2–0
	Mike Caldwell	2–0
ERA	Joaquin Andujar	1.35
Strikeouts	Mike Caldwell	6
	Bruce Sutter	6
Innings Pitched	Mike Caldwell	$17^{2}/_{3}$

NINETEEN
EIGHTY-THREE

★ ★ ★   ★ ★ ★

The 1983 World Series was an east coast affair, with Baltimore triumphing in the American League and the Philadelphia Phillies emerging a victor in the National League. The Orioles were back to the title-tilt for their sixth time; the most recent being 1979, when they lost in seven games to the Pittsburgh Pirates. The Phil's last appearance in 1980 had been more successful, setting down the Kansas City Royals four games to two. 1983 marked the Philadelphians' fourth Series engagement.

The Orioles, an especially well-balanced team, took the American League East with relative ease. Their record of 98–64 (.605) stood them six games ahead of the Detroit Tigers and seven above the New York Yankees. Among the most valued of their assets in 1983 was the hitting of Cal Ripken and Eddie Murray. Ripken batted .318, fourth highest in the American League, got 209 hits, and led the circuit in doubles (47) and runs scored (122). Eddie Murray's 33 home runs were the third most in the league, his 111 RBIs fifth best, and his 114 runs scored were second only to Ripken. Murray batted .307. Other respectable hitters in the Oriole line-up included Dan Ford (.280), designated hitter Ken Singleton (.277), and Al Bumbry (.273).

Baltimore also had one of the

league's most admired pitching staffs. Scott McGregor won 18 games and lost just seven, and Mike Boddicker triumphed in 16 while going down to defeat in only eight. Tippy Martinez chalked up 21 saves.

Standing between Baltimore and the World Series was a formidable object, the Chicago White Sox. They had not captured a flag since 1959 but totally dominated the AL West in 1983. The White Sox finished 20 games ahead of the second-place Kansas City Royals. The ChiSox also won more games than any team in the majors that year (99) and produced the best won-lost percentage (.611). They did it on the arms of Cy Young Award winner Lamarr Hoyt (24-10), Rich Dotson (22-7), and Floyd Bannister (16-10), supported by the bullpen back-up of Dennis Lamp and Salome Barojas. Chicago also had enormous power, chiefly provided by Rookie of the Year Ron Kittle, who hit 35 homers and drove in 100 runs. Hulking designated hitter Greg Luzinski belted another 32 four-baggers, Carlton Fisk added 26, and Harold Baines 20. And the Sox had speed on the basepaths with Rudy Law stealing 77 bases and Julio Cruz snatching 57.

Despite the regular season bril-

liance of the White Sox, the Orioles were rated a slight favorite by the oddsmakers. It looked like they were wrong, however, when the teams matched up in Baltimore for Game 1. The Sox took it, 2-1, with Lamarr Hoyt controlling their destiny from the mound. And back in Chicago there was indeed pennant fever.

But then along came youthful Mike Boddicker for Baltimore. The strong righthander shut out the normally hard-hitting Sox, giving up only five hits and tying a playoff record by striking out 14 White Sox batsmen. The final was 4-0.

The next day the two teams convened at Comiskey Park in Chicago where Oriole hurler Mike Flanagan and reliever Sammy Stewart combined to hold the Sox to a single run and only six hits. It was also the site of a Baltimore batting explosion: 11 runs, three of them scoring on a first inning home run by Eddie Murray.

The White Sox offense fizzled the following day as well. It took 10 innings but Tito Landrum, off the bench, iced it with an extra-inning home run, the final, 3-1. The vaunted White Sox offense lost the playoffs by a composite score of 19-3 and had to live with the fact that they had stranded 35

Joe Morgan made his fourth World Series appearance in 1983, although it was his first in a Philadelphia uniform. Morgan hit two home runs and a triple—both Series highs—scored three runs, and batted .263.

baserunners during the four games.

In the National League, the Phillies were not the favorite. The Los Angeles Dodgers, so accustomed to World Series play under Tommy Lasorda, were given the edge. The Dodgers had slipped by the Atlanta Braves by three games in the NL West. A lot of the familiar faces under LA caps were gone, notably Steve Garvey, Ron Cey, and Davey Lopes. But the Dodgers still had Fernando "The Bull" Valenzuela (15–10), Bob Welch (15–12), and Jerry Reuss (12–11) to throw the ball for them.

Pedro Guerrero was the most dangerous Dodger at the plate, his 32 home runs the third most in the league. He also accounted for 103 RBIs and posted a team-high average of .297. There was consistent hitting and power from Mike Marshall (.286, 17 homers). Youthful Steve Sax batted .281 and was the third most successful base thief in the league with 56 to his credit.

The Phillies found their utmost strength in the arms that hurled for them. Strikeout wizard Steve Carlton, who has fanned more batters than any pitcher in baseball history, led the majors with

Holder of the all-time major league strikeout record, Steve Carlton was the arm on which the Phillies relied in 1983. But this was not to be his Series. Carlton lost in his one appearance.

Ever-hustling Pete Rose, diving for second here, had a dismal first two games of the 1983 Series and was benched for the third. But the old pro turned it around after that and ended up batting .313. It was Rose's sixth World Series.

Gary Matthews provided some clutch hits for the Phillies in the 1983 Series, including a home run in Game 3. He hit .250.

275 in 1983, although his record was a disappointing 15-16. On the other hand, John Denny posted a mark of 19-6, the most wins and the best won-lost percentage (.760) in the National League.

Phillie slugger Mike Schmidt clouted 40 home runs, the most in either league, and his 109 RBIs were third best in the NL. Garry Maddox had the highest batting average (.275).

The National League playoffs got underway at Dodger Stadium with what promised to be a classic pitching confrontation, Steve Carlton going for the Phils and Jerry Reuss for the Dodgers. And it turned out to be just that. Carlton mystified the Los Angeles hitters, shutting them out, 1-0, with the winning run coming on a Mike Schmidt home run.

The Dodgers rebounded the next day under the fabled southern California sun. Fernando Valenzuela gave up only one run in eight innings and Tom Niedenfuer came on for the save in the ninth. The Dodgers tallied four runs for Fernando, two of them driven in by Pedro Guerrero's fifth inning triple.

The fates were not as kind to the Dodgers in Philadelphia

Baltimore Oriole John Lowenstein goes after a hit to left field. He collected a home run, a double, and a single in four at-bats in Game 2 of the World Series.

Mike Boddicker got the Orioles going on the right track in Game 2 when he hurled a three-hitter to even the Series and launch the Baltimore express. He did not give up an earned run in his nine innings on the Series mound.

Scott McGregor won one game and was charged with the Orioles' only loss in the 1983 Series. At the same time, he led in both strikeouts (12) and innings pitched (17). McGregor dominated Game 5 and shut the Phillies out.

where the two teams met for Game 3. Behind the irrepressible bat of Gary Matthews, who hammered a home run and two singles, accounted for four RBIs, and stole a base to boot, the Phillies pleased the hometown fans with a 7-2 mauling of the Dodgers. Pete Rose also got three hits for the day and scored two Philadelphia runs. And Charles Hudson was magnificent on the mound, going the distance and allowing the Dodgers a mere four hits.

In Game 4, it was Matthews again. In the first inning, he destroyed a Jerry Reuss fastball, turning it into a three-run homer and, as it would later prove, clinching the NL pennant for the Phillies. Sixto Lezcano also whacked a two-run homer for Philadelphia while Mike Schmidt contributed three hits and Pete Rose another two. The final was 7-2.

Baltimore had the home field advantage for Game 1 of the World Series, but it did not help a bit. Oriole batters could produce only one run on a homer by Eddie Murray while Oriole pitchers gave up a pair of solo home runs to Joe Morgan and Garry Maddox.

From there, however, it was all Baltimore. The Orioles rallied in Game 2, winning it behind the

---

Only four teams in the history of the World Series have rebounded from a one-game deficit to win it, four games to one.

1983 Baltimore Orioles over Philadelphia Phillies
1969 New York Mets over Baltimore Orioles
1942 St. Louis Cardinals over New York Yankees
1915 Boston Red Sox over Philadelphia Phillies

---

masterful hurling of Mike Boddicker, who allowed only one run and three hits in nine full innings.

A close, come-from-behind win for Baltimore in Game 3, 3-2, gave them the edge, and another one-run squeaker in Game 4, 5-4, turned it into a commanding three-games-to-one advantage.

The fifth game was not close, however, not even remotely so. Behind the eruptive bats of Eddie Murray and Rick Dempsey and the flawless pitching of Scott McGregor, the Orioles shut out the Phillies, 5-0, and captured the 1983 world championship of baseball.

It was only the third world title to be claimed by Baltimore, the others in 1966 and 1970. And it was manager Joe Altobelli's first.

Keys to the Oriole triumph were the productive bats of John

The MVP award of the 1983 World Series deservedly went to Rick Dempsey. Toting a batting average of .385, he also established five-game Series records of most extra-base hits and most doubles (the latter tying Eddie Collins).

Everybody's All-Star, Eddie Murray, lived up to his reputation in the Series of 1983, whacking two home runs and driving three Orioles across home plate. This was Murray's second World Series appearance; his first was in 1979.

Shelby (.444), Rick Dempsey (.385), John Lowenstein (.385), and Jim Dwyer (.375). Eddie Murray's power was a distinct factor (two homers, three RBIs), as was Rick Dempsey's output of extra-base hits (four doubles and a home run, a Series record). Equally essential were the fine pitching performances of Scott McGregor, Mike Boddicker, and Storm Davis.

1983

Baltimore Orioles   4
Philadelphia Phillies   1

Line-ups

	Baltimore Orioles		Philadelphia Phillies
1b	Eddie Murray	1b	Pete Rose
2b	Rich Dauer	2b	Joe Morgan
3b	Todd Cruz	3b	Mike Schmidt
ss	Cal Ripken	ss	Ivan DeJesus
lf	John Lowenstein	lf	Gary Matthews
cf	John Shelby	cf	Garry Maddox
rf	Dan Ford	rf	Sixto Lezcano
c	Rick Dempsey	c	Bo Diaz
mgr	Joe Altobelli	mgr	Paul Owens

Best Efforts

Batting

Average	John Shelby	.444
Home Runs	Eddie Murray	2
	Joe Morgan	2
Triples	Joe Morgan	1
Doubles	Rick Dempsey	4
Hits	(six players)	5
Runs	Rick Dempsey	3
	Jim Dwyer	3
	Joe Morgan	3
RBIs	Eddie Murray	3
	Rich Dauer	3

Pitching

Wins	(five players)	1
ERA	Mike Boddicker	0.00
Strikeouts	Scott McGregor	12
Innings Pitched	Scott McGregor	17

Records Set or Tied in 1983

Individual Batting

- Most long hits, series, five—Rick Dempsey, Baltimore.
- Most two-base hits, series, four—Dempsey. (Ties record set by Eddie Collins, Philadelphia [AL], 1910.)

Club Batting

- Most pinch hitters used, both clubs, eight—Baltimore, four; Philadelphia, four (Game 4).
- Most consecutive pinch hitters used, four—Baltimore (Game 4, sixth inning).
- Fewest triples, one club, zero—Baltimore. (Ties record held by many, last by Oakland, 1974.)
- Fewest sacrifice bunts, both clubs, zero—Baltimore vs. Philadelphia. (Ties New York vs. Brooklyn, 1941.)

Individual Pitching

- Fewest hits, rookie, complete game, three—Mike Boddicker, Baltimore (Game 2). (Ties record set by Rollie Fingers, Oakland [AL] vs. New York [NL], October 12, 1912, and Dickie Kerr, Chicago [AL] vs. Concinnati, October 3, 1919.)
- Most saves, two—Tippy Martinez, Baltimore. (Ties record set by Rollie Fingers, Oakland [AL] vs. Los Angeles [NL], 1974.)
- Most games lost, two—Charles Hudson, Philadelphia. (Ties record held by many, last by Andy Messersmith, Los Angeles [NL] vs. Oakland, 1974.)
- Most home runs allowed, four—Hudson. (Ties record set by Gary Nolan, Cincinnati vs. Baltimore, 1970.)

Club Pitching

- Fewest bases on balls, game, both clubs, zero—Philadelphia at Baltimore (Game 1). (Ties four others).

General Records

- Largest attendance, 304,139—Baltimore vs. Philadelphia, 1983.
- Largest net receipts—$7,652,103.89, Baltimore vs. Philadelphia, 1983.
- Largest net receipts, one game—$1,722,515.46 (Game 5).
- Largest player's pool—$6,109,306.62.
- Most players, both clubs, 46.

Fielding

- Most putouts, pitcher, inning two—John Denny, Philadelphia vs. Baltimore (Game 4). (Ties four others.)

Orioles Series Averages

Batter	BA	G	AB	R	H	2B	3B	HR	RBI	GW RBI	SB	E
Ayala	1.000	1	1	1	1	0	0	0	1	0	0	0
Shelby	.444	5	9	1	4	0	0	0	1	1	0	0
Dempsey	.385	5	13	3	5	4	0	1	2	1	0	0
Lowenstein	.385	4	13	2	5	1	0	1	1	0	0	1
Dwyer	.375	2	8	3	3	1	0	1	1	0	0	0
Murray	.250	5	20	2	5	0	0	2	3	1	0	1
Dauer	.211	5	19	2	4	1	0	0	3	0	0	0
Ripken	.167	5	18	2	3	0	0	0	1	0	0	0
Ford	.167	5	12	1	2	0	0	1	1	0	0	0
Cruz	.125	5	16	1	2	0	0	0	0	0	0	2
Bumbry	.091	4	11	0	1	1	0	0	1	0	0	0
Roenicke	.000	4	7	0	0	0	0	0	0	0	0	0
Nolan	.000	2	2	0	0	0	0	0	0	0	0	0
Sakata	.000	1	1	0	0	0	0	0	0	0	0	0
Singleton	.000	2	1	0	0	0	0	0	1	0	0	0
Landrum	.000	3	0	0	0	0	0	0	0	0	0	0
Totals	.213	5	164	18	35	8	1	6	17*	3	1	4

Pitcher	W	L	ERA	G	GS	CG	SHO	SV	IP	H	ER	BB	SO
Boddicker	1	0	0.00	1	1	1	0	0	9.0	3	0	0	6
Stewart	0	0	0.00	3	0	0	0	0	4.0	1	0	2	6
Palmer	1	0	0.00	1	0	0	0	0	2.0	2	0	1	1
McGregor	1	1	1.06	2	2	1	1	0	17.0	9	2	2	12
T. Martinez	0	0	3.00	3	0	0	0	2	3.0	3	1	0	0
Flanagan	0	0	4.50	1	1	0	0	0	4.0	6	2	1	1
Davis	1	0	5.40	1	1	0	0	0	5.0	16	3	1	3
D. Martinez	0	0	0.00	0	0	0	0	0	0.0	0	0	0	0
Stoddard	0	0	0.00	0	0	0	0	0	0.0	0	0	0	0
Totals	4	1	1.60	5	—	2	1	2	45.0	30	8	7	29

*Pitcher Boddicker accounts for seventeenth RBI; hit in Game 2.

Phillies Series Averages

Batter	BA	G	AB	R	H	2B	3B	HR	RBI	GW RBI	SB	E
Virgil	.500	3	2	0	1	0	0	0	1	0	0	0
Diaz	.333	5	15	1	5	1	0	0	0	0	0	1
Rose	.313	5	16	1	5	1	0	0	1	0	0	0
Morgan	.263	5	19	3	5	0	1	2	2	0	1	0
Matthews	.250	5	16	1	4	0	0	1	1	0	0	0
Maddox	.250	4	12	1	3	1	0	1	1	1	0	0
Perez	.200	4	10	0	2	0	0	0	0	0	0	0
Lefebvre	.200	3	5	0	1	1	0	0	2	0	0	0
DeJesus	.125	5	16	0	2	0	0	0	0	0	0	1
Lezcano	.125	4	8	0	1	0	0	0	0	0	0	0
Schmidt	.050	5	20	0	1	0	0	0	0	0	0	1
G. Gross	.000	4	6	0	0	0	0	0	0	0	0	0
Hayes	.000	4	3	0	0	0	0	0	0	0	0	0
Samuel	.000	2	1	0	0	0	0	0	0	0	0	0
Dernier	.000	1	0	1	0	0	0	0	0	0	0	0
Garcia	.000	0	0	0	0	0	0	0	0	0	0	0
Totals	.195	5	159	9	31	4	1	4	9*	1	1	3

Pitcher	W	L	ERA	G	GS	CG	SHO	SV	IP	H	ER	BB	SO
Holland	0	0	0.00	2	0	0	0	1	3.2	1	0	0	5
Hernandez	0	0	0.00	3	0	0	0	0	3.0	0	0	1	4
Bystron	0	0	0.00	1	0	0	0	0	1.0	0	0	0	1
Andersen	0	0	2.25	2	0	0	0	0	4.0	4	1	0	1
Carlton	0	1	2.70	1	1	0	0	0	6.2	5	2	3	7
Reed	0	0	2.70	3	0	0	0	0	3.1	4	1	2	4
Denny	1	1	3.46	2	2	0	0	0	13.0	12	5	3	9
Hudson	0	2	8.64	2	2	0	0	0	8.1	9	8	1	6
K. Gross	0	0	0.00	0	0	0	0	0	0.0	0	0	0	0
Totals	1	4	3.47	5	—	0	0	1	44.0	35	17	10	37

*Pitcher Denny accounts for ninth RBI; hit in Game 4.

Box Scores for Individual Games

		R	H	E	Pitching
Game 1	Philadelphia	2	5	0	John Denny (W), Al Holland (8th)
	Baltimore	1	5	1	Scott McGregor, Sammy Stewart (9th), Tippy Martinez (9th)

PHILLIES (2)

	ab	r	h	bi
Morgan, 2b	4	1	2	1
Rose, 1b	4	0	1	0
Schmidt, 3b	4	0	0	0
Lezcano, rf	3	0	0	0
Hayes, ph-rf	1	0	0	0
Matthews, lf	3	0	1	0
Maddox, cf	3	1	1	1
Diaz, c	3	0	0	0
De Jesus, ss	3	0	0	0
Denny, p	3	0	0	0
Holland, p	0	0	0	0
Totals	**31**	**2**	**5**	**2**

ORIOLES (1)

	ab	r	h	bi
Bumbry, cf	4	0	1	0
Stewart, p	0	0	0	0
T. Martinez, p	0	0	0	0
Dwyer, rf	3	1	1	1
Ford, rf	1	0	0	0
Ripken, ss	4	0	1	0
Murray, 1b	4	0	1	0
Lowenstein, lf	3	0	1	0
Roenicke, ph	1	0	0	0
Dauer, 2b	3	0	0	0
Cruz, 3b	3	0	0	0
Dempsey, c	2	0	0	0
Shelby, ph-cf	1	0	0	0
McGregor, p	2	0	0	0
Nolan, ph-c	1	0	0	0
Totals	**32**	**1**	**5**	**1**

Game-Winning RBI—Maddox (1). E—Cruz. DP—Orioles 1. LOB—Phillies 2, Orioles 4. 2B—Bumbry. HR—Dwyer (1), Morgan (1), Maddox (1). Attendance: 52,204

Highlights

- All three runs scored were the result of solo home runs: Joe Morgan and Garry Maddox for the Phillies and Jim Dwyer for the Orioles.

		R	H	E	Pitching
Game 2	Philadelphia	1	3	0	Charles Hudson, Willie Hernandez (5th), Larry Andersen (6th), Ron Reed (8th)
	Baltimore	4	9	1	Mike Boddicker (W)

PHILLIES (1)

	ab	r	h	bi
Morgan, 2b	4	1	1	0
Rose, 1b	4	0	0	0
Schmidt, 3b	4	0	0	0
Lefebvre, rf	2	0	0	1
Matthews, lf	3	0	1	0
Gross, cf	3	0	0	0
Diaz, c	3	0	1	0
Samuel, pr	0	0	0	0
Virgil, c	0	0	0	0
DeJesus, ss	3	0	0	0
Hudson, p	1	0	0	0
Hernandez, p	0	0	0	0
Hayes, ph	1	0	0	0
Andersen, p	0	0	0	0
Perez, ph	1	0	0	0
Reed, p	0	0	0	0
Totals	**29**	**1**	**3**	**1**

ORIOLES (4)

	ab	r	h	bi
Bumbry, cf	2	0	0	0
Shelby, cf	2	1	1	0
Ford, rf	3	0	1	0
Ripken, ss	3	0	1	1
Murray, 1b	4	0	0	0
Lowenstein, lf	4	1	3	1
Landrum, lf	0	0	0	0
Dauer, 2b	4	1	1	0
Cruz, 3b	4	1	1	0
Dempsey, c	3	0	1	1
Boddicker, p	3	0	0	1
Totals	**32**	**4**	**9**	**4**

Game-Winning RBI—Dempsey (1). E—Murray. DP—Orioles 1. LOB—Phillies 2, Orioles 8. 2B—Lowenstein, Dempsey. HR—Lowenstein (1). SB—Morgan (1), Landrum (1). SF—Lefebvre, Boddicker.

Attendance: 52,132

Highlights

- Mike Boddicker went the distance for Baltimore, allowing only three hits, all singles, and striking out six Philadelphia batters.
- John Lowenstein homered to center in the fifth inning for the Orioles to tie the game at one run apiece.
- Rick Dempsey doubled to drive in Rich Dauer, and Todd Cruz scored on a sacrifice fly to add two more runs to the Oriole fifth inning.
- Cal Ripken singled in the seventh to drive in John Shelby for Baltimore.
- John Lowenstein collected a home run, a double, and a single in four at-bats for the Orioles.

		R	H	E	Pitching
Game 3	Baltimore	3	6	1	Mike Flanagan, Jim Palmer (W, 5th), Sammy Stewart (7th), Tippy Martinez (9th)
	Philadelphia	2	8	2	Steve Carlton, Al Holland (7th)

ORIOLES (3)

	ab	r	h	bi
Shelby, cf	4	0	2	0
Ford, rf	3	1	1	1
Ripken, ss	3	0	0	0
Murray, 1b	4	0	0	0
Roenicke, lf	4	0	0	0
Dauer, 2b	4	0	0	0
Cruz, 3b	3	0	0	0
Dempsey, c	4	1	2	0
Flanagan, p	1	0	0	0
Singleton, ph	1	0	0	0
Palmer, p	0	0	0	0
Ayala, ph	1	1	1	1
Stewart, p	1	0	0	0
Martinez, p	0	0	0	0
Totals	**33**	**3**	**6**	**2**

PHILLIES (2)

	ab	r	h	bi
Morgan, 2b	3	1	1	1
Lezcano, rf	4	0	1	0
Hayes, rf	0	0	0	0
Schmidt, 3b	4	0	0	0
Matthews, lf	3	1	1	1
Perez, 1b	4	0	1	0
Maddox, cf	4	0	0	0
Diaz, c	3	0	2	0
Lefebvre, ph	0	0	0	0
Rose, ph	1	0	0	0
DeJesus, ss	3	0	2	0
Carlton, p	3	0	0	0
Holland, p	0	0	0	0
Virgil, ph	1	0	0	0
Totals	**33**	**2**	**8**	**2**

Game-winning RBI—None. E—Cruz, Schmidt, DeJesus. DP—Philadelphia 1. LOB—Philadelphia 7, Baltimore 6. 2B—Dempsey 2. HR—Matthews (1), Morgan (2), Ford (1).

Attendance: 65,792

Highlights

- Gary Matthews belted a solo homer in the second inning for the Phillies.
- Joe Morgan homered with no one on base in the third for Philadelphia, his second round-tripper of the Series.
- Dan Ford hit a home run for Baltimore in the sixth inning.
- Rick Dempsey doubled in the seventh for the Orioles and scored on Benny Ayala's single. Ayala scored later in the inning when Ivan DeJesus made an error on a ground ball hit by Dan Ford.
- Dempsey hit two doubles in his four at-bats for Baltimore.
- Pete Rose of the Phillies was benched by manager Paul Owens.

		R	**H**	**E**	**Pitching**
Game 4	Baltimore	5	10	1	Storm Davis (W), Sammy Stewart (6th), Tippy Martinez (8th)
	Philadelphia	4	10	0	John Denny, Willie Hernandez (6th), Ron Reed (6th), Larry Andersen (8th)

ORIOLES (3)

	ab	r	h	bi
Bumbry, cf	3	0	0	0
Ford, ph	1	0	0	0
Stewart, p	1	0	0	0
T. Martinez, p	0	0	0	0
Dwyer, rf	5	2	2	0
Landrum, rf	0	0	0	0
Ripken, ss	5	1	1	0
Murray, 1b	4	0	1	0
Lowenstein, lf	4	1	1	0
Roenicke, lf	0	0	0	0
Dauer, 2b-3b	4	1	3	3
Cruz, 3b	2	0	1	0
Nolan, ph-c	1	0	0	0
Dempsey, c	1	0	0	0
Singleton, ph	0	0	0	1
Sakata, pr-2b	1	0	0	0
Davis, p	2	0	0	0
Shelby, ph-cf	1	0	1	1
Totals	**35**	**5**	**10**	**5**

PHILLIES (2)

	ab	r	h	bi
Morgan, 2b	5	0	0	0
Rose, 1b	3	1	2	1
Schmidt, 3b	4	0	1	0
Lefebvre, lf	3	0	1	1
Perez, ph	1	0	1	0
Samuel, pr	0	0	0	0
Lezcano, rf	0	0	0	0
Matthews, lf	3	0	1	0
Gross, cf	3	0	0	0
Maddox, ph	1	0	0	0
Diaz, c	4	1	2	0
Dernier, pr	0	1	0	0
DeJesus, ss	4	0	0	0
Denny, p	2	1	1	1
Hernandez, p	0	0	0	0
Reed, p	0	0	0	0
Hayes, ph	1	0	0	0
Andersen, p	0	0	0	0
Virgil, ph	1	0	1	1
Totals	**35**	**4**	**10**	**4**

Game-winning RBI—Shelby (1). E—Lowenstein. DP—Baltimore 2, Philadelphia 1. LOB—Baltimore 8, Philadelphia 6. 2B—Lefebvre, Diaz, Rose, Dauer, Dwyer. SF—Shelby.

Attendance: 66,947

Highlights

- Rich Dauer singled to drive in two runs for Baltimore in the fourth inning.
- Joe Lefebvre doubled to score Pete Rose for Philadelphia in the fourth.
- Phillie hurler John Denny singled to drive in Bo Diaz in the fifth and tie the game at two runs apiece.
- Pete Rose doubled, driving in Denny, in the fifth to give Philadelphia the lead, 3–2.
- With the bases loaded in the sixth, John Denny walked Ken Singleton of the Orioles to tie the game. Rich Dauer also scored in the same inning on a sacrifice fly from the bat of John Shelby to give Baltimore the lead.
- Dauer drove in Jim Dwyer with a single in the seventh for Baltimore.
- Ozzie Virgil got an RBI in the ninth for the Phillies when Bob Dernier scored on his single.
- Rich Dauer collected a double, two singles, and three RBIs for Baltimore.
- Tippy Martinez made his third appearance in relief in four games for the Orioles.

		R	**H**	**E**	**Pitching**
Game 5	Baltimore	5	5	0	Scott McGregor (W)
	Philadelphia	0	5	1	Charles Hudson, Marty Bystrom (5th), Willie Hernandez (6th), Ron Reed (9th)

ORIOLES (5)

	ab	r	h	bi
Bumbry, cf	2	0	0	1
Shelby, cf	1	0	0	0
Ford, rf	4	0	0	0
Landrum, rf	0	0	0	0
Ripken, ss	3	1	0	0
Murray, 1b	4	2	3	3
Lowenstein, lf	2	0	0	0
Roenicke, lf	2	0	0	0
Dauer, 2b	4	0	0	0
Cruz, 3b	4	0	0	0
Dempsey, c	3	2	2	1
McGregor, p	3	0	0	0
Totals	**32**	**5**	**5**	**5**

PHILLIES (0)

	ab	r	h	bi
Morgan, 2b	3	0	1	0
Rose, rf	4	0	2	0
Schmidt, 3b	4	0	0	0
Matthews, lf	4	0	0	0
Perez, 1b	4	0	0	0
Maddox, cf	4	0	2	0
Diaz, c	2	0	0	0
DeJesus, ss	3	0	0	0
Hudson, p	1	0	0	0
Bystrom, p	0	0	0	0
Samuel, ph	1	0	0	0
Hernandez, p	0	0	0	0
Lezcano, ph	1	0	0	0
Reed, p	0	0	0	0
Totals	**31**	**0**	**5**	**0**

Game-winning RBI—Murray (1). E—Diaz. DP—Baltimore 1. LOB—Baltimore 2, Philadelphia 6. 2B—Dempsey, Maddox. 3B—Morgan. HR—Murray 2 (2), Dempsey (1). SF—Bumbry.
Attendance: 67,064

Highlights

- Scott McGregor went the distance to shutout the Phillies, allowing only five hits and striking out six.
- Eddie Murray homered with nobody on base in the second inning for the Orioles.
- Rick Dempsey clouted a solo home run for Baltimore in the third.
- Murray hit a two-run homer for the Orioles in the fourth.
- Dempsey doubled in the ninth and then scored Baltimore's final run of the Series on a sacrifice fly by Al Bumbry.
- Eddie Murray pounded two home runs and a single in four at-bats for Baltimore and accounted for three RBIs.

APPENDIX

World Championships

New York Yankees	22
St. Louis Cardinals	9
Boston Red Sox	5
New York Giants	5
Philadelphia A's	5
Pittsburgh Pirates	5
Los Angeles Dodgers	4
Cincinnati Reds	4
Detroit Tigers	3
Baltimore Orioles	3
Oakland A's	3
Chicago White Sox	2
Chicago Cubs	2
Cleveland Indians	2
Brooklyn Dodgers	1
Milwaukee Braves	1
Boston Braves	1
Washington Senators	1
New York Mets	1
Philadelphia Phillies	1

MVPs

In 1955, an award for the World Series Most Valuable Player was instituted. The following are the players who have been voted MVP each year:

1955	Johnny Podres	Brooklyn Dodgers
1956	Don Larsen	New York Yankees
1957	Lew Burdette	Milwaukee Braves
1958	Bob Turley	New York Yankees
1959	Larry Sherry	Los Angeles Dodgers
1960	Bobby Richardson	New York Yankees
1961	Whitey Ford	New York Yankees
1962	Ralph Terry	New York Yankees
1963	Sandy Koufax	Los Angeles Dodgers
1964	Bob Gibson	St. Louis Cardinals
1965	Sandy Koufax	Los Angeles Dodgers
1966	Frank Robinson	Baltimore Orioles
1967	Bob Gibson	St. Louis Cardinals
1968	Mickey Lolich	Detroit Tigers
1969	Donn Clendenon	New York Mets
1970	Brooks Robinson	Baltimore Orioles
1971	Roberto Clemente	Pittsburgh Pirates
1972	Gene Tenace	Oakland A's
1973	Reggie Jackson	Oakland A's
1974	Rollie Fingers	Oakland A's
1975	Pete Rose	Cincinnati Reds
1976	Johnny Bench	Cincinnati Reds
1977	Reggie Jackson	New York Yankees
1978	Bucky Dent	New York Yankees
1979	Willie Stargell	Pittsburgh Pirates
1980	Mike Schmidt	Philadelphia Phillies
1981	Ron Cey	Los Angeles Dodgers
	Pedro Guerrero	Los Angeles Dodgers
	Steve Yeager	Los Angeles Dodgers
1982	Darrell Porter	St. Louis Cardinals
1983	Rick Dempsey	Baltimore Orioles

Career Records

Service

Series

Batter	Yogi Berra	14
Pitcher	Whitey Ford	11
Manager	Casey Stengel	10

Games

Batter	Yogi Berra	75
Pitcher	Whitey Ford	22
Manager	Casey Stengel	63

Batting

Average*	Pepper Martin	.418
	Lou Brock	.391
	Thurman Munson	.373
	Hank Aaron	.364
	Home Run Baker	.363

*Based on a minimum of 50 at-bats.

Home Runs	Mickey Mantle	18
	Babe Ruth	15
	Yogi Berra	12
	Duke Snider	11
	Lou Gehrig	10
	Reggie Jackson	10
Triples	Tommy Leach	4
	Tris Speaker	4
	Billy Johnson	4
Doubles	Frankie Frisch	10
	Yogi Berra	10
	Jake Barry	9
	Pete Fox	9
	Carl Furillo	9

Hits		
	Yogi Berra	71
	Mickey Mantle	59
	Frankie Frisch	58
	Joe DiMaggio	54
	Hank Bauer	46
	PeeWee Reese	46

Runs		
	Mickey Mantle	42
	Yogi Berra	41
	Babe Ruth	37
	Lou Gehrig	30
	Joe DiMaggio	27

RBIs		
	Mickey Mantle	40
	Yogi Berra	39
	Lou Gehrig	35
	Babe Ruth	33
	Joe DiMaggio	30

Walks		
	Mickey Mantle	43
	Babe Ruth	33
	Yogi Berra	32
	Phil Rizzuto	30
	Lou Gehrig	26

Stolen Bases		
	Eddie Collins	14
	Lou Brock	14
	Frank Chance	10
	Phil Rizzuto	10
	Honus Wagner	9
	Frankie Frisch	9

Pitching

Wins		
	Whitey Ford	10
	Red Ruffing	7
	Allie Reynolds	7
	Bob Gibson	7
	Chief Bender	6
	Lefty Gomez	6
	Waite Hoyt	6

ERA*	Jack Billingham	0.36
	Harry Breechen	0.83
	Babe Ruth	0.87
	Sherry Smith	0.89
	Sandy Koufax	0.95

*Minimum of 25 innings pitched.

Strikeouts	Whitey Ford	94
	Bob Gibson	92
	Allie Reynolds	62
	Red Ruffing	61
	Sandy Koufax	61
	Chief Bender	59

Shutouts	Christy Mathewson	4
	Three Finger Brown	3
	Whitey Ford	3

Innings Pitched	Whitey Ford	146
	Christy Mathewson	101$\frac{2}{3}$
	Red Ruffing	85$\frac{2}{3}$
	Chief Bender	85
	Waite Hoyt	83$\frac{2}{3}$

Complete Games	Christy Mathewson	10
	Chief Bender	9
	Bob Gibson	8
	Red Ruffing	7
	Whitey Ford	7

Managers

Series Won	Joe McCarthy	7
	Casey Stengel	7
	Connie Mack	5
	Walt Alston	4
	John McGraw	3
	Miller Huggins	3

Games Won	Casey Stengel	37
	Joe McCarthy	30
	John McGraw	26
	Connie Mack	24
	Walt Alston	20

Single Series Records

Batting

Average	4 games:	Babe Ruth	.625	1928
	5 games:	Joe Gordon	.500	1941
		Bobby Brown	.500	1949
		Larry McLean	.500	1913
	6 games:	Billy Martin	.500	1953
		Dave Robertson	.500	1917
	7 games:	Pepper Martin	.500	1947
		Phil Garner	.500	1979
	8 games:	Buck Herzog	.400	1912
Home Runs	4 games:	Lou Gehrig	4	1928
	5 games:	Donn Clendenon	3	1969
	6 games:	Reggie Jackson	5	1977
	7 games:	Babe Ruth	4	1926
		Duke Snider	4	1952, 1955
		Hank Bauer	4	1958
		Gene Tenace	4	1972
	8 games:	Patsy Dougherty	2	1903
Triples	4 games:	Lou Gehrig	2	1927
		Tommy Davis	2	1963
	5 games:	Eddie Collins	2	1913
		Bobby Brown	2	1949
	6 games:	George Rohe	2	1906
		Bob Meusel	2	1923
		Billy Martin	2	1953
	7 games:	Billy Johnson	3	1947
	8 games:	Tommy Leach	4	1903

Doubles	4 games:	Hank Gowdy	3	1914
		Babe Ruth	3	1928
	5 games:	Eddie Collins	4	1910
	6 games:	Chick Hafey	5	1930
	7 games:	Pete Fox	6	1934
	8 games:	Buck Herzog	4	1912
		Red Murray	4	1912
		Buck Weaver	4	1919
		George Burns	4	1921
Hits	4 games:	Babe Ruth	10	1928
	5 games:	(eight players)	9	
	6 games:	Billy Martin	12	1953
	7 games:	Bobby Richardson	13	1960
		Lou Brock	13	1968
	8 games:	Buck Herzog	12	1912
		Shoeless Joe Jackson	12	1919
Runs	4 games:	Babe Ruth	9	1928
		Lou Gehrig	9	1932
	5 games:	(six players)	6	
	6 games:	Reggie Jackson	10	1977
	7 games:	(seven players)	8	
	8 games:	Freddie Parent	8	1903
RBIs	4 games:	Lou Gehrig	9	1928
	5 games:	Danny Murphy	9	1910
	6 games:	Ted Kluszewski	10	1959
	7 games:	Bobby Richardson	12	1960
	8 games:	Tommy Leach	8	1903
		Pat Duncan	8	1919
Walks	4 games:	Hank Thompson	7	1954
	5 games:	Jimmy Sheckard	7	1910
		Mickey Cochrane	7	1929
		Joe Gordon	7	1941
	6 games:	Willie Randolph	9	1981
	7 games:	Babe Ruth	11	1926
		Gene Tenace	11	1973
	8 games:	Josh Devore	7	1912
		Ross Youngs	7	1921

Stolen Bases	4 games: (eight players)	2	
	5 games: Jimmy Slagle	6	1907
	6 games: Davey Lopes	4	1981
	7 games: Lou Brock	7	1967, 1968
	8 games: Josh Devore	4	1912

Pitching

Wins	4 games: Bill James	2	1914
	Dick Rudolph	2	1914
	Waite Hoyt	2	1928
	Red Ruffing	2	1938
	Sandy Koufax	2	1963
	5 games: Christy Mathewson	3	1905
	Jack Coombs	3	1910
	6 games: Red Faber	3	1917
	7 games: (six players)	3	
	8 games: Bill Dinneen	3	1903
	Deacon Phillippe	3	1903
	Smokey Joe Wood	3	1912
ERA	4 games: (seven players)	0.00	
	5 games: (fourteen players)	0.00	
	6 games: Rube Benton	0.00	1917
	Jack Kramer	0.00	1944
	Gene Bearden	0.00	1948
	7 games: (eight players)	0.00	
	8 games: Waite Hoyt	0.00	1921
Strikeouts	4 games: Sandy Koufax	23	1963
	5 games: Christy Mathewson	18	1905
	6 games: Chief Bender	20	1911
	7 games: Bob Gibson	35	1968
	8 games: Bill Dinneen	28	1903
Shutouts	4 games: (seven players)	1	
	5 games: Christy Mathewson	3	1905
	6 games: (twelve players)	1	
	7 games: Lew Burdette	2	1957
	Whitey Ford	2	1960
	Sandy Koufax	2	1965
	8 games: Bill Dinneen	2	1903

Innings Pitched	4 games:	Dick Rudolph	18	1914
		Waite Hoyt	18	1928
		Red Ruffing	18	1938
		Sandy Koufax	18	1963
	5 games:	Christy Mathewson	27	1905
		Jack Coombs	27	1910
	6 games:	Christy Mathewson	27	1911
		Red Faber	27	1917
		Hippo Vaughn	27	1918
	7 games:	George Mullin	32	1909
	8 games:	Deacon Phillippe	44	1903

Game Records

Batting

Home Runs	Babe Ruth	3	1926, 1928
	Reggie Jackson	3	1977
Triples	Tommy Leach	2	1903
	Patsy Dougherty	2	1903
	Dutch Ruether	2	1919
	Bobby Richardson	2	1960
	Tommy Davis	2	1963
Doubles	Frank Isbell	4	1906
Singles	Paul Molitor	5	1982
Hits	Paul Molitor	5	1982
Runs	Babe Ruth	4	1926
	Earle Combs	4	1932
	Frankie Crosetti	4	1936
	Enos Slaughter	4	1946
	Reggie Jackson	4	1977
RBIs	Bobby Richardson	6	1960

Walks	Fred Clarke	4	1909
	Dick Hoblitzell	4	1916
	Ross Youngs	4	1924
	Babe Ruth	4	1926
	Jackie Robinson	4	1952
	Doug DeCinces	4	1979
Stolen Bases	Honus Wagner	3	1909
	Willie Davis	3	1965
	Lou Brock	3	1967, 1968

Pitching

Strikeouts	Bob Gibson	17	1968
Most Innings	Babe Ruth	14	1916
No-hitters	Don Larsen	1956	
One-hitters	Ed Reulbach	1906	
	Claude Passeau	1945	
	Floyd Bevens	1947	
	Jim Lonborg	1967	
Two-hitters	Ed Walsh	1906	
	Three Finger Brown	1906	
	Eddie Plank	1913	
	Bill James	1914	
	Waite Hoyt	1921	
	Burleigh Grimes	1931	
	George Earnshaw	1931	
	Monte Pearson	1939	
	Mort Cooper	1944	
	Bob Feller	1948	
	Allie Reynolds	1949	
	Vic Raschi	1950	
	Warren Spahn	1958	
	Whitey Ford	1961	
	Nelson Briles	1971	

INDEX